Improving Literacy
at KS2 and KS3

Improving Literacy at KS2 and KS3

Edited by

Andrew Goodwyn

P·C·P
Paul Chapman
Publishing

Editorial Material and Introduction © Andrew Goodwyn
2002
Chapter 1 © Andrew Goodwyn and Kate Findlay 2002
Chapter 2 © Andrew Goodwyn and Kate Findlay 2002
Chapter 3 © Kate Findlay 2002
Chapter 4 © Michael Lockwood 2002
Chapter 5 © Winston Brookes 2002
Chapter 6 © George Hunt 2002
Chapter 7 © Lionel Warner 2002
Chapter 8 © Cynthia Martin 2002
Chapter 9 © Margaret Perkins 2002

First published 2002

 Paul Chapman Publishing
A SAGE Publications Company
6 Bonhill Street
London EC2A 4PU

SAGE Publications Inc
2455 Teller Road
Thousand Oaks, California 91320

SAGE Publications India Pvt Ltd
32, M-Block Market
Greater Kailash - I
New Delhi 1 10 048

Library of Congress Control Number: 2002105548

A catalogue record for this book is available from the British Library

ISBN 0 7619 4722 1
ISBN 0 7619 4723 X (pbk)

Typeset by Anneset, Weston-super-Mare, Somerset
Printed and bound in Great Britain by Athenaeum
Press, Gateshead

Contents

Dedication

We should like to dedicate this book to the many teachers who have generously given to us their time and demonstrated so clearly their expertise. We hope the book does some justice to them.

Introduction

Andrew Goodwyn

This book sets out to accomplish the especially difficult task of reviewing the issues of transition and of literacy, principally as they affect teachers and pupils. The task is difficult because the transition from primary to secondary school is notoriously problematic and pupils find the shift of cultures at the least very challenging and often traumatic. In the past, communications between the secondary and primary phases have been at best strained and there is no evidence that the National Curriculum has been of much benefit in this respect. And then we have literacy, a term once used as a simple marker of those who could read and write and those (the illiterate) who could not. Now it is, quite rightly, both a much more complicated concept and a somewhat elusive one like 'intelligence' that is recognized to be something we are still grasping to define and understand.

The book thus acknowledges these difficulties and seeks wherever possible to offer help and advice. Some of this takes the form of reviewing research and previous forms of advice, some, concerned with the more uncertain future, is necessarily speculative.

Certain issues are the focus of our discussion. The first must inevitably be the National Literacy Strategy (NLS). The enormity of the National Literacy Strategy is hard to grasp. There has been no single policy initiative like it. It might be compared to the comprehensive movement perhaps, but even there a proportion of the secondary schools were unaffected and the impact on primary schools was essentially to remove the constraint of the eleven-plus. The key point is that every teacher, every pupil and every local education authority (LEA) has been or soon will be, fundamentally affected by this initiative on a daily basis. At least that is what is intended. And who can dispute that possession of literacy is simply a good thing? The writers of this book do not dispute that, but they would be failing all teachers and pupils if they did not point out that this monolithic policy is based on very little research evidence, that its evaluations seem to have been insignificant or disregarded and that the only measures of its success are narrowly focused tests that most teachers find of dubious validity. Our first issue is therefore that we are supportive of changes where we can see their rationale but critical and questioning where we cannot. We feel essentially that there has been very little time or opportunity to critique the whole Juggernaut and it is far too important for such an unreflective approach.

A second key issue entails making sense of this initiative in relation to the past and the future. Criticisms of the lack of literate school leavers are as old as school itself and the tendency for politicians to blame teachers just as ancient. More specifically in the Language Across the Curriculum movement of the 1970s and early 1980s we have a minor precedent, discussed, if briefly in Chapter 2. Overall we intend to help readers place the whole policy and its impact on transition and continuity in a historical context where this will help to reveal what is significant. This is especially important as all members of the profession from the 'trainee' to the head teacher are involved.

Our next issue concerns the active role of teachers, and in the face of such large-scale and remotely constructed change it is hard for any participant to feel much agency. However, we are convinced that agency is not only possible but crucial and that it will very much enhance those elements within the Strategy that are essentially worthwhile. One feature of the text is its constant reference to teachers themselves, and their views as revealed through surveys, interviews and classroom observations. Their voices and opinions come through very strongly and their pros and cons are evident. Often they do feel very 'put upon' and that their cherished autonomy and professionalism are once more further eroded, especially the nature of the training which they have endured. However, they are equally clear that there are things to be done for their own sake as well as for the policy or its appearances; they show that agency is a reality.

Finally this book is about transition and specifically three of its many connotations. The first meaning is perhaps also the simplest, referring to that long-acknowledged difficulty as children move from primary to secondary. This move and the 'dip' in performance associated with it in Year 7 has long vexed teachers and parents. First the National Curriculum was going to solve this problem, now the NLS is asked to do so. We are clear that this is a naive view. That transition is also between school cultures and, more profoundly, between childhood and adolescence. We would rather acknowledge the significance of the change and argue for various ways of minimizing the difficulties and maximizing the opportunities. In this sense the NLS can be made to help.

Our second element in relation to transition is that the acquisition of literacy is an inextricable part of it, of growing up in fact. The secondary school has huge specific demands about literacy, and life outside has many more. Sometimes these demands are confusing and conflicting for young people and their teachers. We hope that secondary schools in particular will conceptualize literacy in this way as a part of adolescence and early adulthood, not as something that should be over by an age or a supposedly acquired 'level'.

Our last point about transition is perhaps more of a play on that term. The phrase 'in transit' suggests a starting point and a place to arrive. The architects of the NLS long for the achievement of nicely quantifiable percentages of children with the 'right levels' of literacy, then we will all have arrived. Unfortunately, such an approach is unsound. Paradoxically we feel sure that those statistics will emerge; too much political capital has been invested for failure to be conceivable. The important point is that we can probably assess literacy but we should not pretend to measure it. Fundamentally literacy is always in transition and will not stop long enough to be simplistically measured. Assessing children's literacy is vital and highly productive, best done by experienced and well-practised professionals. Tests can play a useful, but usually modest, part in the process. For literacy itself is surely changing more rapidly now than at any time and this is an exciting opportunity, not a problem in itself. We can see the evidence all around us and so can our children. Accepting that literacy is now and always in transit, allows us to reject simplistic nostalgias about, for example, former golden ages of spelling and to enjoy the benefits of the spellchecker. We acknowledge that schools are under enormous public pressure to produce quantifiable measures of literacy and we must accept that they will have to do so. However, our argument offers them support in their own view that their professional judgement and experience will be more important in the long run and more in touch with literacy's ongoing transitions.

The majority of contributors are researchers but every one has been a teacher and the author of Chapter 7, 'the' practising teacher, is also a researcher. The book has a strong research base made all the more powerful as the majority of that research belongs to the writers and their recent work in schools. Teachers themselves are increasingly embracing classroom research and also recognizing its importance as they are asked to analyse their 'performance'. The book provides many insights into how research provides some possible answers to our problems but also where it exposes and poses problems for which more research will be needed. The National Literacy Strategy is most certainly not certain, for all its frequently dogmatic assertions; rather its dogmas reveal its insecurities. We hope the book provokes some questions as well as offering at least some suggested solutions.

Making the most of the National Literacy Strategy

This book puts forward a strong argument about literacy, about transition and about literacy in transition. It will review the National Literacy Strategy, offer ways that we can work with it but also provide a critique of both its 'theory' and its somewhat formulaic practice. The research at the heart of the book demonstrates that the majority of teachers can be seen to support what might be called the spirit of the NLS, that is, the admirable aim to make all our future citizens highly literate and articulate in their adult lives. However, teachers also make it clear that the 'letter' of the NLS is often oppressive, it ignores their autonomy and creativity as professionals and it is overdetermined by narrow forms of testing. Finally, unless it is constantly revised and made more flexible it will become even more a prisoner of the past. The obsession with 'teacher proof' manuals, overhead transparencies (OHTs), videos and consultants and co-ordinators still seem more like the trappings of some fundamentalist, even evangelical, cult than anything else. They suggest a constant fear of subversion, demanding that everyone is so busy 'delivering' the NLS message that they will not have time to utter that heretical thought, 'Is this really about improving literacy, and what, in the twenty-first century, actually is literacy?'

Other chapters, especially Chapter 1, grapple with the elusive quality of literacy as it exists in print and multimedia, local and global environments and explore how in the last hundred years or so we have been offered an escape from a narrow, fixed and ultimately exclusive and elitist definition of literacy, and instead have discovered a much more human, humane and inclusive vision. In this formulation we must recognize difference, context and the flux of constant change. The example of text messaging is a wonderfully illustrative example of the power of literacy as a creative engine, able to defy the authority of the academy and its obsessions with language control. Literacy must therefore always be seen as in transition, manuals can be useful in the way they should be; they help with the current model but not the one being invented as the print dries.

So this Introduction is concerned with reviewing where we have got to on this endless journey and with ideas and suggestions about the future. The National Literacy Strategy looks set to run for a number of years and, because of its domineering scale, we have nothing really that can be compared to it. Its companion initiative, the National Numeracy Strategy, is clearly important, but it is being treated as if from a very different and relatively junior league. Chapter 2 will consider to what extent the NLS could be compared to the Language Across the Curriculum movement with the suggestion that there were some lessons from that time to be learned and that the next few years would tell. One purpose behind this book as a whole is to contextualize the NLS and to offer readers some real perspective; the shape of a mountain is best judged from a distance.

The book's other main purpose is to review the problematic transition of pupils from primary to secondary schools. This is always going to be a key issue but is made dramatically so as the NLS itself makes that transition. Therefore, it will have a huge impact on transition issues themselves. Some of the time it is possible to treat pupil transition as a kind of discrete issue; equally literacy and its constant flux can usefully be viewed in a distinctive way. However, at times, and especially now, the issues are entwined and must be considered in that complex formation. The impact of the NLS may well have some significant benefits for transition between schools as long as at least some of the criticisms of the strategy are listened to and the role of teachers is afforded more autonomy and respect. As this may or may not happen, so these suggestions about the future must be tentative but they are informed by a number of patterns that should be helpful.

Literacy as transition

Chapter 1 will explore in more depth how our current obsession with literacy is an outcome of our need in societies with specialized occupations to communicate across distance and time. To that extent every generation since the late nineteenth century has more or less agreed with this impetus and tended to add elaborations both to forms of communication and the literacies that they subsequently generate. Literacy, then, has a history of its own and a future, Margaret Meek's *On Being Literate* (Meek, 1995) provides an excellent account of this whole concept.

One thing missing from the NLS is an interest in literacy *as* transition, that old proverb, 'not seeing the wood for the trees' seems very apt. Children need help to acquire the literacy of yesterday because it has the current status afforded it by the previous generation, i.e., their parents and teachers. This literacy is already dated. However, the great majority of it is worth having and will be extremely useful so there is no tension there for teachers or parents. However, secondary school children also need help to put literacy in perspective. For example, the generation that has 'invented' text messaging may not be very immediately interested in the fact that something called the telegram actually got there first, but good teachers can help them become interested; pupils need to understand, as well as employ, literacy. We have been codifying language to make it more transmittable for longer than we can universally remember, we might possibly track this back through hieroglyphics to cave paintings. This idea brings us to two important points for teachers and schools to consider for the future. First, students should leave school not only literate but with a perspective on Literacy itself. Secondly, as they approach the age of being eligible to vote, they should be ready to participate in the future of a democratic society where literacies will be contested and changing; literacy is always a political issue.

To gain that crucial perspective involves a number of recognitions that schools can help their students to acquire. First, in this process literacy acts as a transition towards the adult world that 'we' have constructed. In that sense it is at least as much about adolescence as childhood. The child that is acquiring yesterday's literacy is developing identities that inevitably are in some tension with it; this is not a problem – it is the beginning of critical literacy. Young people should question the past and consider the future; literacy allows them to do both. Secondary schools must therefore provide some space, probably in Key Stage 4 (KS4), for their students to reflect on literacy and to critique it in a conscious way. This can only be done if teachers offer them some perspective on the history of literacy.

In itself this is not an entirely new activity and might be seen as the culmination of a series of curricular experiments. Previous initiatives have included the change in English teaching brought about by the emergence of the London School in the 1960s, experiments with Language in Use and Language Awareness in the 1970s, Knowledge About Language as a result of the Kingman Report and the ill-fated Language in the National Curriculum project of 1990–93 (see Carter, 1990, for an account). All these projects attempted to help students understand the power of language to liberate but equally to be oppressive and imprisoning. What might be considered new is the exclusive attention to the word 'literacy'. While the NLS prevails it may be best to accept this partly reductive use of the term because students can be asked to reflect on its dominance. After all, the generation born in the mid-1990s will eventually have experienced approximately 10 years of 'doing literacy' as they themselves increasingly describe it. They surely deserve the right to the question, 'What have we learned from all this?' This critical examination of literacy, its history and its constantly changing definitions should be closely linked to another term with a new spotlight of attention, 'Citizenship'; more about this below.

The key aspect for students must be to consider that their struggle with Literacy is intrinsically 'worth it' but that no definition of literacy is neutral. Much of the history of literacy is about elitism and exclusivity. Surely well-educated students in a democratic society ought to know the name of Paolo Freire, to appreciate a model of literacy that was driven by egalitarianism and democratic principles and demanded that citizens use their literacy to be politically active, never apathetic (see, for example, Freire and Macedo, 1987). This focus on a reflection on Literacy should certainly take place in English but equally certain elements are at home in other subject areas such as History or within Citizenship itself. English, as suggested in Chapter 1, is the curriculum area where the concept of discourses is examined and for the foreseeable future retains a key role in broadening pupils' thinking about all forms of language. English also increasingly has a somewhat paradoxical role as a kind of antidote to capital L Literacy, a curriculum space where interesting things about language, not just literacy hours, can occur.

The second point for schools builds on this perspective on Literacy. The general election in the United Kingdom in June 2001 had the lowest turn-out of voters since 1918. A full explanation of this would require a book on its own but the fact that it occurred at exactly the same time as 'Citizenship' was being introduced to the compulsory curriculum is a powerful symbolic conjunction. The explanation most frequently offered has been that the dominant political party is now firmly of the Centre, most people are in work and voters are now cynical about political 'spin'. However, another explanation, or at least important factor, concerns 'schooling', i.e., that process by which future citizens are 'schooled' (Buckingham, 2000). Since the mid-1980s teachers have not been losing control of their classes they have been losing control over their work. In the census of 2001 teaching became a 'second tier' profession, principally because of the lack of autonomy teachers now experience. This topic is equally deserving of a book but the point for readers actually relates to literacy.

Teachers and the curriculum have been increasingly controlled and also policed by Inspection and, therefore, so have children and young people (Goodwyn, 2001b). Citizenship for most people is a somewhat worthily remote term and it is no accident that students have to wait until they are at least 16 to study something called Politics or Sociology. In England and Wales teachers are forbidden by law from expressing strong views on controversial issues, i.e., things that actually matter to them and their students. The link with Literacy is simple, what do you do with it once you have it? One major advantage in being literate is that you can argue a case in writing or in speech. If young people are increasingly politically apathetic, perhaps the curriculum they experience at least in part engenders it?

In 2002 schools and teachers remain straitjacketed, the most common form of protest by teachers has been, increasingly, to leave the profession. The report of the Chief Inspector for Schools (OFSTED, 2001), received much media attention because it highlighted the problem of retention of the profession. Many teachers (figures claimed vary from 40 per cent to 25 per cent) tend to leave after about three years, i.e., just as they are becoming genuinely effective. There is no evidence that the teachers who leave are in any way the ineffective minority. Chapter 2 does stress that there are significant opportunities for agency and Chapter 5 illustrates how thinking professionals refuse to be merely instrumental, however these latter figures are highly experienced and have already survived endless reforms and initiatives. When engaged in a small-scale piece of research about curriculum change (Goodwyn, 1997) I was struck by how consistently highly experienced senior managers in schools reflected on the early years of their careers as full of excitement and challenge. They felt that schools were now much better organized and far more account-able but that much of the enjoyment had gone out of teaching. My own anecdotal experience of the retention crisis is of a similar nature, young teachers in particular are not leaving because they have become cynical or materialistic, they are leaving to find opportunities for more creativity and autonomy, and to escape excessive bureaucracy and endless exter-nally imposed demands. Of course more money helps, but it is less sig-nificant than it used to be.

There are no neat and simple solutions but literacy and politics are inextricably linked by ideology. Literacy should be about change not about the maintenance of the status quo. If young people are to be com-mitted citizens, then schools have to challenge their thinking not con-stantly direct it. One very significant danger in the NLS is that it will further diminish the enjoyment of teaching and deaden the curriculum for teachers and pupils alike. This is especially true in secondary schools where English teachers in particular feel that the curriculum feels like a 'cage' (Goodwyn and Findlay, 1999).

Ultimately, then, students should be encouraged by schools to use their advanced literacy skills in critical and engaged ways. Curriculum 2000 at least provided a little more flexibility and there are indications that GCSEs might be reformed early in the twenty-first century. Whatever space opens up to allow schools and teachers to select what they feel is right for their students should be used as an opportunity to challenge all students to be critically literate. One role for Citizenship then will be to engage students' literacies in social critique. At least some aspects of this challenge are potentially available through the opportunities offered by the new technologies.

ICT and some real opportunities

Chapter 2 examines the current uses of information and communications technology (ICT), productive and unproductive, in schools and reflects on the almost complete absence of computer use from the whole NLS initiative so far. There is a striking paradox in this unintentionally anti-ICT initiative happening in parallel with teachers' in-service training (the

New Opportunities Fund, NOF training) in the use of ICT. The review of the research in this area suggests that we would need a much expanded definition of literacy in order to at least make sense of the impact of ICT on a whole range of aspects of our everyday lives. Many of the suggestions in the next section assume the availability of good hardware and software and plenty of access, conditions that are by no means common as yet. However, there seems little point in endlessly repeating the phrase 'if you have access to', the evidence from schools (BECTa, 2001a; 2001b) is that teachers are learning to maximize ICT opportunities for their pupils and will increasingly do so. Equally there are other problematic issues about confidentiality and data protection that will be especially challenging for schools in the future. If a National Grid for Learning is ever to be a reality then some of these problems must be solved by a managed system and not be a constant distraction for individual schools. Again therefore, and with these cautions in mind, it seems best to review what longer-term benefits ICT can bring.

The other factor to be considered in Chapter 2 is the current convergence of computer and media technologies and its implications for schools at present; this section will speculate about how such convergence may (and should be) truly transforming. Our starting point is the primary secondary transition itself.

The transfer of electronic data

At a simple level electronic transfer makes pupil data immediately available, i.e., as soon as it is prepared it can be transmitted simultaneously to as many recipients as need it, for example to all the teachers in school not just the key figures. This still relies entirely on the quality of human input of that data. If the quality is there then the data is extremely manipulable and can be represented in ways that can make sense to different audiences. The data is also importantly provisional. It can be questioned and interrogated. For example, secondary schools should not just receive such data; they should consider it critically. If a primary school's test scores have risen or fallen then there will a story behind the figures that will involve the actual experience of the children and teachers themselves; finding out the story makes the figures meaningful. In other words, such data is a part of a dialogue about transition; it can never replace that dialogue.

In the spirit of that dialogue such data can also be enhanced and returned to its creators. Primary schools have long been frustrated by the lack of reciprocity between themselves and secondary schools; the latter get lots of their information and they receive nothing back. Secondary schools are very keen to claim how many of 'their' pupils go on to university for example, with individual pupil records it will be much easier to let primary schools have such information. Of more immediate practical value will be the chance to review pupil progress across Key Stages 2 and 3 (KS2 and KS3) and to plot pupil development, record interventions and then to evaluate what has made a difference. This makes the data a resource for research and long-term planning. Primary schools need to do this themselves so that they can see how children fare at different secondary schools. For example, if one of their successful pupils turns out to be struggling at secondary school they may have suggestions to make to the secondary school. This would at last make use of their intimate knowledge of a child's development, something almost entirely lost under current arrangements.

Data is obviously not knowledge, certainly not the kind that in itself provides an understanding for teachers of individual children making the physical and psychological transition between schools. So, although the transfer of data in electronic form provides swathes of raw information, there is some danger of losing sight of the students themselves. Current good practice has some well-established routines that include visits by pupils, visits by staff in both 'directions' and the transfer of physical records, often including children's work. The evidence is that relatively little use is made of these records (see Chapter 2) principally because teachers lack time to absorb them. The *Framework* document, to its credit, is adamant that 'Teachers need to know what their pupils can already do ... The "clean sheet" approach is too slow and allows pupils to fall back when they need to be challenged' (*Framework*, p. 20). Can ICT make a difference to communication about individual pupils and their actual personalities and achievements? The answer is potentially 'yes' but it will need careful co-ordination. There is space here for only a few ideas, each suggestion covers a different aspect of transition.

Pupil to pupil communication

School web sites offer a perfect opportunity to create genuine and active links between primary and secondary schools. Each school can literally develop a virtual transition part of their web site, the responsibility for which could lie with Year 6 and 7 pupils for maintenance and updating. One challenge for Year 6 is research based, they need to know what life at secondary school will be like. A second is to prepare to present themselves to their new school. What do they bring with them, what do they feel they will need? Year 7 can build up a 'virtual tour' of the school designed specifically for Year 6, every year this will need revising and improving. Individual pupils can also create an electronic diary of life during their first year. In all this it may be possible to create electronic pairs of Year 6 and 7 children who can exchange information via email whenever they want. The Year 7s might be made responsible, at certain points in the year, for initiating the dialogue, putting them in a mentorship type role. Year 7 classes might be asked to select examples of good work and to send these to primary to help Year 6 develop a greater awareness of what secondary tasks 'look like' and some of the subject literacy issues that they involve. All these ideas are focused on real communications between real people, in themselves they demand and encourage the use of sophisticated literacy skills.

Pupil to teacher

I suggested above that pupils could consider how to 'present themselves' to their new school. One of the great advantages of electronic texts and images is their provisionality. If each Year 6 pupil is made responsible for developing an electronic profile they are given enormous scope to reflect on themselves, to develop their profile over time (unlike so many school literacy tasks) and to revise and extend it. Such a profile might include a selection of appropriate images, e.g. portraits of myself, my family, my school etc., a range of texts produced during the year, perhaps even 'messages to my future teachers' in which each future subject teacher is addressed. Secondary schools will often not be sure who each teacher will be until late in the school year, or even beyond it, but because the profile can be transferred to the school it can be accessed at the point of need.

Teacher to teacher

Some advantages of electronic data transfer are considered above, one being that classroom teachers can have access to the data at the point of need. Equally important, however, are the opportunities for teachers to communicate in the spirit of dialogue as opposed to the more traditional 'handing on' model. The huge advantage of email is that it can be written and sent instantly but is not time dependent for the recipients; they respond when they are ready. The telephone, even the mobile, apparently more authentic as dialogue, is a problem as far as teachers are concerned because the nature of their work makes arranging telephone calls an elaborate and time wasteful activity.

A primary teacher's records and comments can be emailed to the Year 7 form tutor and/or pastoral head. Such records can then be rapidly distributed to subject teachers, learning support assistants, the librarian and so on. Equally they might be better simply stored in an instantly accessible form so that tutors and teachers can search them at the point of need.

The Year 7 staff, particularly the form tutor in the first term, is in a strong position to tap into the expertise of the former Year 6 teacher of any student. One of the major problems with transition is the exchange of knowledge (as opposed to inert records), which could thus be minimised. Equally students can know that their pastoral care is continuous. There are now very few teachers who think arriving at secondary school should be a naively fresh start, a 'clean sheet'; rather it should be a kind of renaissance and so each child is entitled to the excitement of a new environment but should not be hampered by being treated as if a recently arrived alien.

Many teachers may consider these ideas as desirable but impractical chiefly because of lack of time; the enormous burden of bureaucracy imposed on schools by successive regimes has taken its toll. However, the point is that ICT can do two things extremely well. First, it can improve speed and efficiency and, as it does so, it can return some time to every user and to the whole system. Secondly, and ultimately far more important for schools, it can provide information when teachers (and others) want it and this gradually leads to a feeling of agency. Teachers want to help children and if they can achieve this partly because ICT supports them, then they will use it systematically and consistently. This point applies to all teaching not just to the transition phase but the particular relevance to that phase is so obvious because of the physical nature of the move to secondary school. Our use of ICT is so new and so rapidly evolving that there may be many benefits as yet not thought of, as well as a few more problems but its value to schools engaged in transition will be increasingly significant.

Parents and the wider community

There have been so many claims made about the schools of the future and how the computer will make them community resources that one hesitates to consider this area. Equally there has been an increasing trend to suggest that schools and teachers will rapidly become redundant, everything will happen in the high-tech home. My view is that neither extreme is likely to materialize just yet. The current situation is such that there have been sufficient developments on a number of fronts in the last five years to make a consideration timely. It brings to the fore the need to consider issues about data protection and also child protection, but they are not 'new' in themselves. I will focus on a few, relatively straightforward opportunities that are well within the reach of most schools, or certainly will be within two years.

Currently, parents receive frequent generalized communications from schools and, perhaps, twice a year the 'report' on their child. As schools devise systems to make maximum use of electronic data so they can provide more regular information to parents about each child's progress. Equally, they can make available to parents more information about the curriculum, about policies and about the link between school and national policies. It will be a rare parent who pores over such information, but most interested parents are likely to find such material of relevance at certain times. Many parents will not have state-of-the-art computer access for some time but the evidence from domestic trends suggests that some parents may be much more likely to 'read' information in this form than in some school handbook. Ideally, parents and children might read such information on screen together. As interactivity develops it is even conceivable that parents can be consulted by the school with some hope of genuine response. Even mundane reminders about the school fête might be communicated with speed and minimum effort.

There is certainly scope for some improvement to transition. For example, a primary school web site can offer parents links to all the potential secondary schools that a child might move on to. Each secondary can offer its own links to primaries so that parents can be aware of the wider community that it serves.

It is harder to envisage how the cause of literacy as envisaged by the NLS might be advanced, except to say that many parents are actively engaged in the literacies of the twenty-first century on a daily basis and may themselves become increasingly critical of the narrow conception offered in school. However, one idea may help in coping with school literacy itself. The emphasis on almost all assessment in schools is through writing, in secondary schools this writing is frequently set for completion as home work. What a school (or linked body, e.g. examination board, commercial revision site, etc.) might provide is essentially models of writing, linked to particular ages and tasks. For example the History department might provide three examples of variously successful essays completed by pupils in term 1 of Year 7, giving teacher comments to show how well each piece had been realized. Such exemplar could be useful to a local primary school, to parents and to Year 7 pupils about to attempt their own assignment. The key point is the principle that such models and exemplars of writing are made available and accessible. The various internet based revision sites for GCSE have been extremely popular and this provides some evidence of how such domestic-based interaction with educational support may soon flourish.

Multimedia environments

Later chapters explore the limitations of the NLS in a number of ways and offer suggestions about how schools might go beyond its narrow focus.

They also consider, as earlier in this Introduction, how the absurd pre-scriptions of the whole curriculum are at least partly to blame for pupil and teacher disaffection. At the same time the NLS attention to 'whole-school' literacy is warmly welcomed as essentially about developing good teaching although even that has one very serious limitation, its lack of attention to the multimedia world we all inhabit. It might seem that attention to ICT is the answer and that the increasingly sophisticated skills of children and of teachers will produce the essential multi-literacies needed by all adults.

Unfortunately this view is part of the problem, not the solution. An increase in skills seems very likely but there is a real danger that the school environment will not be the place in which such skills become a part of a genuine set of literacies. One reason is that the teaching of ICT is still in its infancy and has been frequently criticized as relatively, and not surprisingly, inadequate. For example, I observed an ICT lesson taught by a highly competent ICT teacher in which Year 9 pupils exer-cised all kinds of ICT skills. They had to demonstrate their skills by designing some web pages about a topic of their choice, the topic had to be researched on the internet and had to include word-processed text, word art and captured images. The pupils did indeed demonstrate sophis-ticated skills but not a sophisticated grasp of what they were doing or why they were doing it. They had selected all kinds of foci but the major-ity of pupils had chosen rather self-indulgent topics such as the latest boy band or a premiership football club. There was no process of critiquing choice or rationale. In constructing their web information pupils were only thinking of themselves as audience and so were equally indulgent in this respect. As far as I could tell, the class were using their ICT skills but were learning nothing new. The task should have been an activity that made high demands on their literacy. The key point is that ICT skills in themselves are simply that, isolated skills.

A multimedia world demands a variety of literacies that complement each other. If schools are to make transition a success then their model of whole-school literacy must be based on this fundamental principle. All teachers should not only be teachers of language in the strict and literal sense, they should also be media teachers. This does not require them to become Media Studies experts but it does demand an engagement with their pupils', and their own, experience of media-intensive environments.

It is absolutely clear that increasing amounts of time will be spent with a screen acting as the centre of attention from the infant to the pensioner. This attention may be entirely recreational, watching certain kinds of television for example, or it may be watching an interactive white board as part of a formal lesson. It would be possible to list hundreds of educa-tional, work, entertainment and domestic functions that now involve attention to a screen (Goodwyn, 1998; 2001a); the mobile phone has become a screen in ways that very few developers would have predicted. Given this centrality, the argument for what is essentially media education becomes irresistible and its centrality to successful transition becomes vital.

The only place where Media Education has some formal status in England is at Key Stage 4 and almost entirely in English. There is a brief section about 'teaching about the moving image' in Curriculum 2000 and GCSE syllabuses require the majority of students to undertake a piece of media-related course work. In Key Stage 3 most English departments have units of work that directly or indirectly focus on media topics. However, a major problem is a lack of progression, students are frequently asked to write newspaper articles or to analyse advertisements with almost no attempt to develop this knowledge into increasing levels of sophistication. There are some teachers able to achieve this but they are certainly not helped by the nature of either the curriculum or the Literacy Strategy. There is some irony in the notion that we start work on media literacy as late as Key Stage 3 when the media are a far more influential source of knowledge for most children than formal school. In the multimedia world this must change.

One complex problem is that the teaching of Media Education still has no real place in the primary school. In one way this is not surprising. The last 15 years have been dominated first by a National Curriculum and then by an equally prescriptive Literacy Strategy. Curriculum delivery, not curriculum development, has been the order of the day. As 'Standards' of literacy are rising some might argue that there is no problem and that media-related work is merely a distraction from the more serious business of traditional print literacy. This book argues vehemently that this is a contradiction in terms. Literacy is much more than decoding and making print but we spend far too much time and money testing to make sure that schools are forced to ignore this fundamental point.

We certainly do not assess pupils' media understanding in the primary school so we have very little in the way of 'standards' to relate to. However, we do have plenty of evidence of two other important factors. First, pupils do show media understanding and a keenness to develop and enhance it, and we have had evidence of this for some time (see, for example, Buckingham, 1990; 1993). Such an understanding increasingly includes the practical dimension of making media as well as analysing it (Buckingham, Graham and Sefton Green, 1995). Part of this practical aptitude comes through the convergence of technologies, the digital camera providing an excellent example. Secondly the literacy practices of young people, as discussed in Chapter 1, are rapidly changing and schools are simply in danger of neglecting these and of ignoring their potential to make students fully engaged in formal education. We are perfectly happy for teachers to intervene constantly in developing children's print literacy so why do we almost entirely ignore their other literacies, especially in an age when their (and our) lives are dominated by media? The argument here is that both Key Stage 2 and Key Stage 3 teachers should be developing children's media literacies and that this book is suggesting that this will further improve transition and progression for pupils. This argument, more extensively developed elsewhere (Goodwyn, 1998) can be summarized as key points.

First, a vast amount of our knowledge and understanding now comes through the media; this is indisputable. However, the term 'through' is potentially misleading. All messages must be codified and so knowledge is mediated, it never passes neutrally 'through' anyone or any 'thing'. All teachers should spend some of their time enabling children to move from decoding to deconstructing. In secondary schools 'whole-school literacy' is nonsense without this fundamental principle.

Secondly, education has been conceptualized as fundamentally concerned with 'cultural capital', that is, the form of knowledge that societies give high status to even if not material reward. For the purposes of this argument, that might be simplified as 'academic' knowledge. A great deal of the knowledge brought into school by children is from the media environment that they (and we) inhabit. Occasionally this knowledge is allowed into the classroom when it coincides with academic content. However, such knowledge could and should play a consistent part in teaching and learning. Unless we bring our own views into play we cannot question them, we cannot test our knowledge and therefore deepen our understanding. Of course, much of this pupil knowledge does fit quite neatly with academic knowledge, such as a documentary about animals (Science) or a profile of a leading politician (History). Other elements, for example the concepts of character and narrator in fictions have absolute links with 'normal' work in school. But far more of this 'knowledge' is problematic and provisional. What do, for example, 10-year-old girls learn from the magazines and comics addressed directly to them? What do 12-year-old boys learn from watching MTV or from playing Tomb Raider games? Certainly these media artefacts are all powerfully engaging for children and young people, and they require all kinds of literacies in order for them to interact with them. The well-managed classroom is the forum for reflection and discussion, it should not exclude some of the fundamental influences on all our lives.

Thirdly, Citizenship is now a secondary 'subject'. Whatever benefits this innovation may bring, one disadvantage is its implicit message that secondary schools will take care of it and that it fundamentally 'belongs' there. A 'common' sense reaction might be that young people approaching the voting age are the natural targets for citizenship. However, Citizenship need not be conceptualized as like the driving test, something to pass to make sure you are safe on the roads. The critically literate citizen, as advocated above, cannot be tested and passed 'safe'. It is rather obvious to state that primary school children have shown themselves passionately committed to many 'causes' but in the rush to create Citizenship as a school 'subject' it needs stating. Key Stage 2 teachers in particular can engage with children's emerging sense of rights and responsibilities and their very deep concerns about justice. As all future citizens are interacting with the media on a daily basis, so they need to be educated about the media just as much as the topics being mediated.

Overall then schools can greatly enhance their pupils' learning by engaging with a broad definition of literacy that both includes media literacy and so requires media education. Through formal attention to media work children's own knowledge can be brought into the curriculum and employed and tested. Key Stage 2 work can provide a sound basis for Key Stage 3, promoting genuine progression and offering another curriculum strand that crosses from primary to secondary. In the transition to the adult world nothing could be more important than making young people literate in the broadest possible way.

The NLS therefore has a very serious weakness in its fixation with an outmoded version of literacy. Ironically it is at odds with the other strategy aimed at increasing the ICT competence of the whole teaching profession. For example, the whole of the *Framework* for Key Stage 3 makes hardly a reference to ICT or to any form of media-related activity. It might be argued that this specificity of definition is intended so that the rest of the curriculum, or at least the English curriculum, can address these 'other' areas. This entirely misses the point that a genuine definition of literacy would have these 'other' areas at its heart, not as alternatives. For teachers the other effect will be to frustrate them, as they wish to make maximum use of their ICT capabilities in their teaching. Once more it will be vital for schools to have the courage to be better than the official policy.

The teachers and pupils of the future

As far as teachers are concerned perhaps the most pragmatic stance to take is that, whatever they do, literacy will always be perceived as either 'in crisis' or having a brief lull, whilst political attention is elsewhere, and so the next crisis is already on its way. It seems most unlikely that we will achieve a future golden age as nostalgia has far more emotional hold than rationalized Strategies; nostalgia certainly has levels but seems to set its own standards. This view is not cynical it is a realistic reflection on the history of education which is subsumed within the history of politics. The key point is that the evidence (see, for example, the Literacy section of the Department for Education and Skills web site, 2001) suggests relatively minor fluctuations in reading standards since the 1950s. Examination results have steadily risen in quality and quantity, and it seems feasible that 50 per cent of the population will eventually have some experience of higher education. Teachers and their pupils have achieved an enormous amount but good news is weak news, a crisis is much more attractive to politicians and the media.

Realism, in this instance, is not a rejection of principle. If we accept that the sound and fury regularly generated around literacy in the public domain will always be with us to lesser or greater degrees then we can get on with the real challenge which is that, as we are ahead of society's model of literacy, we must embrace the constancy of change. Society's sense of crisis seems to stem from a fear that the literacy of tomorrow looks threateningly different to the comforts of yesterday. For example the constant cry that GCSEs are not really like O levels is, ironically, absolutely right. They were designed for a broader purpose and a much more diverse population; they are evidence of intelligent change. They should be treated by teachers, whatever others say, as one sign of society's increasing levels of literacy. Of course, even they have not been designed to assess the range of literacies that our pupils currently enjoy. We can only keep up with the real literacy of the world by paying it constant attention in the classroom; this is essentially a daily activity. We can only assess it, in an approximate way, by finding new means to that end; tests will always have a place in our repertoire but they are not much use once they become the purpose of teaching. If testing or working towards tests is the daily activity then there is not much time left for learning by pupils, and perhaps even less by teachers. The evidence of this book is that teachers neither value the current testing regime nor do they feel they are learning much from it.

Developing literacy is not simply a daily activity because this may give rise to simplistic notions of a Literacy hour or something similar. Literacy is a constant and it needs constant attention. Hence the role of all teachers is, in every sense, to *take care of* their pupils' literacy. This is the paradox and the challenge of the future. We want to take as much care as possible of children as they make that transition from the relative security of the primary school to the overwhelming and alien landscape of the secondary. In this area (see above) there are real signs of better means to this end.

Literacy, as this book illustrates in abundance, is far more problematic. It is something of a paradox in that our taking care of children's literacy means we cannot fully endorse the grand design of the National Literacy Strategy. All its folders, manuals, videos and armies of consultants do not make it right, indeed its relentless insistence on its own certainties reveals both its insecurities and its lack of trust in experienced professionals. This point is consistently made throughout the book. However, the attention to literacy is likely to bring positive benefits to teachers and pupils. Their attention to literacy will expose the narrowness and exclusivity of the NLS model, and secondary schools will do a better job then their restrictive brief. Teachers talking to each other about literacy, the literacies of their subjects and about the relationship between technology and changes to literacy, will inspire some genuinely exciting conversations. It is these conversations that lead to school 'improvement'; when teachers talk about learning, they learn. This book is dedicated to them and the following chapters have all been written to help them in that crucial process.

References

British Educational Communications and Technology Agency (BECTa) (2001a) *Primary Schools of the Future – Achieving Today*, Coventry, BECTa.

British Educational Communications and Technology Agency (BECTa) (2001b) *The Secondary School of the Future*, Coventry, BECTa.

Buckingham, D. (1990) *Watching Media Learning: Making Sense of Media Education*, London, Falmer Press.

Buckingham, D. (1993) *Children Talking Television: The Making of Television Literacy*, London, Falmer Press.

Buckingham, D. (2000) *After the Death of Childhood: Growing up in the Age of Electronic Media*, London, Polity Press.

Buckingham, D., Graham, J. and Sefton Green, J. (1995) *Making Media: Practical Production in Media Education*. London, The English and Media Centre.

Carter, R. (ed.) (1990) *Knowledge about Language and the Curriculum: The LINC Reader*, London, Hodder and Stoughton.

Department for Education and Skills (2001) *The Standards Site*, www.standards.dfes.gov.uk/literacy.

Freire, P. and Macedo, D. (1987) *Literacy: Reading the Word and the World*, South Hadley, MA, Bergin and Garvey.

Framework for Teaching English: Years 7, 8, and 9, DfEE, London.

Goodwyn, A. (1997) 'Signs of growth but not of status: management and media education', *English and Media Magazine*, **37** (Autumn), pp. 36-9.

Goodwyn, A. (ed.) (1998) *Literary and Media Texts in Secondary English:*

New Approaches. London, Cassells.

Goodwyn, A. (2001a) 'Cultural rights in the convergence', in C. Durrant and Beavis (eds), *P[ICT]URES of English: Teachers, Learners and Technology*. Kent Town, Australian Association for the Teaching of English, Wakefield Press.

Goodwyn, A. (2001b) 'Second tier professionals; English teachers in England', *L1: Educational Studies in Language and Literature*, vol. 1 (forthcoming).

Goodwyn, A. and Findlay, K. (1999) 'The Cox models revisited: English teachers' views of their subject and of the National Curriculum', *English in Education*, 33(6), pp. 19-31.

Meek, M. (1995) *On Being Literate*, London, Bodley Head.

Office for Standards in Education (OFSTED)(2001) *The Annual Report of Her Majesty's Chief Inspector of Schools, 1999–2000: Standards and Quality in Education*, London, OFSTED.

1

Literacy in transition

Andrew Goodwyn and Kate Findlay

This opening chapter expands on the Introduction and explores the broad issues of transition and of literacy, setting the scene for the chapters that follow. It undertakes a review of much of the research and practice in both areas, offering readers the chance to review these sources for their own development.

'Literacy' and 'transition' are two issues which have been the focus of attention for educationalists for a number of years; both are regarded as problems which must be alleviated. 'Transition' is frequently used as a term to describe the move from one stage of education to another, and our focus is on the important transition between primary and secondary schooling. Since the 1970s this has attracted the attention of numerous official and independent research studies which, taken together, provide evidence of a hiatus and frequently a dip in pupil progress, particularly in the first year of secondary school.

Whilst earlier studies included assessments of reading and 'language' skills, the current drive to improve literacy standards has encompassed the transition issue, and this focus on literacy has provided common ground for teachers and pupils in the separate phases of education. In September 2001 the National Literacy Strategy, in place in primary schools for three years, was extended to Key Stage 3 and one of its main objectives is to provide continuity and ensure progression in pupils' literacy learning between the phases.

On the face of it, this policy initiative does make matters simpler. Yet the concept of 'literacy', what it is and how it should be taught and assessed, is not a simple matter. The problem of transition has been aligned with a hotly debated issue. For literacy, once conceived unproblematically as an ability to read and write, has been complicated to the extent that the concept itself is in transition, at a time when government policies are intent upon pinning it down to standardized tests and benchmarks.

Research over the past 20 years has developed a more complex understanding of literacy which profoundly challenges the 'basic skills' model. Literacy is seen to be located in social practices which are formed and function in particular social contexts. The idea of a literate (or illiterate) individual can only therefore make sense in relation to some context, and the notion of a single literacy gives way to a plurality of literacies (Heath, 1983; Street, 1984). This broader concept is potentially very powerful for educationalists as the basis for recognizing that pupils need to develop a repertoire of literacy practices in order to access both the school curriculum and the complexities of contemporary life. In addition to developing this schooled literacy, it makes it imperative for teachers to be sensitive to the literacy practices and events pupils experience outside school and the relationship between home and school literacies. And above all it moves beyond a simplistic, or what Street calls an 'autonomous', model of literacy to recognize that some literacies are more powerful than others and all are inherently ideological. They contain within them world views, which can never be neutral and imply differential power relations, in ways that are often taken for granted and invisible. The ideological effects of literacy are transparent but nowhere are they more powerful than in educational settings.

This social view of literacy problematizes the validity of standard assessment tests as reliable indicators of pupils' literacy ability. It is very striking how the voices of teachers who speak in this volume consistently criticize test validity. These tests carry the risk of reducing the rich variety of language uses to a set of discrete skills. And premised, as current Standard Assessment Tests (SATs) are, on print literacy, they do not adequately engage with the new kinds of literacy practices which pupils already experience outside school, and need to participate in if they are to make meaning and communicate effectively in a world permeated by new information and communication technologies. Teachers are themselves in transition as they adapt to the challenge of the National Grid for Learning and to developing innovative pedagogies which incorporate literacy practices associated with new technologies, yet it is axiomatic that what counts as literacy in the school context is what gets tested.

This chapter reflects some of the issues and debates which surround these various understandings of the idea of transition. Whilst much of the research we present lies within the official discourse on literacy, our analytical work rests on an understanding that literacy is too important to be confined to frameworks and the parameters of policies, and that schools have a responsibility to pay attention to the literacy competencies pupils, in all their cultural and linguistic diversity, have and need to develop if they are to maximize their learning potential and life opportunities.

The transition from primary to secondary schooling

In order to understand the current relationship between literacy and transition, it will be useful to summarize the most significant research studies which have attended to the two issues. Taken together, these studies identify three main causes for a lack of progression over the transition period:

- different teaching styles in the two phases
- secondary schools adopting a clean slate/fresh start approach rather than focusing on continuity
- poor liaison between the phases, in terms of professional co-operation and the transfer of information about pupils.

Before the National Curriculum

The first and still the most comprehensive study to investigate the 'transfer' issue was the ORACLE (Observational Research and Classroom Learning Evaluation) Project, carried out between 1975 and 1980. The study of transfer to two schools for 9–13-year-olds, two schools for 11–14-year-olds and two schools for 12–18-year-olds revealed that there was 'something of a hiatus in their progress on the basic skills'.

> All classes and almost all children in the primary school made progress (in the basic skills). However, this was not so in the first year of transfer to secondary education. Not only were average levels of progress a good deal lower in the first year after transfer ... but for the first time substantial members of pupils made losses in absolute terms. (Croll, in Galton and Willcocks, 1983, p. 81)

Results suggested that 40 per cent of pupils do less well in the first year of secondary than in the last year of primary school. This conclusion rests on evidence from tests in Maths, language skills and reading administered during the final term at the feeder school and at the end of the first year in the transfer schools. Validity of tests notwithstanding, the study remains interesting because it attempts to categorize pupil 'type' and teaching 'styles', adopting an American-style process-product orientation. Primary school teachers were seen to work closely with individuals and groups, with whole-class teaching occupying twice as much time in the secondary school as in the primary classroom; this change was associated with increased pupil engagement with the work. The 'class enquirer' category of teachers who used a high percentage of whole-class teaching was more effective in bringing pupils on in language and mathematics, but not in reading. The study reported a striking difference between boys and girls, with girls performing better in their first year, particularly in reading where under half the boys but three-quarters of the girls made progress. One interesting finding was that a fifth of the pupils, predominantly boys, proved the exception to the rule, making progress after standing still in their last year at primary school.

Subsequent studies took from the ORACLE Project the basic assumption that the 'hiatus' in pupil progress should be a matter for concern. Many focused on pastoral concerns, the social and emotional aspects of transition (Benyon, 1985; Measor and Woods, 1984). Others were concerned with academic progress and contributing factors were proposed, such as the 'fresh start' approach adopted by secondary schools (Gorwood, 1986; Steed and Sudworth, 1985) which fail to use assessment and other information from feeder primary schools. Arrangements were often unsystematic and 'personal', with primary schools varying a great deal in what they chose to report about transferring pupils.

The National Curriculum

The introduction of a National Curriculum, a common curriculum for 11–16-year-olds organized around a framework of attainment targets with SATs in the core subjects, was based on the understanding that pupil progress should be continuous and that curriculum continuity would facilitate it. A uniform system of assessment would provide test results for Key Stage 2 pupils available to secondary schools, thus safeguarding the reliability of assessment and providing a solution to the liaison problem. The transition problem would be alleviated, ensuring 'progression within and between primary and secondary education and will help the continuity and coherence which is too often lacking in what they are taught' (DES, 1987, p. 4).

Yet the new arrangements did little to bridge the divide; subsequent studies reported that transfer continued to be a problematic area leading to a decline in pupil performance (Nicholson, 1990; Taylor, 1994; Williams and Howley, 1989). Secondary schools distrusted and frequently ignored Key Stage 2 results, regarded them as unreliable as baseline information and continued to adopt a 'clean-slate' approach administering their own tests to new pupils (Brookes and Goodwyn, 1998; DfEE, 1997a, 1997b; Huggins and Knight, 1997; Lee, Harris and Dickson, 1995; Shagen and Kerr, 1999). In 1996, the School Curriculum and Assessment Association (SCAA) produced a booklet, *Promoting Continuity between Key Stage 2 and Key Stage 3* which assumed that secondary schools should be able to 'plan on the basis of pupils having a more common experience across the subjects of the National Curriculum' (SCAA, 1996, p. 13), and that the problems could be solved through improved communication and administration. Despite the more secondary-type subject-based curriculum now imposed on primary schools, however, there was little evidence that this had facilitated a higher degree of curriculum continuity and progression. The most recent study (Hargreaves and Galton, 1999), which replicates the ORACLE study (albeit on a much smaller scale), reports that 42 per cent of the pupil sample failed to make progress in English language and 38 per cent in reading after transfer to secondary school. For most pupils these differences were small. However, 7 per cent (of pupils) at Year 7 made significant losses of somewhere between a quarter and a third of the possible marks.

Studies into the general issue of transition are likely to continue. However, with the National Literacy Strategy moving into secondary schools, the concern over the language/reading performance of pupils in transition is likely to be subsumed into this drive to improve literacy standards.

The National Literacy Strategy

In August 1997, the Literacy Task Force, set up in May 1996 by David Blunkett whilst he was Shadow Secretary of State for Education and Employment, published its final report, *The Implementation of the National Literacy Strategy* (DfEE, 1997a). The new government (the first Labour government for 17 years) made literacy a priority with the promise to raise standards so that 80 per cent of 11-year-olds would reach level 4 and above in Key Stage 2 English tests by 2002. (In 1996, 57 per cent of pupils had reached this standard.)

Whilst the National Curriculum provided detailed prescription of curriculum content and assessment, it had never intruded in any significant way upon teaching methods. By contrast, the *Framework for Teaching* (DfEE, 1998) represents a direct intervention pedagogy. Setting out termly teaching objectives for the 5–11 age range, teachers are expected to deliver a dedicated Literacy Hour to all pupils during each school day. The structure of time and class management details both content and how it should be taught. Teaching objectives are divided into three strands, at word level (sounds, spelling and vocabulary), sentence level (grammatical knowledge and punctuation) and text level (comprehension and composition) work. A mixture of whole-class teaching and guided, shared and independent reading and writing activities is prescribed, with a clear emphasis on direct teaching both the whole class and groups. The notion of the nurturing, facilitating, child-centred primary practitioner is challenged and teachers are required to 'teach for 100 per cent' of the hour. In addition, the *Framework* suggests that literacy work should happen outside the hour, linked to work in other curriculum areas, and that additional time may be needed for reading to the class, independent reading and extended writing.

From the start, it was clear that secondary schools were implicated in the measure; the final section of the Literacy Task Force report, *The Implementation of the National Literacy Strategy,* stated that:

> Every secondary school should specialise in literacy and set targets for improvement in English. Similarly, every teacher should contribute to promoting it . . . In shaping their plans it is essential that secondary schools do not see work on reading and writing as exclusively the province of a few teachers in the English and learning support departments. (DfEE, 1997a, para. 112)

The recommendations for secondary schools included a specific focus on transition:

> Because it is vitally important to ensure that there is continuity between primary and secondary schools in the efforts to improve literacy, we recommend that in their strategy for literacy, local education authorities give deliberate attention to creating and maintaining co-operation between secondary schools and their feeder primary schools. (Ibid., para. 119)

The recommendations began to impact upon secondary schools and the idea of 'language across the curriculum' (see Chapter 2) was informally resurrected, informing the series of booklets produced by the School Curriculum and Assessment Authority (SCAA) in 1997 outlining the use of language in secondary subjects (*Use of Language: a Common Approach*, SCAA, 1997). An Her Majesty's Inspectorate (HMI) survey of 49 literacy-focused schools, conducted in the Autumn term of 1997, reported that secondary schools were at an early stage in their policies and practice and that most failed to monitor and evaluate their efforts (DfEE, 1997b). Whilst many schools were developing their own initiatives, as our research at the time revealed, in September 1998 22 LEAs began Key Stage 3 Literacy Initiatives financed by the DfEE Standards Fund; bids were favoured if they 'focused on literacy development in year 7 and the crossover from primary to secondary'. In 1998, the first Summer Literacy Schools (SLSs) were provided, and the following year, host schools were presented with a follow-on programme to include a co-ordinated literacy curriculum for Year 7, planned around objectives from the National Literacy Strategy and lessons based on the Literacy Hour. All these measures were specifically designed to address the needs of pupils 'with significant deficiencies in their skills as readers and writers' as they transferred to secondary school (DfEE, 1999a).

The evaluation of the Summer Literacy Schools (Sainsbury, Whetton, Mason and Shagen, 1998) revealed that there remained a significant 'dip' in pupils' reading levels between the May of the final year at primary school and the following September, irrespective of whether they had attended an SLS or not. Speculating on the reasons for this, Sainsbury et al. suggested that the motivational factor, high for both pupils and teachers at the time of Key Stage 2 tests, is absent at the start of secondary school, and that the easing off of pedagogical input in the last few months of primary school followed by the summer holiday are important factors. The anxiety of moving to a new school may also, it is suggested, lead to a decline in attainment. They conclude that 'a major research programme to investigate this issue and its bearing upon standards should be undertaken' (ibid., p. 80).

No major research project has happened. However, the pilot projects were inspected by HMI and, looking back at the process which has resulted in the Key Stage 3 Strategy, this was the crucial point at which a spirit of enquiry and a serious attempt to confront the issue of literacy in transition in all its complexity might have produced some meaningful answers. The HMI report identified 18 issues arising from the inspections of the pilot projects which schools would need to address, some of which have been side-stepped in the Strategy (Hertrich, 1999). Most importantly, HMI were ready to regard the concept of literacy in a broad sense: 'Literacy development is inextricably connected with the development of the whole young person and is linked to pupils' perceptions of themselves and their place in the world'; 'There are other "literacies" besides reading and writing which schools need to develop, for example pupils' information literacy' (DfEE, 1997b).

Our own research into secondary schools' views about literacy and the initiatives they have developed over this period will be presented in Chapter 2. What is striking is the time that has lapsed between the first serious official attention to secondary schools and literacy and the implementation of a policy. Schools have been left largely to their own devices for three years. Our experience over the period suggests that schools lost momentum and were unwilling to go too far with their own policies once it became clear that something would be imposed from above.

In September 2000, a national pilot in 150 schools from 17 LEAs of a Key Stage 3 Strategy began (*Transforming Key Stage 3: National Pilot*, DfEE, 2000). Building on primary achievements and promoting continuity between Key Stage 2 and Key Stage 3 were key objectives of the pilot strategy. However, the term 'pilot' hardly seems appropriate as the decision to introduce the *Framework* had clearly already been taken. Our research has not been able to identify any genuine evaluation leading to any significant adjustment in the move from 'pilot' to implementation. The first annual report of the team evaluating the whole Numeracy and Literacy Strategy project (Earl et al., 2000) does not mention evaluation, choosing the more organic sounding word 'evolution' (ibid., p. 6) instead, this report is discussed in more depth below.

The *Key Stage 3 National Strategy: Framework for Teaching English: Years 7, 8 and 9* was published in March 2001 and introduced in all schools from September 2001 (DfEE, 2001). Essentially an English *Framework*, it is structured around the word, sentence and text-level organization of the primary *Framework* and advocates approaches to teaching and learning which replicate the structure and styles of teaching in the primary Strategy. 'Literacy across the curriculum' is a key informing principle, and with the new National Curriculum Orders literacy objectives are expected to be included by all subject teachers in planning their lessons.

How will the Key Stage 3 Strategy be implemented by secondary schools? Will the idea of literacy implied by its stipulations speak meaningfully to secondary teachers? Will it provide a solution to the problem of 'literacy in transition'? What does the available research tell us about the ways in which secondary schools conceptualize literacy and engage with the issue of pupils' literacy learning? In this light Chapter 5, where experienced English teachers critique the whole initiative, makes especially powerful reading.

Literacy in context

The current drive to improve literacy standards is underpinned by a concern to improve teacher effectiveness and school effectiveness (Beard, 2000; Reynolds, 1998). The recently DfEE commissioned Hay McBer Report is the latest attempt to delineate the characteristics of the prototype 'effective teacher'. However it is also important to note the whole NLS project is not actually a response to yet another crisis. For example, the review of research available on the Standards website (DES, 2001) is emphatic: 'standards in literacy among British primary school children have largely remained stable over the period between 1948 and 1996'. The Strategy is therefore designed 'to raise these standards substantially' and the argument is based more on the fact that several other countries perform consistently better in international comparative tests and that British performance also has 'a long tail of underachievement'. This latter point is especially of concern in relation to transition. This overview is somewhat problematic in itself. The term 'British' must be a loose one as the education systems of Scotland and Northern Ireland are distinctively different to those of England and Wales; the latter country is now devolving rapidly and has already abolished school league tables in a radical departure from English policy.

Overall the Standards site does provide a wealth of information about research into literacy (and school effectiveness) but it suffers from a combination of 'officialese' and 'web site vagueness'. It is unclear when sections have been written, who has summarized the research, whether any updating has ever taken place and so on. It is not surprising, given the NLS's initial concentration on Key Stages 1 and 2, that the vast majority of cited evidence concerns primary schooling, but it is of concern that there is very little evidence at all cited to help secondary schools as they face a huge challenge.

The National Literacy Strategy embraces many of the recommendations from the growing body of academic research in this field, together with the characteristics of effective literacy teachers outlined in various Office for Standards in Education (OFSTED) Inspections. However, as Reynolds (1998) observes, any attempt to 'map' these onto existing practice by way of a one for all policy ignores the crucial consideration of context. At school level, Reynolds summarizes various research studies which point to a number of contextual factors, relating to:

- the socio-economic status of the catchment area
- the level of effectiveness of the school
- the trajectory of effectiveness of the school (improving, static, declining)
- the region of the school
- the urban/rural status of the school
- the religious status of the school
- the culture/history of the school
- the primary/secondary status of the school.

In addition to these complicating factors, every classroom is a further subcontext, and Reynolds' research review suggests that the within-school variation (by department in secondary school, by teacher in primary school) on pupils' levels of achievement or 'value added' may be four times greater than the variation between schools. This suggests that there may be problems with universal measures such as the NLS and that they must work at the level of the teacher, not just the whole school. A full consideration of this context specificity of literacy provides a useful vantage point for evaluating the NLS.

The most vulnerable groups of pupils at the time of transition are those on free school meals, those with special educational needs and pupils with bilingual backgrounds (Galton et al., 1999) The Strategy includes provision for Special Educational Needs and English as a Second Language pupils (Section 4 'Additional guidance on inclusion'). 'Inclusion' is a recognition that all pupils are entitled to equal access to the school curriculum, but it should not ignore the contexts of pupils' lives which extend beyond the school gates, into literacy domains which are either validated and valued in school or wished away by applying more schooled literacy. Matters of class, gender and ethnicity are intricately connected to literacy learning, the 'whole young person' that HMI are concerned with. If the official discourse on literacy is a gendered discourse, or if it excludes the literacy experiences which, for example, bilingual learners encounter in their homes and communities, then there are important implications in terms of equal access to school literacy. From this perspective, the years of research into the problem of transition has rested on a false divide between, on the one hand, personal and social effects, and, on the other, the impact of transition on academic progress. A social and contextual understanding of literacy collapses the categories into each other so that the pastoral concerns (such as pupils' self-identity [Measor and Woods, 1984]; friendships [Benyon, 1985]; motivation and enjoyment [Galton et al., 1999]) cannot be regarded as separate from the concern for pupils' literacy development.

Research into secondary teachers' views about literacy

The Key Stage 3 *Framework* has been devised without any specific reference to evidence which might inform its objectives and strategies. Training is available to teachers for implementing the measures, but any questioning of the fundamental reasons for doing so (see Chapter 5) are not invited. Any drafting, consultation and evaluation processes seem to have happened behind closed doors. Based on a particular conception of literacy, it may or may not be congenial to the variety of contexts in which it will operate.

The evidence of how secondary teachers conceptualize literacy and their role in teaching it within their subjects is indeed patchy. One useful study is reported in *Managing the Literacy Curriculum* (Webster, Beveridge and Reed, 1996). The book is the outcome of a research study and project working with secondary schools to develop a whole-school approach to literacy, regarding the transition phase as an 'issue of fundamental importance'. What is particularly interesting is the attempt to map teachers in terms of their concepts of literacy, in both primary and secondary schools, and the results suggest that teachers do generally have an intricate and consistent understanding of literacy. However, this did not translate easily into any understanding on the part of secondary teachers that literacy is an integral part of their subject teaching and only English teachers were used to 'thinking of literacy' in this way. Lesson observations suggested that pupils experience a 'culture shock' as they 'move from the more interactive settings of the primary school where literacy is constructed, or scaffolded within lesson contexts, and on to the loosely coupled, content-driven secondary curriculum where literacy competence is expected or dealt with peripherally' (ibid., p. 97) Getting closer to the heart of what school literacy is about, and beyond the reductive accounts of test scores, they note that, 'The function of texts, in both written and read formats, change markedly between school subjects', and, 'children need to be actively prepared for this shift' (ibid., p. 97).

A smaller-scale study by David Wray and Maureen Lewis (1999) was conducted over a two-year period to ascertain secondary teachers' views about literacy. Whilst they did not find any resistance from teachers who indicated that they accepted their role in pupils' literacy development, they found teachers unsure of what they should do, and a high proportion were not using well-established strategies to support literacy. What they describe as a 'culture of blame' was seen to prevail, with almost half of teacher respondents agreeing that, 'If primary teachers did their job correctly regarding literacy we could get on with teaching our subject specialism' (ibid., p. 273–82).

The overall picture suggests that, prior to the *Framework*, there has been little meaningful co-operation between the two phases, and Year 7 teachers have remained ignorant of the changes in primary practice brought about by the National Curriculum and the Literacy Hour in primary schools (Shagen and Kerr, 1999). Our most recent research, reported in Chapter 2, suggests that the situation is changing, that secondary practitioners are more aware of the need to be informed about primary practice, and the Key Stage 3 *Framework*, which is close to the primary *Framework* in terms of teaching structures and strategies, will accelerate this process. However, it would be naive to think that secondary teachers are ready to regard themselves primarily as literacy teachers, and their subject 'specialisms' will not change overnight. There is evidence that even in English, teachers from the two phases operate very different subject models (Marshall and Brindley, 1998) which result in discontinuities in pupils' experience.

School-centric literacy

We suggest that there is an increasingly consensual definition of what we call school-centric literacy. This term follows on from work done by Street and others (see above) who use the term 'school literacy'; we have added the 'centric' to emphasize and clarify in the way 'logocentric' does how absolutely and exclusively this literacy belongs in school. We argue that this definition informs the thinking of both the agents of the strategy and of the increasingly important school agents (see Chapter 2). It is not therefore the definition of, for example, all teachers. Indeed, interview data in particular reveals the myriad ways that agents plan to overcome anticipated 'resistance'. We feel that most of the agents see resistance as essentially ignorance rather than knowledgeable subversion; there is a constant tendency in their discourse which reveals their mission to enlighten. Part of their mission is to help teachers adopt the consensual definition of school-centric literacy.

We argue that this definition, outlined below, is not that of much of the research community (or of practising teachers) which has increasingly adopted the concept of *literacies,* sometimes *multi-literacies.* There the debate has often centred on how many *literacies* we might identify, e.g. visual, print, computer, media, etc., and on to what extent these literacies overlap or compete with each other. There has also been much work on the value positions and status of these various literacies with the general suggestion that the former dominance of print literacy is now under threat and that the new literacies, especially those associated with technology will soon supplant print literacy in every sense including status. A point often made there, and relevant to this discussion, is that schools remain technologically primitive whilst the real world and the domestic space are often sophisticated omni-tech environments (whilst acknowledging that many homes are not). We feel that our research (see Chapter 2) suggests that ICT not only remains outside the school-centric definition but, as we analyse it, actually reinforces the essentially traditional notion specified in the NLS; this is more fully discussed below.

What exactly is the NLS definition of literacy that secondary schools should at least consider? Rather interestingly it was *not* in the general Guidance to Schools entitled *Transforming Key Stage 3: National Pilot* (DfEE, 2000). Within the pack was the *Framework for Teaching English Years 7–9* (DfEE, 2001) which has since moved from draft to 'official' status with no obvious changes. Here in the section entitled 'Rationale' we have these two paragraphs:

> The notion of literacy embedded in the objectives is much more than simply the acquisition of basic skills which is sometimes implied by the word: it encompasses the ability to recognise, understand and manipulate the conventions of language, and develop pupils' ability to use language imaginatively and flexibly. The Framework also encompasses speaking and listening to support English teachers in planning to meet the full demands of the National Curriculum, and to tie in the development of oral skills with parallel demands in written text.
>
> English teachers have the leading role in providing pupils with the knowledge, skills and understanding they need to read, write, speak and listen effectively, but this document also addresses other subject staff. Language is the prime medium through which pupils learn and express themselves across the curriculum, and all teachers have a stake in effective literacy. A set of cross-curricular Language

for Learning objectives has been identified to support the co-ordination of departments working together on literacy (Ibid. pp.9-10).

In order to reinforce the idea that these skills are not basic, the next section outlining the 'overall aim of the framework' (ibid., p. 10) states that it is 'to enable all pupils to develop sophisticated literacy skills' and as result at the end of Year 9 each pupil is expected to be:

A shrewd and fluent independent reader:
- orchestrating a range of strategies to get at meaning in text, including inferential and evaluative skills;
- sensitive to the way meanings are made;
- reading in different ways for different purposes, including skimming to quickly pick up the gist of a text, scanning to locate specific information, close reading to follow complex passages and re-reading to uncover layers of meaning;
- reflective, critical and discriminating in response to a wide range of printed and visual texts.

A confident writer:
- able to write for a variety of purposes and audiences, knowing the conventions and beginning to adapt and develop them;
- able to write imaginatively, effectively and correctly;
- able to shape, express, experiment with and manipulate sentences;
- able to organise, develop, spell and punctuate writing accurately.

An effective speaker and listener:
- with the clarity and confidence to convey a point of view or information;
- using talk to explore, create, question and revise ideas, recognising language as a tool for learning;
- able to work effectively with others in a range of roles;
- having a varied repertoire of styles, which are used appropriately.
  (Ibid., p. 10)

Clearly the emphasis is on what a pupil can do, and with the current policy emphasis on Citizenship this is not surprising. There are some interesting words to highlight. Readers should be shrewd, independent, reflective, critical and discriminating: this sounds rather like critical literacy of the Freirian variety. However, it does not exist in a vacuum. These readers will, for example, be displaying these critical capacities on the narrow cultural heritage model of the English National Curriculum, they will be assessed on their literary powers at the end of Key Stage 3 on two scenes from a Shakespeare play. An examination of the content to be covered in Key Stage 3 reveals a very heavy emphasis on linguistic terminology and language rules. In this respect the content certainly displays continuity with the existing Key Stage 2 Literacy Hour. We are suggesting therefore, that the critical element is severely blunted by the wooden content of the curriculum. Some of our previous work, investigating the views of English teachers, has revealed how frustrated they are by the extremely narrow and conservative nature of the English curriculum (Goodwyn and Findlay, 2000).

Our essential point is that this school-centric definition of literacy remains just that, a means of succeeding within a traditional academic curriculum. In one significant way this is to be welcomed as it is an honest acknowledgement that schools, secondary ones especially, place enormous demands on children and the literacy they require is a very particular one. The Qualifications and Curriculum Authority (QCA), following from the now defunct School Curriculum Authority (SCA), is busy reinventing the Language Across the Curriculum wheel by offering lots of guidance about literacy across the curriculum and reinforcing this with statutory requirements that teachers of all subjects should demonstrate their awareness in their planning and teaching. This will also be a feature of Initial Teacher Training. OFSTED can then check that all parts of the system are compliant. Essentially this emphasis, if not the process adopted to create it, mirrors what Barnes, Britton and Rosen were asking for in the 1970s (see Chapter 2). It is also further evidence of how the NLS is affecting literally every teacher. Pupils should become very effectively trained in school-centric literacy and one would expect Standards that test this literacy to rise quite dramatically and rapidly.

Literacy in the twenty-first century

The element missing from this current definition is a simple one. As the curriculum is essentially preservative, this school-centric literacy remains singularly divorced from the social experience of children. It pays very little attention, for example, to the whole area of media and electronic text, especially to the multi-modal world of the Internet and interactive technologies. It states at the general level that it at least acknowledges these areas, e.g. 'a wide range of printed and visual texts' (see above) but at the level of classroom detail this breadth disappears. It would be interesting to ask what 'word' and 'sentence' level are in a film? There are answers to that question but the framework is not interested in them. Equally, any attention to multi-modal literacy, however superficial is placed within the reading context. Under 'writing', every phrase is strictly about writing in its most traditional form; where, one might ask, does producing a web page come in?

This issue is neatly illustrated by examining one complete section from the review of research on the Standards site, the section entitled 'Literacy and Information', as follows:

> The words of the Bullock Report also had a prescient ring in relation to the reading and writing of information. The Report argued that dealing efficiently with information should be recognised as one of the major problems in modern society (DES, 1975, p. 95).
>
> The subsequent growth in information and communications technology adds further support to the Report's suggestions for educational practice. Individuals need not only to cope with information efficiently but to organise their own use of it. This involves several interrelated processes: identifying information needs; knowing where relevant sources are and how to access them; using appropriate criteria to judge their value; and selecting the limited number of sources which suit individuals best. In this way, individuals are more consciously able to cope with the demands of the 'information age'.
>
> Literacy education has more recently been influenced by studies of the different genres in which non-fiction texts are written. Drawing upon earlier work by Gunther Kress (1982) and Michael Halliday (1985), a number of Australian writers have developed theories which have linked different kinds of texts to the social purposes they fulfil (e.g. Martin, 1989). Learning to read and write in particular genres is linked to certain realms of social interaction, influence and power (Cope and Kalantzis, 1993, p. 7).

It is quite extraordinary that the most recent citation here is 1993 and that there is not even a mention of the British Educational Communications and Technology Agency or its predecessor the National Council for Educational Technology. It is not that the sentiments expressed in these three paragraphs are not valuable, it is simply that they are so utterly out of date. And that is the complete section on literacy and information in the 'information age'.

Equally, one might take the example of text messaging and ask what is its relationship to this framework? Not because text messaging in its current form should be compulsorily taught in schools but because it is a perfect example of the interplay between technology and written language. The quill, the biro, the typewriter, the word processor, and now the mobile phone, liberate and constrain the 'writer' and human ingenuity comes into play. Is there such a thing as an 'accurate' text message? The answer is definitely yes if we mean one that communicates an effective meaning to its recipient. Text messaging is a highly conventionalized and codified linguistic and symbolic rule bound system which has evolved from the 'normal' expectations of current written language. So, the place of text messaging in school (apart from under the desk) is as an object of reflection and investigation. Pupils and teachers can consider it together as a phenomenon of literacy and might well employ it and try it under that heading considering why it lies outside school-centric literacy.

Text messaging also illustrates a further key point. It can only be described as a form of discourse and, like all such forms, it tends towards the exclusive. One of the chief values of the subject English is that it is that place within the formal curriculum where discourses themselves are the subject of study. In this sense the focus on English as the key subject for literacy is absolutely right. Chapter 3 looks at how within the larger curriculum the discourses of, for example, Geography and History, in some ways closely related, are yet exclusive of each other. As argued above all teachers need to teach explicitly the discourse of their subjects, enabling pupils both to be literate in each subject domain and to cope with the transition to the narrowly specialized environment of the secondary school.

However, within English and possibly other areas of the curriculum, there is an absolute need to explore the much broader issues of literacy that are grounded in the complex world of social discourses. Here, issues to do with power, race, gender, class, community and culture come to the fore as part of a much deeper examination of the literacies available at any point in history. The formal literacy of school is enormously powerful and therefore it is all the more important that schools reveal that power rather than merely being exploited by it. There will clearly be huge pressure on English to 'deliver' high test scores, narrowly gauged on school literacy. This pressure is likely to be at its greatest in schools where socio-economic and cultural factors make it the hardest to achieve. Therefore English itself will be under pressure to justify its existence or be replaced by capital L Literacy; this will be an irony to members of the profession who always believed that the capital L came before Literature (and of course Leavis).

English will have a corner to fight and its professional community should be under no illusions about that. The tendency of the literacy hour format has been to reduce attention to whole texts, whether 'literary fiction' or other, and this tendency will increase in the next few years. Pupils deemed below the expected literacy level are especially likely to spend their time separated from the pleasures of reading any books apart from the dubiously designated 'progress units'. English needs to argue the case then for the much broader view of literacy which includes what the 'academy' expects but resolutely resists its tendency to exclusivity. Ironically the original conception of the National Curriculum for English adopted just such an inclusive approach in 1989.

The current, emphatically explicit focus on literacy in school, is one more reminder about the transitoriness of definitions of literacy. Literacy is necessarily always in transit. One of the great benefits of more than a century of what might crudely be called mass literacy is just that understanding, although myths about golden ages of literacy, just like spelling and grammar, are always in vogue amongst politicians and the media. Schools should at least try to debunk such myths and should argue for the much more humane and enlightened concept of literacies; it is a quintessentially democratic notion.

It is also a much more honest recognition that technology and literacy now have an inextricable relationship. Once we invented a symbolic language the possibilities became infinite. The 'original' computers were conceptualized purely in relation to numbers but the human drive to communicate has mutated them into just another tool for making symbolic meanings, numbers are still allowed but at a minimum for most users. Chapter 2 will explore this issue in more depth but the essential point here is that school literacy, currently conceived, is in historical terms unusually out of touch with the kinds of literacies both prevalent and highly valued in many prestigious work environments.

For example, it might be argued that the school curriculum should devote considerable time to teaching pupils how to 'read' the internet. In fact many schools are tentatively engaging with this issue. Research by BECTa (2001a and 2001b) and work by OFSTED are both investigating how schools are adjusting to the development of the National Grid for Learning and the impact of the New Opportunities Funding training scheme for teachers. Other factors under consideration are the marked increase in personal/home use by teachers themselves and the general trend towards 'wired' households with regular Internet access. In some schools teachers are expecting their pupils to use a whole range of sophisticated software, to communicate regularly by email, to research topics chiefly through the Internet and present their academic work in multimedia formats, sending in assignments as attachments. This description parallels a very normal office environment in the 'adult' world.

This recognition that pupils and teachers are dealing with many and variable literacies also acknowledges that not only do we need expanded definitions of the term literacy but a realization that we are working with a much more complex and demanding scenario. To be literate in any democratically participatory way in the twenty-first century makes many demands on each citizen. So we can welcome genuine attention to this area whilst arguing constantly that a nineteenth-century model of reading and writing will create problems not solutions.

The end of the beginning

The transition from the relatively intimate primary school to the generally large-scale and intimidating secondary school is always going to be difficult. The experiment with middle schools (see Chapter 4) remains interesting but marginal. Some might argue that transition occupies a necessary place of ritual significance in the move from child to adolescent. Others might argue that instead of lamenting the 'academic dip' we should simply accept it as an inevitable effect of an appropriately demanding change. These views are not mutually exclusive. What the research of the last 20 years makes clear is that our identification of the problems of transition has not yet led to satisfying solutions. However, several chapters in this book do offer either evidence of changes that look promising and may give possible ways forward or speculations based on that evidence that schools may need some courage to adopt: the Introduction in particular looks ahead.

The research evidence certainly suggests that current patterns are not actively improving transition. The obsessive pressure on schools to raise 'achievement', measured only by SAT results, is hardly likely to encourage teachers to value a more balanced assessment of each pupil's real capabilities and needs. This obsessive pressure is providing some benefits but also creating renewed tensions between primary and secondary schools (see Chapter 2) as disagreements emerge about the validity of level scores and about the value (or otherwise) of current record systems transferred between schools. Chapter 2 has much to say about some resolutions to these problems.

We hope that this opening chapter has made clear that the literacy issue is a genuinely complicated and vexed challenge and that the National Literacy Strategy is still more of a recognition of this challenge than a panacea. The main job of evaluating both Strategies, Numeracy as well as Literacy, has been given to the Ontario Institute for Studies in Education and to a team which includes Michael Fullan, an expert in the field of educational change. Their first annual report, *Watching and Learning* (Earl et al., 2000), is available in summary form (11 pages). We have not been able to trace either the full version or their second summary report which would have been anticipated in January 2001. Their opening remark 'Large-scale educational reform is difficult to do well ...' (ibid., p. 1) is typical of their cautious and relatively cool appraisal of the Strategies. The views expressed are based on work carried out in 1999 in which they 'interviewed approximately 200 people, observed over 20 meetings and conferences, visited 20 schools and/or LEAs, reviewed documents and reports and conducted extensive reviews of the international research literature on large-scale education reform' (ibid. p.1). This account is vague by any standards, 'visited 20 schools and/or LEAs' is particularly woolly, making it sound as though they were looking for a cup of tea rather than hard evidence. However, this is perhaps tending towards the unfair if one presumes that this summary was written for all-purpose use and the point being made is that they have been 'watching and learning'. The report itself is well balanced and is clear about the initial success of National Literacy and Numeracy Strategies (NLNS, their acronym) but extremely cautious about its long-term impact and sustainability. They consider NLNS as 'comprehensive and fully developed . . . policy levers for large-scale reform' (ibid., p. 4), characterized by 'explicit performance standards', 'explicit focus on changing teaching practices linked to student learning', 'massive commitment to the infrastructure, training and capacity building to support teacher development and strategy implementation', 'significant new financial resources' and the alignment 'of the Strategies and other policies' (ibid., p. 4) We would have to question the last point as we see schools as massively overloaded by competing initiatives. Also we find the conflation of Numeracy with Literacy extremely misleading, the scale of the NLS is enormously different to the NNS. The main body of the report is concerned with the development of the NLNS and very much adopts the spirit of Fullan's other work on educational change. They itemize six 'Challenges' for the future, most of which explain themselves: Changing Practices is Hard Work – Intellectually and Emotionally; Motivation is Important, But it is Not Enough in the Long Run; New Teachers are a Long Term Investment; Assessment Literacy for Wise Decisions (this refers to the need to develop much better understanding about the strengths and limitations of statistical data); The Power of Professional Learning Communities; and Dissenting Voices Contribute to Clear Thinking (ibid., pp. 9-11). On this latter point they argue 'The SEU [Schools Effectiveness Unit] needs to avoid succumbing to false certainty and inappropriately rigid adherence to the Strategies . . . Challenge and debate about ideas can help to clarify both intentions and approaches during the next few years' (ibid., p. 11). This book is offered with that intention and in that spirit.

There are many intelligent aspects to the NLS but it has many blind spots. For example, the whole notion of the Literacy Hour was an intelligent recognition that one major negative effect of the National Curriculum on Key Stage 2 had been to reduce pupils' opportunities for reading and writing. However the almost paranoiac obsession with a literal 60 minutes broken down into ritualized sections produced a parody of good teaching. It seems, however, that primary schools and teachers have done their best to contextualize and refine the hour into something far more sensible and beneficial to pupils. Secondary schools will have several years to undertake their own set of experiments. During that period a very different factor, Information and Communications Technology, will have some real impact on schools for the first time. It would seem that computers have been in schools a long time, since the BBC computer of the 1970s, but in reality their impact has been absolutely marginal. In the next five years there will be a real change and this change will be essentially about literacy. If the NLS, or its equivalent, is to have any long-term importance, then it must embrace this change rather than, as it currently does, treat it as something separate.

It is absolutely clear then that:

- schools must continue their efforts to improve the literacy of their pupils and that discussion of the meaning of literacy is always a part of that effort
- the introduction of the NLS reinforces the need to discuss the concept of literacy; it has not somehow replaced that need
- the NLS is a vast, centrally determined policy, by its nature it cannot be flexible enough to improve practice in every context, schools should exercise their professional judgement
- schools should pay close attention to the specific literacies of their local communities as well as to national and global trends
- transition between primary and secondary will always be difficult for pupils; this should be acknowledged by all parties, there will never be a 'one stop' solution
- we know enough about the challenges of transition to anticipate many, for example which pupils will be most vulnerable, and to plan and act accordingly.

If literacy is always changing, then one cannot really offer a simple all-purpose definition. It might be possible to say how literacy used to be defined and by whom although this would reveal mostly information about the definers. If one also believes that literacy is only truly understood in social terms, then definitions would tend to be typically specific and situated. However, readers may feel that this chapter should offer them some help towards a definition. Margaret Meek's comment, in her excellent book *On Being Literate* (Meek, 1991), seems to us the most helpful:

> To be literate we have to be confident that the world of signs and print, in all the different mixtures and modes of meaning that surround us, is a world we can cope with, be at home in, contribute to and play with. If it is simply mysterious, threatening, unreliable or hostile, then we feel at a disadvantage, victimized and inadequate. There is no guarantee that literacy makes the world a more benign

place, but it helps everyone to consider how it might be different (Meek, 1991, p. 238).

References

Beard, R. (2000) 'Research and the National Literacy Strategy', *Oxford Review of Education*, **26** (3) and (4), pp. 421–36.

British Educational Communications and Technology Agency (BECTa) (2001a) *Primary Schools of the Future - Achieving Today*, Coventry, BECTa.

British Educational Communications and Technology Agency (BECTa) (2001b) *Secondary Schools of the Future*, Coventry, BECTa.

Benyon, J. (1985) *Initial Encounters in the Secondary School*, Lewes, Falmer Press.

Brookes, W. and Goodwyn, A. (1998) 'Literacy in the secondary school', paper presented at the 1998 British Educational Research Association conference, Queens University.

Department for Education and Employment (DfEE) (1997a) *The Implementation of the National Literacy Strategy*, London, DfEE.

Department for Education and Employment (DfEE) (1997b) *Secondary Literacy: A Survey by HMI Autumn Term 1997*, London, DfEE.

Department for Education and Employment (DfEE) (1998) *The National Literacy Strategy Framework for Teaching* London, DfEE.

Department for Education and Employment (DfEE) (1999a) *National Literacy Strategy Guidance for Providers of Summer Literacy Schools and Key Stage 3 Intervention Programmes for Literacy in 1999–2000*, London, DfEE.

Department for Education and Employment (DfEE) (1999b) *The Impact of School Transitions and Transfers on Pupil Progress and Attainment*. Galton, M., Gray, J. and Ruddock, J. Research Report No. 131, London, DfEE.

Department for Education and Employment (DfEE) (2000) *Transforming Key Stage 3: National Pilot*, London, DfEE.

Department for Education and Employment (DfEE) (2001) *Key Stage 3 National Strategy: Framework for Teaching English: Years 7, 8 and 9*, London, DfEE.

Department of Education and Science (DES) (1987) *The National Curriculum 5-16, a Consultation Document*, London, DES.

Department for Education and Skills (2001) *The Standards Site*, www.standards.dfes.gov.uk/literacy

Earl, L., Fullan, M., Leithwood, K., Watson, N., with Jantzi, D., Levin, B. and Torrance, N. (2000) *Watching and Learning: OISE/UT Evaluation of the Implementation of the National Literacy and Numeracy Strategies*, Toronto, OISE.

Galton, M. and Willcocks, J. (eds) (1983) *Moving from the Primary School*, London, Routledge and Kegan Paul.

Galton, M., Hargreaves, L., Comber, C. and Wall, D. (1999) *Inside the Primary Classroom: 20 Years On*, London, Routledge.

Goodwyn, A. and Findlay, K. (1999) 'The Cox models revisited: English teachers' views of their subject and the National Curriculum', *English in Education*, 33(2), pp. 19-31.

Gorwood, B. (1986) *School Transfer and Curriculum Continuity*, London, Croom Helm.

Hargreaves, L. and Galton, M. (eds.) (1999) *Moving from the Primary Classroom: 20 Years On*, London, Routledge.

Heath, S. B. (1983) *Ways With Words: Language, Life and Work in Communities and Classrooms*, Cambridge, Cambridge University Press.

Hertrich, J. (1999) *18 Issues Deriving from HMIs Inspection of the Projects*. www.literacytrust.org.uk

Huggins, M. and Knight, P. (1977) 'Curriculum continuity and Transfer from Primary to Secondary school: the case of history', *Educational Studies*, 23(3).

Lee, B., Harris, S. and Dickson, P. (1995) *Continuity and Progression 5-16: Developments in Schools*, Slough, NFER.

Marshall, B. and Brindley, S. (1998) 'Cross-phase or just a lack of communication: models of English at key stages 2 and 3 and their possible effects on pupil transfer', *Changing English*, 5(2), pp. 123–34.

Measor, L. and Woods, P. (1984) *Changing Schools*, Milton Keynes, Open University Press.

Meek, M. (1991) *On Being Literate*, London, Bodley Head.

Nicholson, J. (1990) 'An extended project looking at the transition of pupils from primary to secondary education', *Links*, 15, pp. 28–32.

Reynolds, D. (1998) 'Schooling for literacy: a review of research on teacher effectiveness and its implications for contemporary educational policies', *Educational Review*, 50(20) pp. 147–162.

Sainsbury, M., Whetton, C., Mason, K. and Shagen, I. (1990) 'Fallback in Attainment on Transfer at age 11: evidence from the Summer Literacy Schools evaluation', *Educational Research Journal*, 40(1), pp. 73–81.

Schools Curriculum and Assessment Authority (SCAA) (1996) *Promoting Continuity between Key Stage 2 and Key Stage 3*, London, SCAA.

Schools Curriculum and Assessment Authority (SCAA) (1997) *Use of Language: A Common Approach*, London, SCAA.

Shagen, S. and Kerr, D. (1999) *Bridging the Gap? The National Curriculum and Progression from Primary to Secondary School*, Slough, NFER.

Steed, E. and Sudworth, P. (1985) 'The humpback bridge', in R. Derricott (ed.) *Curriculum Continuity*, Windsor, NFER/Nelson.

Street, B. (1984) *Literacy in Theory and Practice*, Cambridge, Cambridge University Press.

Suffolk LEA (1997) *A Report on an Investigation into What Happens When Pupils Transfer into their Next School at the Ages of 9, 11 and 13*, Ipswich, Inspection and Advice Division, Suffolk Education Department.

Taylor, N. (1994) 'The primary-secondary transition; a case study of a Midlands comprehensive school', *Education Today*, 44(1), pp. 30–4.

Webster, A., Beveridge, M. and Reed, M. (1996) *Managing the Literacy Curriculum*, London, Routledge.

Williams, M. and Howley, R. (1989) 'Curriculum discontinuity: a study of a secondary school and its feeder primary schools', *British Educational Research Journal*, 15(1), pp. 61–76.

Wray, D. and Lewis, M. (1999) 'Secondary teachers' views concerning literacy and literacy teaching', *Educational Review*, 51(3), 273–82.

2

Secondary schools and the National Literacy Strategy

Andrew Goodwyn and Kate Findlay

Chapter 2 focuses on the secondary school, especially the period of the last few years, as the Literacy Juggernaut has been viewed as approaching, increasingly at speed. It reviews the 'readiness' of schools and their concerns about the Strategy, their relationships with their 'feeder' schools and also the potential role of ICT, something problematized by its absence from the NLS documentation. Where relevant it refers back to the Language Across the Curriculum movement, placing the current initiative within a historical and political context.

This chapter reviews the way secondary schools have reacted to the increasing pressures on them to make literacy a high priority at all levels of the institution. In case schools were in any doubt, OFSTED now inspect schools (including primary schools) with an expectation of finding policies and practices that reflect a school's commitment to raising literacy standards. In one sense secondary schools have always addressed this issue but there have clearly been a series of chronological phases and these are worth reviewing briefly before focusing on the last few years and the current impetus of the National Literacy Strategy itself. Equally, secondary schools have always tried to manage transition but here, as the evidence covered in Chapter 1 reveals, success has been relatively limited. One of the striking things about the research evidence we have compiled (see below) is that secondary schools are now much more aware of this issue of transition as principally their problem, rather than as somehow a failing in the primary sector. Overall the chapter will also review the relationship between policy and practice and the emergence of the role of the local co-ordinators, usually local education authority employees, charged with overseeing the NLS initiative in a group of local schools and also, therefore, key players in overseeing transition.

The background

It has become a cliché to talk about the fast pace of educational change but it is crucial none the less to reflect on the impact of a heavily politicized set of 'reforms' as these help to explain current developments and, potentially at least, to put them into a more comprehensible perspective. Such a review may also encourage teachers to be confident in their own judgement as they observe how frequently top-down reforms prove relatively short-lived and ineffectual.

The abolition of the eleven-plus (for the vast majority of pupils) in the 1970s provided a new challenge for secondary schools both to attend to the full range of ability in their pupils and to develop much closer relationships with neighbourhood schools. However, it was not really until the genuine reform of the examination system, in the mid-1980s, and the introduction of GCSE as a common examination that schools could at least try to accommodate and develop all their pupils equally. The key point for this book is that the GCSE reform was significantly influenced by the Language Across the Curriculum (LAC) movement of the 1970s, a movement with many lessons for current initiatives. In political terms this movement was given momentum by a perceived crisis in reading standards in the early 1970s. The Bullock committee was initially charged with examining just the teaching of reading; eventually it hugely exceeded that brief.

Of course, most of the best writing and research on literacy over the past few years (for example, Lankshear, 1997; Meek, 1988; Millard, 1994; Street, 1984) has consistently pointed out that literacy is always perceived to be 'in crisis' and that someone is always to blame, usually teachers or now 'the educational establishment'. The current 'crisis' seems to stem from the test results accumulated over the last 10 years as part of the assessment of pupil performance within the National Curriculum in England and Wales; these results suggest that many pupils leave primary school with literacy levels that are inadequate for secondary school subject work (see Chapter 3). The 'crisis' also stems from a more intangible lack of confidence in the teaching of reading in primary schools and in the initial training of primary teachers; this latter point was part of a sustained Conservative government and media obsession over about 15 years. 'New Labour', intent on capturing the central political ground of middle-class parents, has picked up this particular gauntlet and put considerable economic resources into it in the shape of the National Literacy Strategy. The NLS was in origin a typically right-wing initiative, introduced by a Conservative government in response to yet another perceived crisis in literacy.

So this current strategy has many parallels with the most important example in recent history of a government-inspired attempt to drive up literacy standards, led by Mrs Thatcher, then Minister for Education, in the early 1970s, who initiated a study into reading standards in schools. However, before briefly reviewing what became the Bullock Report (DES, 1977) it is vital to note that this initiative was only superficially political; fundamentally it derived from an important change in educational thinking, inspired by the work of James Britton, Douglas Barnes and Harold Rosen (1971) who argued for a complete review of educational practice; Britton's *Language and Learning* (Britton, 1970) was unquestionably the key text in inspiring this change. In summary, they argued for placing oral development at the heart of education, for a child-centred rather than subject-centred curriculum and for respect for linguistic diversity in an increasingly multicultural and mobile population. The 1970s were also the era of the reform of the binary secondary system and the introduction of comprehensive schools. Educational and political thinking can be seen retrospectively to be in relative harmony, both parties attempting to generate more egalitarian approaches, the former in the classroom and the latter in the school system.

One element in these changes was that an essentially right-wing inquiry into reading standards turned into the Bullock Report, *A Language for Life* (DES, 1977), a chiefly progressive document arguing that all teachers were teachers of language and advocating the need for a Language Across the Curriculum movement. For a few years this movement dominated many schools, especially secondary schools, leading to a review of curriculum materials, specifically in relation to their accessibility through written language and to the setting up of school working parties and the production of LAC policy documents. Much of the attention of this movement was to reading and this emphasis is perhaps even clearer in Michael Marland's 1977 book, *Language Across the Curriculum*. Two offshoots of the reading standards crisis were the influential work of Southgate et al., *Extending Beginning Reading* (1981), and that of Lunzer and Gardiner, *The Effective Use of Reading* (1979).

The movement has had a lasting and important influence and traces of it can be found in our recent survey, especially where a few schools at least claim to have a Language Across the Curriculum policy. However, in the 1980s the movement was gradually subsumed by the reform of the examination systems, the introduction of Technical and Vocational Educational Initiative (TVEI) and other 'reforms' (Ball, Kenny and Gardiner, 1990). The HMI turned their attention to the perceived disappearance of grammar and their two booklets in the 1980s (HMI, 1984; 1986) paved the way for the Kingman Report (DES, 1988) and then the subject-dominated National Curriculum. The wheel went pretty well full circle from an attempt to look across the curriculum and to bring all subject teachers together to a subject-oriented National Curriculum that pressed subjects well down into the primary curriculum. One aspect of this subject focus was once more to place enormous pressure on English teachers to teach basic skills and to operate more formal approaches to language so that other teachers could, as it were, get on with their job. English teachers have resisted this fiercely, and research (Goodwyn and Findlay, 1997) shows them clearly rejecting the 'cross-curricular model' put forward by Cox (1988) as not a model of English. They accept it as a whole-school model and one for which all subject teachers share a responsibility. Overall, then, LAC has left some lasting and positive changes in schools but it has been overwhelmed by the National Curriculum.

Language across the curriculum or literacy across the curriculum?

As the wheel completes its circle so attention is returning to the idea that all teachers are teachers of language and literacy. The Schools Curriculum and Assessment Authority published a whole set of guidelines for subject teachers on this very point, *Use of Language: A Common Approach* (SCAA, 1997).

The LAC movement, although apparently politically initiated, was taken over and redefined wholeheartedly by teachers and turned into a bottom-up reform. There was no National Curriculum in the 1970s and teachers and senior managers had great scope to interpret LAC in their own terms. There was also a Schools Council that supported excellent research (for example, both reading projects mentioned above). The current NLS remains a centrally controlled, top-down measure, although it has certainly gained much support in primary schools.

The NLS strategy, as articulated so far, adopts the concept of Literacy across the secondary curriculum and the most significant phrase appears to be 'whole-school literacy'. This use of the term 'Literacy' seems to stem from several sources. In education considerable attention and debate has been focused on this term since the LAC movement petered out in the early 1980s with the majority of voices arguing for a redefinition of the term (see Chapter 1). As argued in Chapter 1, literacy is no longer viewed as a basic concept about functional reading and writing. We do not wish to rehash the arguments of Chapter 1 but to review here the connotations of the term, especially in relation to secondary education.

As already discussed, any realistic definition of literacy, especially in relation to adolescents, encompasses much more than 'basics' and must include areas such as 'computer literacy', visual literacy, media literacy and so on (Lankshear, 1997). Equally, the claims made for the intellectual power of western-style print literacy have been much contested (Street, 1984). This latter point is linked to the 'critical literacy' movement of Paolo Freire (Freire, 1972) and others which has argued that most forms of narrowly defined literacy are used oppressively to reinforce unjust social structures and that literacy should be used by educators as a means of empowerment. Literacy has therefore had a high profile in educational circles, which has attracted considerable attention.

However, the use of the term 'literacy' in relation to the teaching of reading and writing, in secondary schools in particular, is relatively recent in England and Wales; its traditional use for most of the twentieth century was in relation to the education of adults with low levels of literacy. For example, the term 'literacy' does not appear, as far as we can tell, in official documents about the National Curriculum for English before 2000. Equally, in the *Initial Teacher Training National Curriculum for Secondary English* (TTA, 1977) it only appears in relation to pupils with low levels of literacy. Overall this change may be summed up as a move from the use of the positive term 'literate' almost always associated with highly educated individuals to a developing definition in which, we would argue, literacy is conceptualized as a lifelong and open-ended process, i.e., a move from an expectation that only a minority will be truly literate to an expectation of a society concerned with literacy for all. However, and not surprisingly, our survey research (see below) reveals a deep confusion in secondary schools about what 'literacy' is. Those responsible for it can include special needs co-ordinators, senior management and heads of English; all three positions we would argue which hold quite different stances on 'literacy'. Only a third of English departments in 1999, for example, claimed to have a policy on literacy. The emergence of the Literacy co-ordinator role in secondary schools may go some way to reducing confusion but the training of these key people seems almost exclusively about instrumental implementation of the strategy (see Chapter 5). The holders of these new posts have come from English teaching and this approach seems commonsensical until one reflects on how many co-ordinators in the LAC period were deliberately selected from other subject areas so that the movement came to be seen as exclusively the province of (and the problem for) English.

There is also a pervasive sense in western societies that the media, especially television, are 'replacing' reading as the key interest of young people. This loss of interest in reading is now being exacerbated, especially amongst boys (Millard, 1997), by the arrival of computer games and the Internet. This linkage to the media is also associated in the public mind with increases in urban violence. Research evidence is conflicting (Buckingham, 1993; 2000); much of this pervasive view is not based on any real evidence and has at least as much basis in nostalgia but also a genuine and anxiety-provoking recognition that society is being changed by technology.

Another key factor is the equally pervasive view that a society's real capital is human. The interpretation of what human capital is leads to further disagreement. Views might be placed on a spectrum from the functional view that our basic workers need more capability to work in technological environments, to the egalitarian view that we are developing a new social structure based around knowledge and creativity and that all citizens are entitled to share in this opportunity.

Even in this brief look at the difficulties in defining 'Literacy' for adolescents it becomes clear that there will continue to be a struggle over meaning in the next few years. In contrast, the LAC movement was not dogged by disputes about what LAC means, although it attracted plenty of media controversy (see Ball, Kenny and Gardiner, 1990) but it is probable that literacy will prove to have incompatible definitions as secondary schools try to get to grips with what they mean by 'whole-school literacy'. Our research has tried to record and analyse this movement as it develops, and looks for ways of helping schools to support themselves and each other.

Secondary schools, the national policy and emerging practice

Our research focusing on secondary schools has investigated a matrix of relationships. We began with a survey in 1998 (Brookes and Goodwyn, 1998) and followed this up with a second survey (Goodwyn and Findlay, 2000). Both surveys used schools from across the country and from diverse settings. The second survey was complemented by a small-scale qualitative study, geographically within the Southern region of England but with some claim to being nationally representative. This latter study brings together the views and perceptions of the key agents concerned with the concept of literacy, chiefly in the secondary school but with many implications for primaries especially in relation to transition. The term 'agents' is employed because in our view no individual involved in these processes is merely a passive victim of the directives of others.

These agents include the architects of the National Literacy Strategy, what might be termed a pseudo-governmental organization. At this national level, the agents may be divided into the political and the educational policy-makers. These national agents devise strategies, appoint other agents, create documents and thus, they hope, change practice and raise standards. One feature of their work is that documents, being official, have no identifiable author or authors. We accept that this is a traditional practice but it nevertheless elides responsibility and makes it impossible to ask 'what did you mean by that sentence?'

At the regional level are similar agents charged with ensuring that this process is working. Within each region there continue to be local educa- tion authority level agents who come in various guises with differing titles, usually consultant (the term 'adviser' is perhaps now unfashionable and too friendly; 'inspector' too threatening but also too independent?). Broadly, however, they are concerned with groups of schools and with ensuring the impact of all the above on actual schools, usually on key staff. Teachers themselves experience all of this and are expected to mediate it to their pupils, the ultimate 'beneficiaries' of the whole process. OFSTED provides another set of key agents whose role is very visibly to inspect individual schools and local authorities and to check up on them. Somewhere, almost inevitably in this kind of top-down model of change, rather on the fringes, are some researchers, in our case poking our proverbial noses in and asking some awkward questions.

It might be argued that this form of centralist, national strategy is now a well-established and well understood process and we acknowledge this to a degree. However, before establishing our theoretical framework in relation to such policies and their relationship to actual practices, it is worth stressing some distinctive features of the NLS that we find make it especially interesting. The most fundamental of these is that, in a pro- found sense, it cannot be opposed. In simple terms how could any edu- cational professional or politician stand against raising standards in literacy? Chapter 1 demonstrated how little an attempt has been made to evaluate and critique the Strategy. Indeed, one of the factors we shall explore below is what we have called the *fundamentalist tendency* in the strategy. By this we mean its ubiquitous ability to make criticism almost unthinkable, the only question is how to implement this great good and to convert unbelievers. In relation to many individuals we have spoken to this is to do them and their critical powers an injustice; they do, fre- quently express certain kinds of reservation. As we have suggested above, individuals certainly have agency and use it. However, even in these moments of criticality, there is, as yet, no real deep-seated opposition; indeed, there are far more moments of evangelical enthusiasm and even occasional awe. This seems true even in the secondary sector, tradition- ally the point of real resistance to imposed policy, but more research would be needed to substantiate this point.

Another factor that we feel distinguishes the NLS, particularly at present and for the next few years, is its success in creating *phase-related role reversal*. It has broken the implicit belief that primary and secondary schools are actually different planets in an age when interplanetary travel for teachers themselves is just possible but not really very desirable. Even more iconoclastically, secondary schools certainly saw themselves in the past as a very important planet around which smaller moons called primary schools, orbited and annually they received parties of young aliens who had to be taught the ways of the real world by the real, expert teachers. Our research shows very clearly that these big secondary planets are in a state of considerable shock. They find the young aliens alarmingly knowledgeable and their teachers challengingly expert; as a result secondary teachers are discovering how to travel and are returning mightily impressed and not a little daunted at the task they face. So the NLS is fostering meaningful exchanges between primaries and secondaries with the genuinely different element in the upward flow of expertise, hence our term 'role reversal'. We anticipate that this will have real benefits for improving the transition of pupils.

Finally, this strategy will eventually have had some impact on every teacher in every school in the mainstream 5-16 age range. It is worth noting that the Language Across the Curriculum (LAC) movement of the 1970s, which was greeted with real enthusiasm by the teaching profession, is generally seen by the profession to have petered out, with little long-lasting impact; in other words, the evangelicals did not convert the masses. In fact, this is to do an injustice to the influence of LAC whose positive traces are still very visible notably in practices such as oral work and coursework. However, the perception by serving teachers is that LAC 'faded away'. One simple and revealing finding in our research is that LAC was not mentioned directly by any respondent at any point. The NLS, through a variety of means, appears to be reaching all teachers and all their pupils.

We are concerned, then, with the complex and inevitably contradictory nature of a huge national project that is clearly 'working' and simultaneously being transformed and interpreted by its workers. Stephen Ball (Ball, 1994) has summarized this complexity very effectively, explaining how policy discourses may shape individual agency but also emphasizing the possibility of individuals claiming agency within these discourses. The effect of policy is, he explains, primarily discursive, since it changes the possibilities for thinking things 'otherwise' and so limits our responses to change. Yet this totalizing effect is tempered by the policy text which is just that, an encoded representation which must be decoded and enacted on a number of levels:

> Given constraints, circumstances and practicalities, the translation of the crude, abstract simplicities of policy texts into interactive and sustainable practices of some sort involves thought, invention and adaptation. And the more ideologically abstract any policy is, the more distant in conception from practice, the less likely it is to be accommodated in unmediated form into the context of practice ....
> (Ibid.)

This helps us to conceptualize the national project and therefore discuss it as a kind of actuality whilst also treating individuals as encompassed by this actuality and yet not engulfed by it.

Another helpful perspective is that of Croll et al. (1994) who have articulated various ways of defining the agency, or lack of it, of teachers caught up in some large-scale policy initiative. They discuss four models: teacher as either partner, implementer, resister or as 'policy maker in practice'.

> If, either because of similar structural or situational constraints, or because of similar attitudes and ideologies (or because of an interaction of these), teachers interpret and prioritise policy changes in consistent ways, then the outcomes of these individual actions will have a systematic effect on the practical outcomes of policy . . . [which] may effectively re-direct educational activities in a way that makes teachers policy makers. (Ibid. p. 242).

This latter definition fits well with our research, as mentioned above. We see both teachers and others as having agency whilst acknowledging that policy shapes their thoughts and actions sufficiently to lead to what we call 'semi-systematic outcomes'. So our survey responses include very many comments which reveal individual voices, although we are unable to give space to them here. The interview data reveals the sensitivity of LEA personnel in particular as they make subtle judgements about how to interact with individual schools and teachers, to make the NLS meaningful to them. Our research provides clear patterns that we feel are nationally representative, the majority of which fit with the 'fundamentalist tendency' of the NLS. We also note here the limiting effects of questionnaires which tend to smooth over the rougher edges of individual reaction. Teacher comments and interview data provide clearer evidence of where the policy may be seen to be only 'semi-systematic' in its effects.

Our most recent survey (Goodwyn and Findlay, 2000) of 230 schools across 10 LEAs, conducted in June 2000, produced 75 returns, a response rate of about 30 per cent, quite typical of large-scale surveys. The qualitative strand consisted, first, of interviews with representatives of all key agents, regional directors and LEA literacy consultants; secondly, practitioners themselves including many teachers who are also in management roles; thirdly, a small sample of 'literacy' lessons were observed. The lessons were selected by asking an LEA agent to recommend a particular school as a site where exemplary work is taking place. At this point we note that survey findings suggest that many secondary schools, 73 per cent in this case, know that the LEA has a specific post but only 42 per cent consider the post holders to be 'effective', 24 per cent considered them ineffective and 33 per cent did not respond. This shows that there is currently some tension and uncertainty about the value of this role from a school's perspective. However, it may also reveal how important that role will become in the very near future once schools actively seek help, and we discuss this further below. Each LEA representative was interviewed on a semi-structured basis and the tape then transcribed. Interview data is analysed holistically but we are especially interested in exploring the 'fundamentalist discourse' of each text and in particular references to policies, documents and to significant events such as training and encounters with teachers.

To contextualize the case study LEA discussed below, we first present and discuss the two sets of survey findings, The earlier study (Brookes and Goodwyn, 1998) established some trends substantiated by the 2000 survey. Inevitably our sample, on a return of 30 per cent, cannot claim to be fully representative and we also acknowledge that more 'clued up' schools were likely to respond. However, to counter this, the wide geographic and social range of the schools does provide a useful sense of breadth. The same range of schools was surveyed in 1998. In 1998 just over 70 per cent of schools saw literacy as a major priority, in 2000 the figure is 92 per cent. In 1998 many schools seemed unclear what kind of provision they should be making about literacy; this was evident, for example, in confusions over who was responsible for effecting change. In 2000, 80 per cent of schools have a working party or equivalent, 65 per cent have a whole-school policy and 73 per cent know that their LEA has a post for secondary school literacy. Schools show increasing confidence in what they are doing: 62 per cent claim to have raised standards in the last two years; 71 per cent have intervention programmes in Key Stage 3, and 56 per cent say they have methods for monitoring the outcomes of their initiatives. However this leaves 39 per cent with no such methods, suggesting that getting something under way has taken priority over setting up means to evaluate progress.

An area of particular importance is transition but also and very specifically the *relationship* between primary and secondary and we have already commented on the cross-phase role reversal effect. In 1998 most schools thought that the information they received from primary was at best fair and generally inadequate but they also acknowledged that they made little effective use of it. At that time they were expending time and resources on selecting base line tests with the implication that this might correct inadequate primary records. In 2000, 71 per cent of schools state that they are 'sufficiently aware of recent developments in literacy teaching' in primary schools, 48 per cent felt the quality of information from primaries had improved (despite 45 per cent saying 'no' this still shows positive change from 1998), and 48 per cent claimed that they were now making 'effective use of this information'. We suggest that these are the signs of the beginning of a process as secondary schools essentially wake up to the task. For example, schools (65 per cent) reject the NLS model as applied to primary schools and (80 per cent) did not plan to adopt the literacy hour model in Year 7. We feel this does show that they understand what this model actually is (see below). However, it is clear from comments that these schools have yet to decide what they plan to do. The *Framework* itself, only piloted for less than a year and with the clear expectation that non-pilot schools would implement it anyway, is written with very strong elements of the Literacy Hour in mind. Perhaps most significantly, a majority of secondary schools are now sending representatives to visit primaries to observe literacy teaching (79 per cent), organizing liaison meetings occasionally (38 per cent) or regularly (20 per cent), and specifically focus on Literacy, with only a minority (21 per cent) never focusing on the topic. Since 1998 there has clearly been a significant shift in the relationship between secondaries and feeder primaries; the former say they are far more in tune with the literacy activities of the latter and are ready to recognize their need to build on their foundational work.

What about information and communications technology?

Given the huge concurrent governmental drives to improve both literacy and teachers' ICT competence we included a brief section on ICT to probe for schools' emerging views about the role of ICT in improving literacy (in this aspect of the work we are supported by the British Educational Communications and Technology Agency [BECTa]). We deliberately did not offer competing definitions of literacy, and so we have used inference to speculate on how teachers conceptualize the place of the electronic media in school.

Overall these questions produced few surprises, although the responses to the first question suggest a higher usage than we would have predicted. The use of ICT in developing pupils' reading and writing skills is still 'rarely' for 39 per cent but 'frequently' for 39 per cent and 'consistently' for 17 per cent. This puts at over 50 per cent the regular use of ICT in reading and writing. However, in relation to whether the growth of ICT has been significant in improving pupil's literacy development, only 25 per cent agreed, 36 per cent claimed 'quite significant' and 32 per cent 'insignificant'. Again this puts ICT use into the mainstream majority of schooling, particularly when related to the clear frustrations expressed about ICT resources with 52 per cent finding them insufficient, 20 per cent sufficient, 20 per cent good and only 5 per cent excellent.

We feel that this reveals the genuine lack of resources available but also the far greater understanding that schools have of what they could do with more adequate resources. This is also reflected in the fact that 45 per cent use software packages designed to develop pupils' literacy whereas 52 per cent do not, and in judging how useful ICT has been so far in raising standards of literacy in the school only 5 per cent said very, 17 per cent useful, 41 per cent quite useful and 36 per cent an emphatic not useful. In looking into the future and to the use of ICT in raising literacy standards 20 per cent said very useful, 36 per cent useful, 29 per cent quite useful and none not useful. Overall then this places ICT rather more in the useful than the essential category in relation to literacy development. We also asked the respondents to estimate subject teachers' use of ICT on a high, moderate, low scale. The results reveal that no subject is rated at above 21 per cent, Maths is thus rated, other relative highs are Modern Foreign Languages at 17 per cent, English, Science and Geography at 15 per cent, Art at 14 per cent. Most subjects are seen as moderate users, Science 58 per cent, English and Maths 53 per cent, Geography 45 per cent, History 44 per cent, Music 35 per cent and Art 33 per cent. Once some lows are added into the picture, Drama 71 per cent, Music 47 per cent, Art 44 per cent, Languages 47 per cent, History 39 per cent and so on, we feel that this picture fits with our own view of the current state of ICT use in schools. The subjects concerned very directly with written and spoken language, e.g. English, History, Languages, do not seem to be leading the way; this supports our contention that electronic literacy is not conceptualized as part of the school-centric model (see Chapter 1).

Comments suggested that many respondents see ICT as essentially supporting the literacy development of the less able, i.e. as linked to a deficit model in school where it is regarded as a tool rather than an important model of literacy. As we argued earlier we feel that society has already developed a very different model in which electronic literacy carries an absolute premium. Overall we suggest these figures show schools coping with the demands of school-centric literacy whilst recognizing that their resources are inadequate. We feel it likely that if organizations like BECTa and the various NOF training consortia can communicate the contribution that ICT can make at a profound level to a broad definition of literacy, then they can have a very marked effect on teachers' thinking and teaching.

It is clear then that many secondary schools, through their own volition, have been 'gearing up' to prioritize improving standards of literacy. They usually have initiatives under way but have less provision for self-evaluation. They are taking their relationships with primary schools much more seriously and aim to benefit from primary colleagues' experience and information about pupils. However, their relationships with LEAs (see below and Chapter 5) are somewhat confused, although this is almost certainly a result of many years of pressure for schools to treat

LEAs essentially as service providers. ICT is problematic for secondary schools for a host of reasons and the survey supports our contention that the concept of literacy is in transition and has to compete with narrowly defined notions embedded within the NLS.

Policy and practice in action

We will focus on one case study LEA and school in order to give some meaningful detail to this account. No single case study can claim empirical representativeness but it can certainly claim to be illuminatingly characteristic in the current situation. The other case studies certainly complement the one described here whose interviewees include a Primary Literacy Consultant, a General Inspector (English) and a Deputy Head (formerly a Head of English) (LEA W). It is notable that other interviewees, despite their varying titles, e.g. an English Adviser (secondary focus LEA B), an LEA Strategy Manager (LEA S), a Primary Literacy Consultant (LEA WB) and an English and Literacy Consultant (secondary) and Head of English, both from LEA SU, describe similar issues within their context. When discussing literacy here we shall focus on how the NLS is seen to be 'working'. We shall then examine the idea of individual agency in relation to policy.

Case study: LEA W

LEA W is a relatively small authority, with 11 secondary schools (one of which is in 'special measures'), 50 primary schools and one special school. It is principally an area of considerable affluence with generally good results above the national average. Interviews were conducted with the two key 'agents' responsible for implementing the National Literacy Strategy using semi-structured interview techniques.

The Primary Literacy Consultant (A), an experienced primary practitioner, was appointed on a two-year contract in 1998. She described her role as one of 'supporting identified schools in order to implement the Literacy Hour so they can raise their literacy standards'. The General Inspector (English) (B) is an ex-Head of English who became English Adviser for the county in 1990. When the larger structure was dismantled in 1998, she took on her current role which also includes Drama, developing the Arts, monitoring pupils educated at home and acting as Client Officer for the Educational Library Services.

The LEA was not a pilot for the Key Stage 3 *Framework*, so at the time of the research there was no new appointment to develop literacy initiatives in secondary schools. The responsibility lay with these key actors who had worked closely together to implement the NLS in primary schools, and were now turning their attention to the secondary phase.

The interviews focused on how they see their role within the broad framework which exists to translate policy rhetoric into curriculum reality. Since the Education Reform Act 1988 the power of LEAs to work directly with schools in devising curriculum has been eroded, and the imposition of a National Curriculum, together with a requirement that schools be directly responsible to the Secretary of State through OFSTED, has meant that they are at once more accountable but less able to exercise any real powers of intervention. The NLS has arrived without consulting them, and they are required to ensure its successful implementation at school level. How do they respond to this role?

In a simple sense, neither respondent had any fundamental argument with the idea of a NLS or the rationale which underpins it. The need as they see it is to persuade teachers of its value:

> I think we have moved on a lot in two years. When I first started the job there was so much resistance, and it is only through doing it that teachers have come to realise there is value to this. They didn't want to change their ways but having made that move they can see the benefits in the ways children can talk about literacy, the competencies they have and the whole thing. (A)

> I very much like the clarity which encourages the modelling of different text structures. The teaching sequence promoted through the Key Stage 3 materials where you are looking at immersion in a text type, getting them to identify for themselves the features that you are modelling through thinking aloud, through scaffolding, through selecting, through all of those processes you want them to go through on a white board or OHP. You are scaffolding the activity for them and pushing them on to independence. And I like that model. (B)

There is an awareness that they are ultimately accountable to central government:

> I am funded by the Standards Fund and you have to be restricted by what they say . . .

yet they do not see themselves as mere rubber stamps of alien policy texts but perceive a space which allows for a more creative response:

> When I started I didn't know exactly what the role would turn out like but I am happy with the way it has gone. I've been fortunate in being able to make it my own and I've had lots of opportunities to do things that maybe some Consultants haven't because they've kept to a very narrow criteria. (A)

Their official remit is interpreted very much in terms of 'training':

> Implementing the NLS meant that my colleague and I had to lay on the training for primary head-teachers and subsequent to that initial training there has been a lot more at various levels, management issues and courses looking at what heads and co-ordinators should be doing, courses helping people get to grips with target setting, and data handling and analysis . . . (B)

They accept their roles as mediators of state policy:

> I am a mediator of any sensible, useful materials I can get my hands on to help them. (B)

In practice, however, this simple role is more ambiguous since universal directives are not always sensitive to the variety of contexts with which they interact. This was highlighted in relation to the 'materials' provided for the Summer Literacy Conferences held in Summer 1999. Each secondary school in the authority was invited to send the Head teacher, Head of English and Special Educational Needs Co-ordinator (SENCO), and there was an expectation that they would then conduct a Key Stage 3 Literacy Audit in their schools:

> I was annoyed when I looked at the materials because I could see that the audit was so obviously an English Department audit because it had terms in it such as narrative poems, the kind of thing that would switch your Head of Science off. Other colleagues from other disciplines would take one look at it and say this has nothing to do with me. It would need to be re-written. (B)

In the event, she did rewrite it, in consultation with the Literacy Consultant in another LEA who had developed a successful Audit for schools in the borough. What became clear in the course of the interviews was that any impact at school level has happened because the respondents have successfully accommodated the Strategy to suit the needs of individual schools:

> Mainly I go into schools and do staff meetings and address the specific needs of schools . . . I say, what programme do you want to work with, what are the issues, where do we need to concentrate resources. And we plan something from that. (A)

> I realised the global approach I had initially taken in our Education Development Plan which set up a Working Party, promoting various initiatives through that Working Party, was not going to work. To be effective I needed to talk to individual schools about the way in for them. (B)

Faced with resistance at school level, the mandatory nature of initiatives provides them with a powerful persuasive mechanism so enhancing powers of intervention:

> I've been able to draw on the new orders for 2000 which have a very clear statement about the role of literacy in the context of all subjects, and the new inspection framework. And I've read these two pieces out and made it clear that all subjects will be inspected and part of that will be literacy. (B)

But this is tempered by a desire to retain some sense of agency:

> How can I work strategically through the EDP when I have six new initiatives land on my desk and they wipe out my own priorities? (B)

Despite this overload, there is evidence of curriculum developments which go beyond the strictures of the policy remit and suggest a feeling of being responsive to a more local community context:

> I love working with the Arts Development Officer here and the Library Services Manager and between us we have put bids in and have been successful in getting a Literacy Development Officer, so I work closely with her on projects to bring writers into the authority, setting up exciting projects. (B)

In one secondary school with a high ratio of second language speakers, a black performance poet spent two days running workshops with pupils. The Primary Consultant organized a project for Year 5 and Year 6 pupils to 'extend learning in the Literacy Hour' by working with a local poet in the three weeks leading up to National Poetry Day in October 1999; it was funded by the local Rotary Club!

In terms of the impact of literacy initiatives in individual schools, only three of the 11 secondary schools were at the stage of conducting literacy audits following a Literacy Day on the Strategy and the rationale behind it:

> The problem is, given the diversity of my role, it is very hard to be systematic about following up in every school. I do need to go back to them because at a few schools there hasn't been so much of a drive ... It is all very well to write a policy but I am aware that I need to go back and monitor a range of lessons to see how their practice is fulfilling what they say they are doing. (B)

Both respondents expressed a desire to ensure that literacy did not become the responsibility of just the English Department, 'how the science teacher, the maths teacher can teach literacy' (A):

The video I have for the Key Stage 3 English Conference, which I will be sharing with our schools in October on a two day conference, to disseminate, shows an English teacher modelling how to write a recipe. What I am interested in is watching the Home Economics teacher doing that, the Science teacher teaching how to write up an experiment, and the History teacher how to construct a persuasive argument, how those subject specialists can take responsibility for the text types that relate to their own subjects. (B)

Commitment from the senior management team was regarded as the key to success:

Schools are only motivated to do things if their head-teachers and senior managers have the vision that they will improve and see this as a means of doing it and put aside quality time for it, as part of their vision for whole school improvement. (B)

It was striking that most discussion centred on writing, with little mention of reading and no mention of speaking and listening, which is a strand in the Key Stage 3 *Framework*, (absent from the Primary NLS). And no comments were volunteered on the potential of ICT for promoting these skills, or any sense that literacy is changing with the impact of new technologies. Direct questions produced a recognition that ICT has a positive role to play in 'motivating boys and less able pupils' (A) but it was frequently 'used badly, just for word processing', copying work already written by hand rather than 'redrafting and improving writing'. The purpose of the activity was often simply to master the technology:

Unless they've got very good key-boarding skills it's laborious and they don't get far enough quick enough and it's frustrating for them and I don't think it promotes literacy. They are just practising key-boarding skills. (A)

Both respondents made reference to problems of limited access and lack of teacher expertise but were keen to support the idea of new literacies required to use new technologies:

It comes down to the confidence teachers themselves have as to how innovative they are. There is definitely a need with the Internet to learn those sorts of skills. When we think about retrieving information, the traditional way is through books. Now we have to think about those skills through the Internet and they are different so it is changing. You think about children writing letters, well we have a new way, we have emails which don't have the same structure and children need to know how to do these as well. (A)

In reality, however, the NLS appears to have stimulated the use of computer-based software which specifically address the reading and writing objectives in the *Framework*, without challenging the school-centric model which underpins it.

Ball's contention that policy operates as discourse, determining the language and concepts available for responding to the policy text, is very evident in this case study which highlights the extent to which key agents have become powerful spokespersons for the discourse and may be relied upon to represent and implement the policy as efficiently as they can. Their concern is a lack of time to do the job thoroughly, and there is no evidence of any fundamental ideological clash which might produce resistance. Other literacies which fall outside the range of the NLS are not mentioned in the discussions. Respondent A might have been expected to question the model of literacy which some English teachers have criticized for its emphasis on skills at the expense of creativity, but she welcomed the more 'structured' approach:

> I think there have been too many divisions between the different styles of English teaching in the past. The people who put their allegiance to one camp or another. And traditionally there has been a lot of Literature based affective work which is very important, but perhaps there hasn't been the focused look at the technicalities of writing. (A)

Operating in a predetermined field in which literacy is part of a broader discourse on standards and quality of teaching, they perceive their role within these boundaries. It is in the 'wild profusion of local practice' that the real impact of their efforts will be discovered, a site where the policy text confronts 'other realities, other circumstances like poverty, disrupted classrooms, lack of materials, multilingual classrooms' (Ball, 1994).

Looking ahead

We have highlighted the very powerful ongoing impact of the National Literacy Strategy and particularly its ambitions to 'transform' literacy teaching in the secondary school. In many ways, we suggest, it is likely to succeed in its own somewhat narrow and prescriptive terms. Whilst welcoming its aim to demystify subject teaching (see Chapter 3) and to involve all subject specialists, not just English teachers, in helping pupils become literate within each subject, we maintain that there are serious weaknesses in the 'school-centric' definition of literacy involved. The most glaring of these are, first, its pronounced emphasis on the 'autonomous individual' and, second, its failure to acknowledge the ever-changing nature of literacy and specifically current developments in the electronic media. For example, ICT is still seen as a distinct curriculum element in school rather than an integral part of literacy needed to participate in ordinary life.

Whilst we are able to report that our sample of schools are working hard to prepare to accommodate the NLS, we are also concerned about their lack of resources and also the 'fundamentalist' tendency of the discourse of the policy which may straitjacket schools with challenging and diverse contexts. An interesting effect of secondary schools 'gearing up' for the NLS is that they are experiencing 'role reversals', looking towards primary schools for advice and expertise, and this is a very positive development that should improve transition. We are able to illustrate that individuals exercise interpretation and agency and can act as 'policy-makers'. However, the influence of the NLS is such that this agency is decidedly modest and that the dominance of school-centric literacy seems set for a renewed lease of life.

The evidence overall suggests that secondary schools should:

- be aware that policy has a history; the Language Across the Curriculum movement demonstrated how schools can involve their entire staff in such an initiative, the challenge is sustaining the momentum
- make sure that the NLS is not a straitjacket, it is not compulsory and schools need the courage to be creative and distinctive
- build on their recent work in preparing for the Literacy initiative and maintain and extend their own good practice
- question 'official' definitions of literacy that place too much emphasis on narrow school-based assumptions
- make full use of LEA support but on their own terms
- make the most of the developments in ICT to extend pupils' literacy
- continue with their work in building long-term liaisons with feeder schools and look to learn from their recent experiences
- see themselves as agents not recipients and act accordingly
- treat their teachers as agents, building on their judgement and expertise.

References

Ball, S., Kenny, A. and Gardiner, D. (1990) 'Literacy, Politics and English teaching', in I. Goodson and P. Medway (eds), *Bringing English to Order*, London, Falmer Press.

Ball, S. J. (1994) *Education Reform: A Critical and Post-Structuralist Approach*, Buckingham, Open University Press.

Barnes, D. (1976) *From Communication to Curriculum*, Harmondsworth, Penguin.

Barnes, D., Britton, J. and Rosen, H. (1971) *Language, the Learner and the School*, revd edn, Harmondsworth, Penguin.

Britton, J. (1970) *Language and Learning*, Harmondsworth, Penguin.

Brookes, W. and Goodwyn, A. (1998) 'Literacy in the secondary school', paper given at the British Education Research Association Conference, Queens University, 1998, and published in *English and Media Magazine* (NATE, Autumn 1998).

Buckingham, D. (1993) *Children Talking Television: The Making of Television Literacy*, London, Falmer Press.

Buckingham, D. (2000) *After the Death of Childhood: Growing up in the Age of Electronic Media*, Cambridge, Polity Press.

Croll, P. et al. (1994) 'Teachers and education policy: roles and models', *British Journal of Educational Studies, **42**, 4.

Department of Education and Science (DES) (1977) *A Language for Life*, London, HMSO.

Department of Education and Science (DES) (1988) *Report of the Committee of Enquiry into the Teaching of English Language* (Kingman Report), London, HMSO.

Department for Education and Employment (DfEE) (2000) *Transforming Key Stage Three: National Pilot, Briefing Pack for Pilot Schools*, London, DfEE.

Freire, P. (1972) *Pedagogy of the Oppressed*, Harmondsworth, Penguin.

Lankshear, C. (1997) *Changing Literacies*, Buckingham, Open University Press.

Goodwyn, A. and Findlay, F. (1997) 'English teachers' theories of good English teaching and their theories in action' paper given at the BERA conference, York.

Marland, M. (1977) *Language Across the Curriculum*, London, Heinemann Educational.

Schools Curriculum and Assessment Authority (SCAA) (1997) *Use of Language: A Common Approach*, London, SCAA.

Street, B. V. (1984) *Literacy in Theory and Practice*, Cambridge, Cambridge University Press.

3

Subject literacies

Kate Findlay

One highly significant aspect of secondary schools is their subject culture and this chapter explores this complex element. The NLS emphasis on the acknowledgement of subject literacies is welcomed as is the attention schools will have to pay to cross-curricular issues. However, the Language Across the Curriculum movement has shown us that this is a very long-term process and that subject literacies are very like icebergs in that much is hidden below the classroom surface. The chapter reveals this invisibility and complexity and shows how subject literacies are powerful and valuable; schools need to balance their intrinsic importance and give careful attention to how children can acquire them over time.

The transition from an integrated primary curriculum to a fragmented subject-based secondary curriculum represents a significant challenge for pupils, who must negotiate a new way of 'doing school'; it places them in a permanent state of transition as they move, physically and conceptually, from one classroom and subject domain to another in the course of every school day. Literacy is inseparable from this ongoing process in which language is both the means and content of learning different subjects. Teachers use spoken and written language to teach, and pupils use spoken and written language to learn. Success in school depends on an ability to manage the transitions between subjects and their associated literacies.

The idea that literacy is a concern of all subject teachers is a key objective of the government's Key Stage 3 National Strategy, which resurrects the principles underpinning the recommendations for literacy across the curriculum made by the Bullock (DES, 1975) and Kingman (DES, 1988) Reports. The recently published *Language at Work in Lessons. Literacy Across the Curriculum at Key Stage 3* (QCA, 2001) provides a rationale which recognizes the centrality of language use in subject learning:

> Effective teaching strategies across subjects involve pupils in many kinds of learning that require them to use language. They engage in

a great deal of talking and listening, different kinds of writing and reading and the best kind of 'thinking on your feet' . . . The teaching objectives for language are not an alternative to, or an additional load on, the learning of the subject, but the means of supporting key learning skills. (Ibid, p. 5)

Exemplar lessons for Years 7, 8 and 9 in different subject areas are provided with specific 'subject learning' and 'literacy learning' objectives, a useful development of the previously published *Language for Learning in Key Stage 3* (QCA, 2000) and the series of leaflets outlining the use of language in curriculum areas published by the SCAA in 1997 (*Use of Language: A Common Approach*).

The broad objectives of these initiatives are a welcome move in the direction of recognizing that subject knowledge and expertise are not in themselves sufficient, that teachers must use their pedagogical knowledge to communicate their subjects to less expert pupils who are novices in the field. Literacy is being highlighted as central to effective teaching and learning. Identifying the literacy demands of different subjects, making them explicit and embedding them in practice is a goal which, if achieved, would help pupils negotiate the boundaries between subjects and know how to be literate in relation to each domain. The process of knowing *about* a subject is made transparent, and pupils will be given the means of knowing *in* that subject. My intention is not to argue with the objectives, but to suggest that they are based on an inadequate understanding of both teachers and the literacies of school subjects. More thorough classroom-based research is needed to understand the contexts in which these policies will operate. My modest aim in this chapter is to offer some observations from classroom-based studies which provide insights into where teachers are in relation to subject literacies, and the ways in which literacy initiatives have impacted on their thinking and practice. The methodology employed in these observations will be offered, not as a tried and tested way of approaching the task, but as an ongoing process of finding more accurate ways of describing the literacy activities which characterize classroom life.

The overall design of the literacy research project, reported in Chapter 2, provided access to a number of schools nominated by LEA personnel as examples of good policy and practice in relation to literacy. Four of these schools have been visited, key staff interviewed and lessons observed in a number of curriculum areas. Lessons were nominated by teachers as representative of how literacy fits into their respective subjects. Evidence from the research will be presented to suggest that literacy-focused teachers and schools have made a modest start in acknowledging the importance of literacy in subjects across the secondary curriculum, but that they are a long way from translating a sophisticated understanding of the concept into effective changes in practice. School policies have implemented measures such as cross-curricular spelling and marking policies, and attention to 'key words' in subjects, but, as one deputy head observed, the real question of 'what next' is not so easy to answer.

In search of consensus

In one of the case study schools, a literacy focus has been on the school's agenda for five years and the process has reached the stage of attending to the teaching and learning in subject areas. I was invited to observe a lunchtime in-service training (INSET) on Writing in the Humanities led by the Head of History. He used an overhead projector to display examples of writing frames used for various age and ability groups, and participants were given copies of pupils' essays which displayed the cumulative value of using the techniques for supporting and structuring their writing.

The techniques demonstrated were:

- writing frames using 'big points' to start a paragraph followed by 'little points' to support them
- the 'hamburger technique', with the introduction at the top of the burger, the main part of the essay as the filling and the conclusion at the bottom. This model was also used for structuring each paragraph opening point, supporting evidence and concluding point
- sentences cut out on sugar paper which pupils organize into a paragraph
- starter sentences which 'kick them off' so then they can 'run with it'
- question prompts, which 'gives more freedom than filling in the gaps which they find frustrating'
- tables, Venn diagrams, ripple diagrams
- model answers which the teacher and pupils deconstruct together. 'We use highlighter pens to locate the argument, seeing where it might be going wrong if the point at the middle or bottom should be at the top.'

The presenter emphasized the value of these techniques in terms of:

getting them to think and understand by making explicit what you should be doing in the essay. So as they move up the school the structure is taken away and they can do it. The initial thinking before writing is more emphasized, particularly in sixth form, where they have to have a point of view, don't go anywhere until you have a point of view, get that out of the way and then a series of planning points. They start with asking *why are we interested in this as historians* and they must argue their point of view.

In what followed, a number of interesting divergences were apparent in participants' ideas on how writing should be organized.

Geography teacher 1:
Isn't that like coming to a conclusion before you've put the facts for it? With Geography we put the facts from both sides and come to a conclusion at the end.

Presenter (History teacher):
If they do it this way the results are fantastic.

Geography teacher 2:
If they've already made up their minds to begin with, wouldn't their argument be lop-sided and exclude all the elements that back up the other point of view?

Presenter:
What we actually get them to do, okay, that's your opinion, one of the things they have to do is give the other side of the story to show why they think that side's wrong and what the evidence is for their point of view. We get them to dismiss the other point of view so there's a common thread and they're going hell for leather for one thing. I know when I wrote A level essays I didn't know where I was going, I used to perambulate through this essay and form a conclusion thinking I don't know how I got here and that just felt wrong. So what I'm trying to get them to do is think.

English teacher:
In English I plan essays with them and they write the conclusion as an introduction, and doing that they push the level of understanding forward and then they go through the exploration to prove that but in some cases they disprove slightly what they've said and they have to counteract that as they go through but it does push the level of thinking one stage further forward.

Geography teacher 1:
Coming to a conclusion in the introduction goes against the grain somehow.

Presenter:
It's one of those things, it reads more impressively if they know what they are thinking right from the start and pursue it ruthlessly right the way through. Students who do that get the A grades. It does pay off.

The evidence from this short dialogue is interesting in a number of ways:

- It indicates a failure to reach a consensus on what counts as 'good' writing, despite the attempt by the English teacher (the deputy head who had organized the session) to bring the two sides together. Whilst all the teachers agreed that literacy was an important aspect of their respective subjects, the move to concrete specifications revealed subtle but significant differences, which pupils are required to negotiate as they move between curriculum subjects. The rhetorical devices and persuasive techniques appropriate to a History essay are not the same as those in a Geography essay. The session may be regarded as valuable in illuminating these divergent perceptions, making teachers more aware of the literacy/writing demands of their own and other subject areas.
- The session also revealed interesting assumptions in relation to the purpose of writing, which was commonly regarded as a vehicle for *thinking*. Teachers were ready to regard literacy as integral to the learning process and not a subsidiary concern, suggesting that they have accepted arguments for the close relationship between language and learning (Britton, 1970), and particularly the development of higher order thinking skills (Bruner, 1984; Olson, 1984; Wells, 1981).
- The session highlighted the extent to which writing instruction and development is conceptualized in relation to the assessment system which values individual achievement. The presenter of the session 'sold' his techniques on this basis. 'The results are fantastic.'

The session ended with examples of writing produced by pupils in Years 8, 9 and 10. All were answers to teachers' questions which had been evaluated by the teacher, thus replicating the traditional three-part discourse structure of schooling, (teacher) question – (pupil) answer – (teacher) evaluation (Sinclair and Coulthard, 1975):

- What was the most important event which led to the growth in the power of Parliament 1500–1750?
- Why and with what consequences did Britain become a Protestant nation?
- Was Hitler to blame for starting the Second World War?

For the History teacher, writing should display argument, evidence and explanation. Yet the dominant mode, which novices are developing in preparation for becoming experts at A level, is the highly structured, tightly argued essay, and the more exploratory methods employed lower down the school are regarded as preparation for the real thing. The question the teacher thought pupils should increasingly be asking as they progress through the school is, 'why are we interested in this as historians?'

This short exchange between teachers suggests that there are important differences between subjects and their associated literacy practices, even in relation to a single written mode. More importantly, it suggests that there is not a single subject literacy but a variety of literacies which are seen as appropriate for pupils at different ages, and perhaps by different teachers within each domain who may not share perceptions of what they are doing and why they are doing it.

Multiple subject literacies

The presenter of the INSET session was assuming that pupils who study A level History have to think and write like professional historians. They have achieved expert status within the subject domain and have mastered the 'academic' literacy, i.e., the means by which this and other subject communities are represented and maintained as specialist domains of knowledge and expertise. Attention to specialized vocabulary and subject-specific writing genres is an important part of this process, but it only scratches the surface of what is required of pupils.

Discourse is a useful concept in coming to a more comprehensive understanding of the nature of subject-specific literacies. Gee (1990, p. 143) defines Discourse as:

> socially accepted association among ways of using language, of thinking, feeling, believing, valuing, and of acting that can be used to identify oneself as a member of a socially meaningful group or 'social network', or to signal (that one is playing) a socially meaningful 'role'.

Gee makes an important distinction between primary and secondary Discourses. Pupils are members of the primary Discourses which signal their membership of family, community, peer groups and other cultural groups outside school, and these serve as a 'framework' or 'base' for their acquisition and learning of other Discourses. Secondary Discourses are developed in association with social institutions, such as schools.

Initiation into any Discourse requires an understanding of the norms and conventions which govern linguistic but also cultural meaning. Pupils are required to internalize the patterns of Discourse so as to speak, write, think and act as members of the culture. Schools are charged with developing what counts as school literacy and constructing an identity for the 'literate' pupil. In broad terms, this will be reflected in the norms and rituals which guide behaviour and communicate the aspirations, beliefs and values which constitute the school as a literate community. It may be located in overt public forms, such as dress codes, school assemblies and school rules. It is also evidenced in the day-to-day transactions

which constitute school learning and, although these will vary across subjects, there will be commonalities. Writing is used as evidence of learning
and is closely associated with assessment. Reading is more intensive and
task oriented than the reading pupils might engage in outside school.

In addition to becoming literate in relation to the school, pupils enter
the discourses of school subjects, and they need to function within and
across these discourses. Teachers represent, and are spokespersons for,
their respective subject discourses and are responsible for mediating the
subject by engaging pupils in a variety of literate activities. Every school
textbook or worksheet, for example, will have a subject discourse embedded in it which has implications for literacy learning. Some meanings will
be authorized and privileged, whilst others will be marginalized and even
suppressed by the reading, writing, speaking, listening, thinking and
viewing activities which make up the literacy events in lessons. In order
to participate in the discourse, pupils need to understand the rules, which
determine when and how they should speak and listen, and the kinds of
reading and writing practices and positions appropriate to the subject.
These discursive practices are not natural but learnt competencies. The
challenge for teachers is to be in control of the discourse, to be able to
stand outside its parameters and recognize its power, so they can understand the literacy demands it makes on pupils as they participate in the
discourse community. They do not reject it, but consciously 'speak it'
without allowing 'it' to 'speak' them. Gee's distinction between the
primary Discourse of experience outside school and the secondary
Discourses of schooling makes it imperative for teachers to realize that
some pupils will easily adapt to the literacy demands of schooling because
they are closer to what they already know. And pupils see the point of literacy when it is presented as a means of participation rather than decon-
textualized skills which have no practical application to learning.

Morgan (1997, p. 3) makes the point that 'no teacher is circumscribed
entirely by one discourse', and school subjects contain a number of sometimes competing discourses which may be seen to 'converge and argue
with one another'. Goodson and Marsh (1996, p. 33), in their study of
the subject communities, describe them as 'arenas of conflict':

> 'We do not, then, view subjects as continuing homogeneous groups
> whose members share monolithic and similar values and definitions
> of role, common interests and identity. Rather subjects should be
> viewed as comprising a range of conflicting sub-groups, segments or
> factions.'

Differences within subjects are as important as differences between subjects. They suggests three broad traditions which contest the definition of
school subjects:

- the *academic* tradition, which is content focused and stresses abstract and theoretical knowledge for its own sake, closely associated with formal written examinations
- the *utilitarian* tradition which values subject knowledge for its relevance to adult life
- the *pedagogic* tradition which focuses, not on the subject, but on the pupil as active agent in the learning process, favouring discovery methods as a means of personal development.

It is possible to extrapolate from these categories a number of possible *models* of literacy which teachers operate within their subjects. The History teacher cited earlier can be seen to adhere to the academic literacy model when talking about A level writing, but he was aware of the importance of pedagogy in relating content to pupils' individual needs and interests. Any one teacher may subscribe to a number of subject and associated literacy discourses or models, which are not separate but coexist, being constructed and developed through each other.

A fourth model or discourse, is a *critical* literacy, and in one sense this is what is required of teachers if they are to have sufficient distance from their subject to analyse it and recognize its discursive nature. It involves demystifying the subject and how it is selected, interpreted and represented, requiring pupils to read and write against the grain, deconstructing the assumptions which underpin school knowledge. Moreover, it is about reading 'the word and the world' (Freire, 1972), thus making use of both primary and secondary Discourses to develop a critically conscious understanding of the politics of literacy.

The notion of a plurality of literacies within a subject, asking 'which History?' or 'which Science?' and so on, may be a productive way of reflecting on practice, and relating literacy activities to subject content, and teaching objectives and methods. Teaching History for personal growth, in the pedagogic tradition, is likely to invite exploratory methods such as role play, drama, simulations, and local and family studies, with a focus on developing historical imagination and empathy. These may be regarded as part of the historical method and, so, an element of the academic discourse. And the literacy skills involved in the process of enquiry, in recording, judging, selecting, organizing and communicating information, feeds into the utilitarian discourse in developing skills which have wider applicability. A critical literacy would focus on developing an understanding of how the past was, and is, constructed and represented, and in whose interests. Methods and approaches which involve reading different versions of events, analysing sources and detecting bias, have great potential for demystifying the process (and politics) of representation.

The languages of school science

The research project highlighted the fact that, in terms of persuading teachers of the importance of subject literacies, science teaching is the most problematic area. Of all curriculum subjects, science may appear to pupils as something separate from their lives, intent upon transmitting difficult knowledge in the strange context of the laboratory where teachers wear white coats and manipulate tools and apparatus which require an expertise not developed anywhere else. The classroom even smells strange, and the language register expected in science investigations, observations and reports are likely to be unfamiliar to pupils. The transition from the 'cosy' science of the primary classroom to the 'hard science' of the secondary school is likely to be difficult, and OFSTED Inspection speculates that the relatively poor progress made by pupils at Key Stage 3 may be due to the changes in teaching methods and terminology used in science teaching, together with low expectations of pupils and insufficient emphasis on practical and investigative work which could increase pupil motivation.

Lemke (1990) argues that the science curriculum builds a false mystique around science, implying that most pupils are not capable of learning it. The academic discourse is dominant, and science knowledge appears to have little connection to the everyday science experiences of pupils. And it is presented unproblematically as, 'not a way of talking about the world but as the world is'. Yet pupils are exposed to mediations and representations of science, particularly in the media, and it is a fundamental part of life outside the laboratory. 'Science literacy' has become an objective for educators in the US, Canada and Australia, and the ability to understand and criticize science as a human activity is increasingly regarded as necessary for understanding and participating in both our natural and social worlds.

The eight science lessons observed in the research project, nominated by teachers as representing both the subject and its attendant literacy, provided evidence of an increasing understanding of the need to demystify the subject, to make connections with everyday experience and explain specialist terminology in lay terms, but less indication that pupils are to be encouraged to question the truth, value and objectivity of science. Practical experiments are designed to prove scientific facts, analogies are drawn with more everyday concepts, but there is no fundamental questioning of the economic, social, technical and political role of science in society. In short, there was little evidence of teachers developing a critical science literacy.

In one Year 9 Physics lesson, a 'bottom set' of pupils (six boys and six girls) were conducting an experiment to investigate the concept of resistance and how it affects voltage and current, part of a Key Stage 3 scheme of work on 'Electricity and Magnetism'. The teacher, who had been at the school for 11 years, had previously worked in science research and her qualifications included a Bio-Chemistry degree and a doctorate. She felt that the main problem with less able pupils was reading and following instructions, and understanding scientific terminology. She had produced a booklet to introduce the concepts, draw an 'everyday' analogy with a water pump, guide pupils through the experiment, record their results and draw conclusions by completing two sentences:

If the voltage in the circuit is increased without changing the resistance the current will . . . .

The current leaving the power supply is . . . . as the current flowing back into the power supply.

A number of interesting literacy issues emerged from this lesson. The most obvious is that making meaning was not simply a matter of verbal communication. It required practical action, to conduct the experiment. Pupils were required to read and copy a visual representation of the experiment, together with the mathematical symbols (A for ammeter, V for voltage, plus and minus, the symbolic representation for a battery, filament lamp and power supply). They had to copy and complete a table recording their observations of the readings on the two ammeters. Finally, they had to complete the sentences to record their conclusions, integrating the diagrams and numerical representations and putting into words what it all meant. The second conclusion was all but drawn for them – it is not possible to insert any words other than 'the same'. ('Bigger' or 'smaller' cannot be followed by 'as'.) However, a seemingly simple task, carefully structured by the teacher through demonstration and the workbook guide, was in fact a very demanding one in terms of literacy which included not just specialist language but specialist visual, mathematical and quantitative symbols. Although the teacher did much of the talking in the lesson, and little time appeared to be spent on pupils' writing, literacy was a major part of this lesson. The literacy tasks were minimal, the literacy demands of the lesson as a whole were far more complex. It might be characterized as an academic science literacy in that the focus was on learning concepts which are fundamental to the discipline and to becoming a scientist.

Conceptual learning does not have to be divorced from everyday experience. In one Year 8 lesson, a low-ability class of pupils worked in groups to construct a concept map to illustrate the connections between words associated with digestion. The teacher explained that his aim was to encourage them to 'talk science': 'When they do science they sit there and listen to it and write it, they never discuss it. The biggest problem they have is with the science specific word, enzyme, such a strange word.' In the course of the scheme of work on 'Healthy Eating', pupils had engaged in a variety of literacy activities and genres not automatically associated with science learning. Pupils' writing tasks included writing menus, a script for a radio show on healthy eating, a video advertising a healthy product, and a poem. The teacher was in control of the subject discourse, and literacy was serving both the pupils and the subject. This was a personal growth style lesson, but the scheme of work as a whole had potential to develop a critical science literacy in tasks which investigated how science is marketed and mediated in society.

The literacy wasteland

The four case study schools had all allocated English lessons for specific literacy teaching to Year 7 pupils. In one school, this was for all pupils in the year group, in the others for those below level 4 or 3 in their Key Stage 2 English SATs. These 'catch up' programmes are part of the Key Stage 3 Strategy (DfEE, 2001, p. 13):

> The aim is to provide focused and practical methods of catching up for pupils who are out of step with their peers, and to achieve this as early as possible. The emphasis is on applying what has been learnt so that pupils transfer skills into their everyday work in English and in other subjects.

The concept of literacy informing this aspect of the Strategy is a mechanistic notion of literacy skills. These skills are not confined to surface features and include sophisticated reading and writing strategies, such as 'reading between the lines, using inference and deduction', and 'developing a wider repertoire of sentence structures' (ibid., p. 13). They are a well-intentioned move to provide all pupils with 'high expectations and support'. Yet the teaching of literacy in some neutral, autonomous space where pupils are isolated from their peers and offered disembodied skills for no obvious purpose may well be counter-productive. Of all the observed lessons, these provided the least evidence of pupils actively engaged in creative and purposeful uses of language. They were characterized by tightly structured, whole-class, teacher directed exercises in spelling, punctuation, grammar and comprehension. They were low-risk lessons, with pupils performing undemanding tasks in a routinized fashion, and there was more boredom than disruption. There was no apparent connection between the knowledge transmitted to pupils and their everyday experiences, in or out of school. To understand literacy as a social and cultural practice is to recognize that it cannot be reduced to skills but is a dynamic resource for getting things done, socially and culturally. Passive imitation and 'getting it right' does not amount to full and proper literacy, and the effect on pupils engaged in this quality control exercise may be damaging. Research suggests that successful literate pupils see themselves as literate, not a literacy problem, and pupils would be justified in asking the fundamental question, literacy – for what? The answer would be to help them reach level 4, or 5, to reach the standard expected of their age group, and no doubt they will since the tests test what is taught.

In one Year 7 Literacy lesson, a class of 'low ability' (level 3) pupils – 10 boys and two girls – worked on spelling and full stops. They worked in mixed-ability sets for the other four-weekly English lessons, but were 'set' for the Literacy lesson. (This was the next to bottom set.) The teacher, a Special Needs and English specialist, valued the session:

> I think it's a good thing because we teach mixed ability English and there is a huge range of ability, some have reading ages of 6, others 15, and we are trying to set work appropriate to them all. When we're reading together, writing character studies in diaries, they can all work at their own level, but when it comes to literacy teaching, you know, teaching punctuation, some of them need to learn full stops and commas, and some subordinate clauses and the passive tense. The top sets are learning about the philosophy of language, that sort of thing.

The fixed ability groupings for 'literacy' lessons mean that pupils are given access to different models of literacy; those in 'low-ability' sets are confined to a narrow curriculum of basic skills, whilst the 'high attainers' are developing a critical language awareness.

This was an experienced, thoughtful and competent teacher who provided evidence of innovative and creative literacy teaching. Her Year 9 group had recently used the Internet to download short stories, written their own, posted them onto the short story site and were responding to reviews they had received. The social nature of literacy, of sharing ideas and having a sense of audience, was highlighted in this and other activities.

In this 'Literacy' lesson, she began by writing a sentence on the board:

> Sue spilt the stew on the fruit.

Pupils were instructed to copy the sentence in their best handwriting. She then asked them to make three columns, for *ue, ew* and *ui*, and to put the words she would read out in the appropriate column. She placed the words in sentences. The exercise lasted 15 minutes, and pupils were then asked for the correct answers and marked each others work. For the rest of the lesson, they worked independently, writing a sentence to include a word from each column. The teacher reminded them to use capital letters and full stops, 'it's the first thing you learn about sentences. If you haven't learnt the first thing you can't go on to other things. After half term we'll work a bit at developing our sentences using commas, exclamation marks, question marks and other things so we can have a more interesting range of sentences.'

The lesson was based on literacy conceived as a structured, linear process, learning to walk before you can run. The class included one dyslexic pupil who was disruptive on a number of occasions. He was clearly popular with other pupils, the 'clown of the class' in the teacher's eyes. A snippet from the lesson transcript encapsulates the situation:

Teacher
Bruise. I bumped into the wall and I had a big bruise.

Luke
(Gestures to his leg, leans back on his chair and loses his balance).

Teacher
Few. There are only a few people who have been to the moon.

Luke
I've been to the moon.

Teacher
We only have one literacy lesson a week Luke, I know you have your tutor time.

View. There is a lovely view out of the window.

The teacher passed comment on the pupil after the lesson: 'He's bright and he's frustrated so he hates the whole idea of literacy, doesn't want to know about spelling or anything, just thinks he's a failure so he does all this to block it all out I suppose.'

Researching literacy: in search of a method

This designated 'literacy lesson' has been characterized as a 'no literacy' lesson and it highlights the ways in which well-intentioned policies with positive objectives may have unintended outcomes. The lesson could be evaluated as effective on its own terms, through testing the skills transmitted by the teacher, but to view literacy as a social practice, a way of using language for a variety of purposes, supports classroom based research which focuses on literacy *events* and *practices* and how they are constructed by participants (teacher and pupils) in those events through their social interactions.

The aims in observing subject/literacy lessons was to develop some understanding of the literacy demands of different subjects and the teaching strategies which characterize lessons in which teachers are consciously focusing on their subject and its attendant literacy. The design of the project was such that the participant teachers would be likely to provide examples of good practice. This does not mean that they were simply experts in their subjects, or good teachers. If effective literacy teaching is collapsed into the general category of effective teaching, how do you research it? The research literature is slight and much relates to primary practice (see, for example, Beard, 2000; Medwell et al., 2000; Reynolds, 1998).

Literacy teaching and learning may be seen as part of what Shulman (1986, p. 4–14) has called a teacher's 'pedagogical content knowledge':

> [it] embodies the aspects of content most germane to its teachability. Within the category of pedagogical content knowledge I include, for the most regularly taught topics in one's subject area, the most useful forms of representation of those ideas, the most powerful analogies, illustrations, examples, explanations and demonstrations – in a word, the ways of representing and formulating the subject that make it comprehensible to others . . . [It] also includes an understanding of what makes the learning of specific concepts easy or difficult, the conceptions and preconceptions that students of different ages and backgrounds bring with them to learning.

There are certainly absences in this account (the gender identity of students is a striking omission) but it illustrates the extent to which literacy teaching requires an integration of subject content knowledge and pedagogical knowledge to become a fundamental part of the teacher's 'pedagogical content' expertise (see Leach and Moon [1999] and Mortimer [1999] for discussions which focus specifically on teachers'pedagogy).

How to research literacy is not simply an academic question; teachers are increasingly called upon to be researchers, as they observe primary literacy hours and colleagues' lessons, and reflect on their own practice in relation to literacy.

Before deciding 'what to look for', a number of points may be worth considering:

- No research method is neutral.
- The research methods we adopt are likely to embody and reflect our beliefs.

- The research methods we adopt inevitably determine what we see.
- All literacy research must be informed by a theory of literacy.

Schools who are encouraging teachers to observe literacy teaching are, implicitly or explicitly, subscribing to a social model which sees it as an active learning process rather than the handing over of knowledge or skills. The classroom is a complex, multidimensional environment, any lesson a dynamic event. Professional researchers have devised sophisticated methods which confront this complexity (see, for example, Webster, Beveridge and Reed, 1996). It may be useful as a starting point to focus on one or two manageable dimensions identified in the research and literature as having an important effect on literacy.

All the 24 subject lessons were audio recorded to provide a record of oral discourse. These have been placed alongside field notes and an observation schedule completed in each lesson. A number of *categories* were devised for observation; any one of the categories could stand alone as a research focus:

- *The classroom environment* – furniture, seating arrangements, computers, equipment, the positioning and movements of the teacher and pupils. There is a close relationship between these factors and the pedagogy used by the teacher, e.g. whole-class teaching places the teacher at the front of the class and pupils do not move, group work often requires rearrangement of furniture and more teacher mobility. Some of these factors are within the teacher's control, whilst others (such as the positioning of computers) are not. The interaction patterns in the lesson may be determined to a large extent by the opportunities and constraints of the classroom environment.
- *Classroom displays* – the subject is communicated to pupils partly through the way it is represented around the classroom. For example, displays of pupils' work as opposed to, or as well as, posters of professional authors, literacy displays which emphasize the place of literacy in the subject.
- *Literacy tools* – the material technologies available to make and communicate meaning. These are important elements in the learning environment since they shape the activities around them. The availability of resources is not the same as using them.
- *Interaction patterns* in the classroom – individual, paired and group work, whole-class teaching.
- *Texts* read and produced in the lesson.
- *Literate practices – reading, writing, speaking, listening, viewing.* These may be related to the *interaction patterns* (are pupils listening to teacher exposition or instruction/as respondent to a partner or group?); to the *purpose* of the activity (are pupils writing to report, explain, instruct,

describe, narrate, inform, persuade, reflect, argue, analyse?); to the *level of difficulty* or challenge on pupils' literacy. Writing which involves copying or completing set exercises may be regarded as a low level literacy activity, a more open task such as rewriting a text from a different point of view as a high level literacy activity; reading a textbook to reinforce knowledge transmitted by the teacher or to answer set 'comprehension' questions as opposed to using it as a source of information to be critically analysed and evaluated. The quality of the literacy activities and the time spent on them can be noted.

- *The role of the teacher* – the teacher is the most important 'variable' in any lesson. Even in a lesson where the teacher loses control and is wholly ineffective, the course of the lesson is determined by the teacher. The model of effective literacy teaching advocated in the research and literature, which underpins the Strategy, promotes teaching that is 'direct and explicit' and 'highly interactive'. Teachers should make connections with pupils' prior knowledge, have clear objectives explicitly stated at the start of any lesson and consolidated in a plenary at the end of the lesson. There should be an emphasis on scaffolding to support pupils' early efforts and build their confidence, modelling the process of composition or comprehension in shared reading and writing sessions, guided reading and writing in which the teacher attends to a particular group. Pupils should be encouraged to develop a language to talk about language, a meta-language which is made explicit by the teacher.

The observation categories are not exclusive but interacting variables which impact upon literacy teaching and learning. Field notes also considered more elusive categories, such as levels of pupil motivation and interest. Other important non-linguistic elements in the meaning-making process became evident, such as actions (body language, gestures, facial expressions) and the importance of visual representation and communication.

The lessons provide no more than snapshots and it is not possible to generalize from the small sample. However, they suggest that, when teachers are focusing on subject literacy, they adopt very traditional styles of teaching with a high proportion of whole-class teaching 'from the front', based on the initiation/response/evaluation pattern of discourse (Sinclair and Coulthart, 1975). Attention to language focused on the naming of parts of sentences, dictionary word meanings and spellings, with no evidence of developing grammatical knowledge as a tool for critical reading. The 'literacy tools' used are traditional and print based, with the teacher using whiteboard and pens and pupils writing in books or on worksheets being the most common activity. In one school, where

English teachers have adopted the 10-minute literacy 'starter', A4 pieces of laminated card are used as slates and pupils write their answers with marker pens, holding them up for the teacher to check. Other tools included textbooks, a class reader, a poetry anthology, a play text, information books, dictionaries, a board game, all part of the technology of the book. In one lesson a video was shown, in another an overhead projector was used, and computers featured in three lessons.

The role of ICT in literacy learning: in search of a pedagogy

The value of the approach adopted in observing lessons was its ability to focus on the context of the lesson as a whole. In relation to the use of computers, it did not start from a position of advocacy, and regarded the technology as one element in a complex learning environment. The fact that ICT is not generally an element in the observed lessons suggests that the current drive to improve literacy is not linked to the promotion of ICT in schools. A close reading of the Strategy reveals almost no references to the use of ICT in any aspect of literacy teaching. Teachers were interviewed before the observed lessons and, despite the absence of ICT in the literacy-focused lessons, all said that it is an increasingly important and integrated aspect of their subjects. There was a common acceptance of using word processors to compose texts, and English teachers particularly valued the opportunities for redrafting and text transformation. Geography teachers placed high value on using the Internet and developing information retrieval skills. Science teachers make use of software packages for data logging, graphs and spreadsheets. There was ample evidence from pupils' work that computers are increasingly a normal part of classroom routines. Teachers seem therefore to regard ICT as an essential aspect of their subjects but not necessarily of the *literacy* of their subjects.

The interface between literacy teaching, subject teaching and ICT is an important area which is neglected in the Strategy, where there is no specific mention of how new technologies may be harnessed to promote 'traditional' literacy, or the ways in which new literacy practices are being developed through the use of new technologies. Can ICT be integrated into current models of effective literacy teaching? What does scaffolding and modelling look like when ICT is the chief literacy tool employed in a lesson? Are different styles of teaching and lesson structures emerging, or do they need to be developed, in order to maximize the potential of ICT for literacy learning? Literacy is always mediated through a technology of some kind, even if it is simply the voice of the teacher. What is 'new' technology to one teacher may be 'old' technology to another, and using an overhead projector or video may be perceived as radical in some classrooms. Lankshear and Knoebel (1997) make the point which brings us closer to reaching an understanding of the relationship between ICT and literacy:

> Talk of technological literacies seems to arise from the fact that the technologies integral to conventional or 'normal' literacy practices have become 'invisible' as a result of their always having 'been there' in our practice. Hence we take them for granted and they do not stand out as technologies. When new technologies come along, however, they stand out in relief from our conventional practice, and notions of applying them to and incorporating them into literacy practices strikes us as introducing a technological dimension, as constituting 'technological literacies'. (p. 139)

New technologies do not replace but exist alongside older technologies. However, applying computer-based technologies to literacy practices is not simply doing old things in new ways. New literacy practices are developing, and new types of texts are being comprehended and composed, as pupils read, write and think electronically. The National Literacy Strategy is unlikely to promote the idea that managing and producing new kinds of texts is a part of literacy, and while teachers are often engaged in activities involving information genres, multimedia genres and the like, they do not appear to regard them as emergent forms and practices of literacy. The Strategy seeks to teach pupils to 'manipulate the conventions of language' and use it 'imaginatively and flexibly'; where are words more obviously manipulable than on a computer screen?

Teachers were presented with the rationale from the beginning of the Strategy and asked to comment on it. It makes no mention of ICT. Only one teacher made reference to this silence:

> Literacy is a preparation for life and ICT should be there. The technology we have at the moment is our means of communication in the world of work and schools should reflect that, and the danger is that our pupils are ahead already.

Literature, literacy and ICT

One of the observed lessons which involved the use of computers was an English lesson. The current literacy initiatives have adopted a 'base camp' in English, and the Key Stage 3 *Framework* is essentially an English *Framework*. A 'reading' of one lesson may be a useful indication of the ways in which computers affect literacy pedagogy, and how this might impact upon teachers who are planning to meet the objectives of the *Framework* and simultaneously harness the potential of ICT to achieve them.

The lesson involved a class of 17 pupils (11 boys and six girls) investigating the narrative structure of *Wuthering Heights* as part of their first-year A level Literature study. *The teacher* was interviewed briefly before the lesson. She has a degree in English, Drama and Media Studies and has been teaching for three years. She feels very strongly that the 'whole literacy thing' is a 'waste of time' if it does not address teachers in other subjects, and feels that for her it is an unnecessary repetition of what she already practises in delivering the National Curriculum for English:

> Any English teacher would tell you that they teach literacy in every lesson but the idea that we have to prove that . . . is not valuable. Anyone who has been trained in the past five years has been taught the strategies they're bringing in so for me it's nothing new.

She is confident in her own ICT skills and believes that literacy teaching should include teaching these skills to pupils. She described her two *aims* for the lesson as 'word processing, and the narrative structure of *Wuthering Heights*'. Thirteen statements were written on a 'worksheet' entitled 'Why Tell the Story in this Way?', and this was already on each pupil's file on the computers:

> (a) The narrative structure of the novel is more complicated than it needs to be.
>
> (b) Lockwood is not absolutely essential to the novel.
>
> (c) Nelly's conversations with Lockwood are an awkward reminder of the artificiality of the novel.
> etc.

Their task was to open three Word documents entitled 'Agree', 'Disagree' and 'Unsure', and cut and paste the statements into one of the documents, giving a reason supported by a textual quotation for their decision.

> So it's combining discussing in pairs, getting them to look at the text and think about what other pairs think, use their word processing skills, all quite simple stuff. (Teacher)

The lesson took place in the computer suite situated in the school library, a large wood-panelled Victorian room which has tables scattered around the bookshelves with the computers situated along each side of the room. Pupils facing the screens will automatically have their backs to the teacher. The suite has to be prebooked and subject teachers compete for its use. Whilst the English Department has a small annexed suite, it does not have enough machines for a whole class to use at the same time which makes it difficult to integrate computers into everyday classroom activities.

The pupils entered the room and sat around the tables. The teacher spent the first 10 minutes addressing the whole group, delivering instructions about the technical aspects of the task, how to cut and paste, create documents, use bold and italic. They were given the choice of working alone or in pairs.

The pupils then moved to the computers and all chose to work alone, each with their own screen, in clusters of all boys and all girls. For the rest of the lesson they worked on the task and the teacher visited each pupil, working her way systematically down one side of the room and then the other. Pupils interacted with their neighbours, helping each other sort out operational problems, interspersed with general 'chat'. I did not hear any discussion of the subject content as I circulated around the room. On two occasions, the teacher addressed the whole group, drawing their attention to aspects of the text but she did not gain their attention and few turned away from their screens to focus on what she was saying. Her conversations with individual pupils varied: with some she discussed the statements but the majority sought her help in relation to the technical problems they were having.

The lesson ended with the teacher telling the pupils to save their work, and to read the next two chapters of the novel for homework. They would 'come back to this' in the next lesson, which was to be in their classroom without the computers.

This lesson illustrates the problems of utilizing the model of effective literacy teaching enshrined in the Strategy when pupils are working with computers. They had an impact on *pupils' interactions* (with each other, with the teacher and with their learning environment) and the lesson problematizes any assumption that writing at a computer makes it a more collaborative, less private activity. Most interaction occurred between the teacher and individual pupils, through the voice and not the technology. The pupils did not work in pairs and there was little sense of the social nature of literacy; their main focus was not on *what* but *how* they were writing. It also had an impact on the *teacher's role* and pedagogical style. The lesson was in one sense tightly controlled, but without any real structure. She did not have a teaching screen, so the kinds of whole-class teaching, and the modelling and scaffolding activities which she supports were not technically possible. Nor was she able to share some of the strategies in a 'plenary' at the end of the lesson. Some of the pupils found the task technically difficult, others found it easy but struggled with the requirement to keep looking at their hard copy of the text to find supporting quotes and their frustrations were partly a product of having to move from screen to page and back. (No pupil completed the task in the lesson.) They were disinclined to turn away from their screens when the teacher tried to gain their attention, so 'teaching points' were repeated to each individual as she moved round the room.

This was an effective literacy teacher, who is confident in using ICT to promote her subject and plans carefully for opportunities to make that 'link'. Asked whether the lesson could be taught as effectively without the computers, she felt that 'an important dimension would be lost'. Yet there are important issues here, and how to run an effective ICT/literacy/ subject lesson which maximizes learning potential in each is one that needs to be addressed in the light of lessons like this. Pupils did practise their computer skills, and they were learning literacy *for* technology. And the technology was highly motivating, particularly for boys, several of whom said they find handwriting slow and laborious. But there was no real interaction between the ICT objective and the subject objective and it could be argued that the lesson might have been taught more effectively through the use of a whiteboard or an overhead projector.

In this lesson, ICT was employed as a tool, an electronic version of a traditional pen and paper activity. In terms of the subject literacy embedded in the lesson, that is the academic discourse which requires A level pupils to become literary critics, it was a useful tool but not a springboard for developing new ways of reading and writing.

What if?

This was very much a partial study, and the cases discussed represent only a selective sample of lessons which are not necessarily typical or representative, but they are certainly indicative of some of the issues which need to be addressed if literacy across the curriculum is to become a reality. There is a danger that the official attention to the issue will result in a narrowing of teachers' perceptions of what literacy is, and the rich variety of language uses in different subjects will be simplified and levelled in a quest to find commonalities which do not exist. The transition into this new cultural milieu is a challenge but also an opportunity for pupils; discontinuity and variety are only a problem if they are not provided with the necessary guides to traverse this multicultural domain.

Attention to language is always a disconcerting experience. For teachers, it involves consciously thinking about their subjects and how they are represented, presented and communicated. By comprehending the discourses which they operate, they are in a position to analyse, criticise and change them. Model lessons and new ways of approaching literate tasks can help develop teachers' 'pedagogical content knowledge' but changes in practice require more than this. To have a real and lasting impact, literacy thinking needs to confront comfortable certainties and ask not just *how* but *what if* and *why?*

What if teacher exposition, making connections with pupils' experience, at the start of a lesson became a writing task by pupils? What if the practical experiment in a science lesson became a simulation which pupils could play around with on the computer screen? What if pupils' work were assessed according to different criteria other than how well they have reproduced the answers in the teacher's head? What if the aim is to challenge as well as teach subject genres? What if the subject discourse which authorizes certain literate practices is challenged to justify its authoritative status? The anonymous authors of the National Literacy Strategy have constructed an official discourse on literacy, which seeks to change, and also control, teachers' practice, at a time when they are already overworked and overwhelmed by the sheer volume of official directives. If it is to have any more than a superficial impact on literacy in the secondary school, it would do well to start by treating them as thinking subjects and not just passive objects in the discourse.

Overall the evidence suggests that schools should:

- invest time and resources in involving all staff in the literacy strategy, i.e., 'training' is not enough, staff need to feel ownership of the changes
- make selective use of the huge banks of externally produced resources, the resources are no guarantee of teacher engagement
- encourage departments to review the 'literacies' of their subject
- encourage departments to talk to each other about common issues using real examples
- accept that disagreements can be as productive as bland consensus
- link with schools who have developed their own strategies over time to adapt (not copy) them
- recognize that the primary model and the secondary model of a subject may be (and usually are) very different
- recognize that pupils can take a long time to internalize the language of each subject; recursive teaching is therefore very important
- recognize that subjects themselves have internal debates about their purpose and meaning; this is a sign of their health as disciplines
- be careful not let literacy become a mechanistic skills model leading to 'less able' pupils endlessly failing at a 'basic' level
- provide opportunities for colleagues to watch each other teach 'literacy' lessons and to be aware of the literacy environment, e.g. classroom furniture, wall displays, texts, literacy practices, teacher language
- consider that literacy is always related to technology and the 'new' technologies will be making a difference, a difference that is not predictable and needs close monitoring.

References

Beard, R. (2000) 'Research and the National Literacy Strategy', *Oxford Review of Education*, **26** (3–4), pp. 421–436.

Britton, J. (1970) *Language and Learning*, Harmondsworth, Penguin.

Bruner, J. (1984) 'Language, mind and reading', in H. Goelman, A. Oberg and F. Smith (eds), *Awakening to Literacy*, London, Heinemann.

Department of Education and Science (DES) (1975) *A Language for Life* (Bullock Report), London, HMSO.

Department of Education and SCience (DES) (1988) *Report of the Committee of Enquiry into the Teaching of English Language* (Kingman Report), London, HMSO.

Department for Education and Employment (DfEE) (2001) *Key Stage 3 National Strategy: Framework for Teaching English: Years 7, 8 and 9*, London, DfEE.

Freire, P. (1972) *Pedagogy of the Oppressed*, Harmondsworth, Penguin.

Gee, J. P. (1990) *Social Linguistics and Literacies: Ideology in Discourses*, London, Falmer Press.

Goodson, J. and Marsh, C. (1996) *Studying School Subjects: A Guide*, London, Falmer Press.

Goodwyn, A. (1992) 'English teachers and the Cox models', *English in Education*, **28** (3), Sheffield, NATE.

Goodwyn, A. and Findlay, K. (1999) 'The Cox models revisited: English teachers' views of their subject and the National Curriculum', *English in Education*, **33** (2), Sheffield, NATE.

Green, B. (1988) 'Subject-specific literacy and school learning: a focus on writing', *Australian Journal of Education*, **32** (2), pp. 156–179.

Lankshear, C. and Knobel, M. (1997) 'Literacies, texts and difference in the electronic age', in C. Lankshear (ed.) *Changing Literacies*, Buckingham, Open University Press.

Leach, J. and Moon, B. (eds) (1999) *Learners and Pedagogy*, London, Paul Chapman.

Lemke, J. (1990) *Talking Science: Language, Learning and Values'*, Norwood, NJ. Ablex.

Medwell, J., Wray, D., Poulson, L. and Fox, R. (2000) 'The teaching practices of effective teachers of literacy', *Educational Review*, **52** (1), pp. 75–85.

Morgan, W. (1997) *Critical Literacy in the Classroom*, London, Routledge.

Mortimer, P. (ed.) (1999) *Understanding Pedagogy and its Impact on Learning*, London, Sage.

Olson, D.R. (1984) ' "See! Jumping!" Some oral language antecedents of literacy', in H. Goelman, A. Oberg and F. Smith (eds), *Awakening to Literacy*, London, Heinemann.

Qualifications and Curriculum Authority (QCA) (2000) *Language for Learning in Key Stage 3*, London, QCA.

Qualifications and Curriculum Authority (QCA) (2001) *Language at Work in Lessons. Literacy Across the Curriculum at Key Stage 3*, London, QCA.

Reynolds, D. (1998) 'Schooling for literacy: a review of research on teacher effectiveness and its implications for contemporary educational policies', *Educational Review*, **50** (20) pp. 147–162.

Schools Curriculum and Assessment Authority (1997) *Use of Language: A Common Approach*, London, SCAA.

Schulman, L. S. (1986) 'Those who understand: knowledge growth in teaching', *Educational Researcher*, **15**, pp. 4–14.

Sinclair, J. and Coulthard, R. (1975) 'Towards an analysis of discourse', Oxford, Oxford University Press.

Webster, A., Beveridge, M. and Reed, M. (1996) *Managing the Literacy Curriculum*, London, Routledge.

Wells, G. (1981) 'Language, literacy and education', in G. Wells (ed), *Learning through Interaction*, London, Cambridge University Press.

4

Literacy at Key Stage 3

Michael Lockwood

This chapter examines the experience of middle schools, an almost for-gotten territory in terms of the NLS but uniquely placed to offer all other schools a very illuminating perspective. These schools, in their various forms, e.g. 8–12, 11–14, 9–13, etc., have been perceived as *the* transition schools in themselves, designed to avoid the problems of the primary–secondary divide. The chapter is based on recent research into the middle school experience and offers some unique insights.

Introduction

The research in this chapter has its background in my own career in edu-cation. As a grammar school pupil in the West Riding of Yorkshire in the 1960s I missed out on a pioneering 9–13 middle school scheme by just a few years, watching from a distance at university as my old school evolved into a 'high school' in new buildings and its former premises became a new middle school. After university and then a junior/middle PGCE course, I taught in 9–13 middle schools for the best part of 10 years before entering teacher education. My middle school teaching left me with an experience of a model of primary–secondary transition that I have since found to be not widely known.

Since their establishment, middle schools have gained unique experi-ence in continuity and progression in all areas of learning between primary and secondary education. Their collective expertise in teaching English at both Key Stage 2 (KS2) and Key Stage 3 (KS3) has taken on par-ticular and crucial relevance since the implementation of the National Literacy Strategy at KS2 in September 1998 and its extension to KS3 in September 2001. Middle school English teachers already have consider-able experience in attempting to adapt the NLS objectives in the *Framework for Teaching* (DfEE, 1998), and its recommended lesson struc-ture, the Literacy Hour, for Year 7 and often for Year 8 pupils. With the numbers of middle schools rapidly declining for reasons discussed later, this seemed a good moment to see what lessons can be learned from these schools about literacy teaching and learning at KS3 for the benefit of secondary teachers and pupils about to embark on the KS3 National Strategy.

Middle schools

The creation of middle schools was partly a response to the requirement to reorganize secondary education along comprehensive lines which came into force under the Labour government of 1965. Other arguments put forward at the time for their establishment were:

- the earlier maturation of children
- the recognition of the years 8–14 as a period of marked social and emotional, as well as physical, development which needed a flexible educational environment
- the beneficial effects of extending progressive primary education
- the elimination of the eleven-plus examination
- a smoother transition from primary to secondary schooling
- the opportunity to innovate new curricula not tied to public examinations
- in Scotland and other countries transfer to secondary education was later than 11
- in most British private schools the age of transfer was 13 (Blyth and Derricott, 1977; Edwards, 1972).

As well as these educational arguments, it was widely recognized that in practice some LEAs opted for reorganization into a three-tier comprehensive system with middle schools because of administrative convenience: this system made better use of existing buildings and staff. Also the 9–13 option was attractive since that type of middle school could be deemed secondary for funding purposes by its LEA and financed accordingly (Blyth and Derricott, 1977, p. 16). Whatever the motive for founding them, middle schools grew rapidly in number so that by the start of 1983 there were 1,810, including combined 5–12 schools, and 22 per cent of the 11-year-olds in English maintained schools were in some form of middle school (DES, 1983, p. 1), an expansion which has been called 'one of the most remarkable events in the recent history of the British educational system' (Hargreaves and Tickle, 1980, p. 1).

Equally remarkable has been the decline of middle schools in the late 1980s and 1990s. The HMI survey of 9–13 middle schools in 1983 concluded with a warning that: 'if 9–13 middle schools are to continue to provide a transition from primary to secondary modes, as originally envisaged, and to perform, age for age, as well as primary and secondary schools are expected to perform, given the present and likely trend of falling rolls, they will become increasingly expensive' (DES, 1983, p. 130). Middle schools had to expand generalist teaching because of financial cuts at a time when an increase in subject specialist teaching to raise standards in upper primary and lower secondary education was being recommended.

In his later book, *Two Cultures of Schooling: The Case of Middle Schools*, Hargreaves speaks of 'the likelihood of the extinction of the species in some areas', and mentions specifically that 'the winding up of middle school systems has already been announced for Wirral, Stoke-on-Trent and Brighton. Others may follow' (Hargreaves, 1986, pp. 2–3). Others did follow. With the advent of the National Curriculum (NC) in 1988, with its division of schooling into four Key Stages (ages 5–7, 7–11, 11–14 and 14–16), each ending in a nationally reported assessment point, the 1990s has seen a steady increase in the reorganization of middle schools back into primary and secondary schools in many LEAs, including, recently, in Bradford where the 9–13 model first began. As a researcher at the time reflected: 'The NC appears to deny even their [middle schools'] existence and provides further ammunition for those wishing to bring about their end' (Fox, 1990, p. 16). Administrative convenience which led to the advent of some middle schools seems likely to account for many more as the age of transfer is harmonized with the end of Key Stages. Oxford, where I did my own middle school teaching, has become one of the latest LEAs to announce the abolition of the three-tier system, despite strong local opposition. Latest figures suggest just over a fifth of LEAs now have schools where pupils transfer part way through a Key Stage, involving over 500 middle schools (OFSTED, 2000, p. 15). The decline in middle schools deemed primary has been most dramatic. Initially this was the most popular model (Burrows, 1978, p. 221), but there are now only about a quarter of the number existing in 1986, currently making up less than 1 per cent of all primary schools and teaching 1.25 per cent of all primary pupils. Middle schools deemed secondary, mostly 9–13 schools, have proved a more resilient model overall. There are still 60 per cent of the number existing in 1986, when numbers of primary and secondary middle schools were almost exactly equal, which currently represents just over 10 per cent of all secondary schools and almost 5 per cent of secondary pupils (DfEE, 1995, p. 222; DfEE, 2000, pp. 20–22).

Ironically the next major development after the NC, the implementation of the National Literacy Strategy (NLS) in 1998, is one which is now evolving to straddle Key Stages 2 and 3 in a way which middle schools have sought to do through their curriculum for 30 years. This development may be too late to halt the decline of middle schools, but the middle school experience may have much to say to help guide the implementation of this latest curriculum initiative in secondary schools.

The NLS at Key Stages 2 and 3

The National Literacy Project, as it originally was, began as a pilot project in some 250 primary schools between 1996 and 1998, one of a number of literacy initiatives begun under the then Conservative government. The initial evaluations of this pilot were sufficiently encouraging for the incoming Labour administration of 1997 to extend the initiative nation-wide as part of its National Literacy Strategy, a five-year plan aimed at raising standards of attainment in literacy to published target levels. The NLS involved training primary teachers to teach to the objectives laid down in the *Framework for Teaching* through the medium of the Literacy Hour, a daily structured time devoted exclusively to the development of knowledge, skills and understanding in the '2 Rs' of literacy. The revised NC for English implemented in 2000 recognizes that: 'The programme of study for English and the NLS *Framework for Teaching* are closely related. The *Framework* provides a detailed basis for implementing the statutory requirements of the programmes of study for reading and writing' (DfEE/QCA, 1999, p. 46).

The NLS is not statutory but has been almost universally adopted in some form, since the onus has been on primary schools to opt out rather than opt in. The NLS at KS1 and KS2 was an initiative designed to raise attainment in Reading and Writing, as measured by the SATs for 11-year-olds. Speaking and Listening, though clearly involved in most literacy learning activities, was not a main focus of the primary NLS and is not systematically developed through it. Teachers have to find additional opportunities to develop pupils' oral language skills outside of the Literacy Hour. Because of the time constraints of the Literacy Hour, primary teachers have also found that additional opportunities are needed for extended writing especially for older KS2 pupils, and for indi-vidual reading conferences with younger pupils at KS1.

The extension of the NLS to KS3 was a response to government con-cerns about perceived gains in literacy standards at KS1 and KS2 being reduced in the early years of 11–18 secondary schools, a 'dip' not only immediately after transfer but one continuing well into KS3. Evidence for this was inferred (despite teachers' concerns about the validity of such data) from the results of English SATs at age 14, which have not shown the same statistical improvement that the KS2 national tests have over the past few years in terms of the percentage of pupils achieving or exceeding the national standard for the end of Key Stage (between levels 5 and 6 for 14-year-olds). The percentage of pupils achieving level 4 or above at age 11 in 2000 was 75 per cent in English, whereas the corresponding figure for those attaining level 5 or above at age 14 was 63 per cent; also, of pupils who attained level 4 in English at 11 in 1996, 13 per cent were still at that level at age 14 in 1999 (Standards and Effectiveness Unit, 2001). It was felt that greater continuity was needed in order to build on pupils' experience of the NLS at primary school and to avoid the 'clean slate' approach which many secondary teachers were still perceived to be using. However, research has shown that secondary teachers use this 'clean slate' approach, or retest pupils on transfer, because they distrust the KS2 data and the 'dip' it implies (Lewis and Wray, 2000, pp. 10–11).

The draft *Framework for Teaching English: Years 7–9* began with a pilot scheme in secondary schools in 17 LEAs in September 2000. Before this pilot was completed it was announced that the initiative would be extended to all KS3 pupils from September 2001, on the same non-statutory basis as in primary schools. The KS3 version, however, has significant differences from the primary model. The structure of the final *Framework for Teaching English: Years 7, 8 and 9* (DfEE, 2001b) retains the division into Word, Sentence and Text level teaching objectives, although the Text-level ones are presented more clearly as separate columns of Reading and Writing objectives, but there is an additional column which gives Speaking and Listening objectives, including Drama. There is a clear emphasis on making links between objectives in each column and there are also objectives for cross-curricular language for learning. The KS3 *Framework* 'is based closely on' the NC for English and provides 'a framework for progression and full coverage of the English Order' (ibid., p. 9).

The KS3 *Framework* also builds on the experience gained from the National Numeracy Strategy (NNS) and its attendant *Framework for Teaching Mathematics* (DfEE, 1999). The NNS, unlike the earlier NLS, does not dictate a set structure or time for the daily numeracy lesson, instead giving the outline of a typical lesson which 'should not be seen as a mechanistic recipe to be followed' but adapted according to the 'professional judgement' of the teacher (DfEE, 1999, p. 15). The KS3 Framework gives no single Literacy Hour format for lessons, but highly recommends a four-part structure which begins with the kind of 'short lesson starter' used in the primary NNS. The Introduction, Development and Plenary sections that follow are hardly different from the format of most existing secondary English lessons. The expectation at KS3 is not for a daily dedicated Literacy Hour, but for at least three hours per week, possibly more for pupils who need to catch up with their peers (DfEE, 2001b, pp. 17–18).

The middle school experience

The project reported on here involved the use of mostly qualitative research methods to compile data on the teaching of literacy at KS3 in middle schools from a small sample of schools and LEA advisory staff.

Responses from schools

Initial written questionnaires were sent to four 9–13 middle schools in two different LEAs to ascertain how the teaching of English was currently organized at KS3. The returns showed that the pattern of teaching had significant differences from the typical organization of secondary schools. Examples of such differences were: the average amount of time spent on English in Years 7 and 8 was 3.75 hours per week, pupils were not taught in ability sets in the majority of year groups (62.5 per cent), and the average number of teachers involved in the teaching was 4.75, with 1.5 of these being non-specialists. All English Co-ordinators taught Year 8 classes, but most taught other KS2 and KS3 year groups in the school as well. However, on the scale 'Very Strong' to 'Weak', a strong allegiance to subject teams for planning was reported, as in secondary school departments, in contrast to a very strong allegiance to year teams at KS2.

Semi-structured, tape-recorded interviews were then conducted with English/Literacy Co-ordinators in the four middle schools to follow up the questionnaire. The questions asked related to the implementation and impact of the NLS at KS2, its introduction at KS3 and the position of middle schools. For reasons of space, it is not possible to include the full transcripts of the interviews here. Instead, I have reported and summarized the responses of the four interviewees to each question below, though I acknowledge the increased risk of editorial interpretation in using this method.

(i) How far does your school follow the NLS Framework and Literacy Hour structure at KS2?
In all four schools, the NLS was well established at KS2. In school A, the practice was to teach to the KS2 *Framework* objectives and to incorporate all the elements of the Literacy Hour (LH), but not to 'follow the clock'

or the prescribed order of events of the Hour. The Co-ordinator was new to the school, having previously taught in a primary school, and found she had to adjust her teaching of the LH to fit the more inflexible middle school timetable, having to 'condense' her teaching into an hour without the possibility of additional time as in her primary school. School A had set itself the target of raising standards in writing, and to this end had abandoned guided reading in the LH this year and was focusing instead on guided writing, along with shared reading and writing. In school B, the Co-ordinator had previously worked in middle schools in another LEA. The KS2 NLS was followed fully in Years 5 and 6 of school B. The 'rigid' structure of the LH was adhered to, but the timings were becoming less rigid and this year two weeks of extended work from LH lessons was planned.

School C followed the LH format 'loosely' for three out of five lessons per week with Years 5 and 6, but used the other two lessons for extended writing, spelling or speaking and listening activities. The LH structure was usually adapted so that word or sentence level work, not related to a text, came first, followed by work with a text and then activities. The plenary was sometimes difficult to incorporate since pupils became involved with the activities and teachers were reluctant to interrupt them.

School D had fully implemented the KS2 NLS and operated the LH 'very tightly', but put an emphasis on delivering a fully differentiated approach.

(ii) What is your evaluation of the impact of the NLS at KS2?

The newly appointed Co-ordinator of school A did not feel in a position to answer this. Her previous primary school did not follow the NLS fully, so it was not possible to give a judgement based on that experience either.

The Co-ordinator of school B, however, was emphatic that the NLS had had a positive impact: it had raised standards in English, changed teacher expectations, tightened up the curriculum and added more pace to teaching. As far as children's reactions were concerned, she reported that most liked it, but some more able pupils said they found the LHs 'boring' and felt that they 'hadn't got the time to read a book in depth'.

Co-ordinator C was also positive about the NLS with Years 5 and 6: it had raised standards, focused teachers more and made pupils more knowledgeable about language. The only aspect that was disliked was the 'strict timing' of the LH, which in practice the teachers had adapted.

Co-ordinator D had at first found the KS2 NLS 'restrictive', with problems involving work not being finished in lessons and a lack of depth in work completed. The organization of extended writing and guided reading opportunities also caused difficulties. Some of these problems had been alleviated by recent changes to the NLS and NC. The Co-ordinator was now starting to notice an improvement in pupils entering KS3: for example, they were more knowledgeable about a variety of different texts as readers and writers.

(iii) What elements of the primary NLS Framework are currently used with KS3 pupils in Years 7 and 8?

In school A, the Co-ordinator was already using the 'highly recommended' lesson structure from the draft KS3 *Framework for Teaching English* with her Years 7 and 8 pupils. This involved a 10–15 minute starter or warm-up activity, an introduction to the main teaching points, a development of those points and a 5–10 minute 'plenary' to 'draw out the learning'. Although the Co-ordinator was following this structure, she had not insisted that other teachers of English in the school follow it; her advice at this stage (December 2000) was that they 'try bits'. The Co-ordinator of school A felt personally that the approach set out in the KS3 *Framework* was proving successful for most pupils. English in Years 7 and 8 was taught in ability sets and she felt top sets of able pupils were capable of coping with any approach. Lower-ability sets were well suited to the 'short, sharp tasks' and 'little bits of things' in the KS3 *Framework*. However, the Co-ordinator would not like to see English lessons taught to a formula, since it was 'horses for courses' and she would handle the same material in completely different ways with different sets. It was also necessary with KS3 pupils to keep them interested and motivated.

In school B, the teachers of English had looked at the KS3 draft *Framework* as a group and the Co-ordinator had asked them to 'bear in mind' its suggestions for lesson structure, the teaching objectives for years 7 and 8 and the recommendation for pace in teaching. However, a joint decision had been made to introduce 'catch-up' groups in Year 7 for pupils at level 3 in the National Curriculum, as suggested in the KS3 *Framework*. These groups would operate in registration and assembly times and would start after Easter 2001 when the Year 7 Progress Units were to be published.

School B taught English in mixed-ability classes at KS3. Differentiation was seen as built into the group work for the more and less able pupils. Reaction from pupils to the Co-ordinator's use of the KS3 *Framework* to date had been that they 'found it hard' and 'didn't seem to be getting the levels' of KS2 work. However, this was not a representative sample. Also in school B, the Year 5 Co-ordinator commented that she was already conscious of taking over the approach of the KS2 *Framework* into her KS3 English teaching, particularly the focus on language at text, sentence and word level, if not the actual LH structure.

In school C, mixed-ability classes were also used for KS3. The primary NLS had similarly had an influence on teaching style at KS3 in that more whole-class teaching was used and there was more differentiation of work for pupils, including homework tasks, than before. The existing schemes of work for KS3 had been kept, however, though updated for the new NC and influenced by 'an awareness of what additionally we should be doing, for example complex sentences with Year 7'. Year 7 and 8 pupils' reaction to being told 'the government was bringing the LH to KS3' was, predictably: 'Oh no!'

School D had also adapted the KS2 NLS approach to their KS3 English teaching, 'without being too aware of it', for instance in lesson structure and the use of group work. The Co-ordinator felt that the NLS approach 'suits a typical English teacher'. Resources such as Big Books had been borrowed from KS2, in the absence of suitable KS3 material, but not for use in 'carpet time', which was 'impossible and impractical' with this age group. However, the changes so far made to KS3 were informal and nothing was 'set in stone' as yet.

(iv) What advice, guidance or support has been received from your LEA with respect to English/Literacy at KS3?

The Co-ordinator of school A had received training from her LEA about the new *Framework*, along with Co-ordinators and Heads of Department from other local middle and upper schools. Her reaction to watching the training video had been slightly sceptical ('all that energy, time and preparation for a 10-minute starter activity!') and she had advised her staff to 'take it with a pinch of salt', but overall she was positive about the training, although other secondary colleagues had not been. She commented that she had 'got my laminated whiteboards all covered, but haven't used them yet!' As a result of the training, the Co-ordinator intended to go through the English syllabus in the middle school to see if it covered the KS3 *Framework* objectives. Her guess was that whilst the fiction objectives were being covered adequately now, the non-fiction objectives probably were not and would need revising.

By contrast, school B had not yet received any advice from its LEA. However, the LEA had recently produced its own guidelines for English in Years 7 and 8, which the school and other local middle schools were now following. These guidelines were 'good' according to the Co-ordinator, but went against the draft KS3 *Framework*.

The Co-ordinator of school C had attended a Heads of English conference in November 2000 and been introduced to the 'transformation document' (the draft KS3 National Strategy) but had not yet 'cascaded' this to the other English teachers involved with KS3. The Co-ordinator was very positive about the KS3 *Framework* and felt it was 'ideal' for the way school C currently worked through mixed ability teaching. She felt she would not have to change existing practice much since what was proposed was 'so similar to the way we have been operating the LH [at KS2]'. She was 'delighted' about the KS3 *Framework* which she thought was better than the KS2 one, particularly in the lesson structure it proposed. She liked the way the NLS made language knowledge explicit and so empowered children from all backgrounds.

Co-ordinator C was convinced that the cross-curricular language for learning incorporated into the KS3 *Framework* was vital: 'you can't just do it in English. It needs reinforcement across the curriculum.' She felt school C was 'ahead' in this respect since she had already shared literacy targets concerned with complex sentences, adventurous vocabulary and sentence punctuation with all staff at an in-service day in January 2001. She had already had feedback from colleagues in other subjects suggesting that they were developing these aspects through their lessons and pupils' written work.

At school D, the Co-ordinator had received an introductory briefing but no training yet for the KS3 National Strategy. Her view was that there was a need for a new, modernized curriculum at KS3 and she felt that some of the *Framework* proposals were 'great'. She was particularly pleased about the potential for the use of ICT and media which she perceived to be there.

(v) What liaison have you had with your upper school(s)?

School A had had no liaison with its upper schools yet on the subject of the KS3 *Framework*, apart from the shared training.

School B had had more contact with its (neighbouring) upper school. English teachers from the upper school had been invited to observe LHs in Years 5 and 6, which they had found an 'eye-opener'. The Head of English had observed that some of the Year 5 were producing 'a better standard of work than Years 9 and 10' in the upper school. However, there had been no specific discussion of the proposals for KS3 Literacy.

School C had invited its upper schools to visit and observe the LH but they had not as yet taken up the offer. The Co-ordinator was reluctant to put forward her school as a 'perfect example of what should be done' or 'typical LH stuff', but felt that 'what we do is what works' and 'gets results' therefore upper schools would benefit from being aware of middle school practice and policy.

Liaison was getting better for school D, as upper schools became more anxious about the impending changes at KS3. They had attended the same meetings and were planning exchange visits for English staff.

(vi) What advice would you give to secondary colleagues who will be implementing the KS3 Framework for the first time from September?

The Co-ordinator of school A listed these 'dos' for Literacy at KS3:

- Try it, as KS2 teachers had had to do! Don't reject it out of hand.
- Rather than jumping straight in, do little bits. Pick out elements and see what works and what does not.
- Remember to share teaching objectives with pupils.
- Tweak the model and use it to suit you.

The following were definite 'don'ts':

- Don't use Big Books for teaching at KS3. Use class sets of texts.
- Don't put pupils into groups for guided work. They work perfectly well individually.
- Be aware of the huge danger of killing off creativity.

School B's Co-ordinator was also positive and saw the forthcoming extension of the NLS as a good thing. She advised:

- It needn't damage what are your/our current strengths.
- Some of the expectations for Drama, for example, are tough and demanding.
- Have objectives in mind and share them with children.
- Be clear about your expectations for each child and each group.
- The plenary is important at the end of the lesson.
- Have a less rigid structure at KS3.
- The time structure can be valuable. Year 6 pupils who've followed the LH can achieve more in the hour than a Year 8 class who haven't.
- Additional assessments should not be resented as they make the teacher accountable.
- There are vast implications for the texts used at KS3 from pupils encountering extracts from these books at KS2 in the LH.

Her 'don'ts' were similar to school A:

- Don't seat pupils on the carpet.
- Only use Big Books for illustrative purposes not as the main texts of the lesson.

The Co-ordinator of school C advised from her experience and that of her English teachers:

- Get any support you can.

- Plan for it: a total change in planning habits will be needed.
- Pool resources and planning, share work, work in pairs.
- Watch each other.
- Make learning objectives explicit at the start of a lesson and keep returning to them; keep pupils as informed as possible about what they are doing.
- Make sure you have other lessons not in the NLS format.
- Do not jettison the class reader: experience of whole narrative texts is important.
- Try to have lessons timetabled for the morning.

Aspects of the primary NLS which had not worked at KS3 were:

- Having all the pupils gathering round and using big books (partly due to problems with classroom accommodation).
- Independent working in groups and guided group work (possibly due to pupils' lack of experience of this).
- Having a plenary at the end of *every* lesson (it was more effective to have one every two or three lessons).

Co-ordinator D still had concerns about the 'depth' of work covered in Years 5 and 6, and advised KS3 teachers to revisit some of the KS2 work 'at greater depth'. She also advised:

- Just using setting is not enough; differentiation is needed within sets.
- Experiment – don't worry if children are not sitting on their chairs all the time.
- Speaking and listening needs to be developed, especially since it may not have been emphasized at KS2; oral work can be as important as what's in the books.
- KS3 teachers will need to look for different resources; they will be surprised at the amount of stuff children have covered at KS2.
- Get children to write down learning objectives and discuss them at the start and end of lessons.
- Be tightly focused on what to cover in a week, rather than over a half-term.

(vii) What do you think is distinctive about the middle school in terms of English/Literacy teaching?

For Co-ordinator A, the strengths of the middle school lay in giving children access to subject specialists from an earlier age. However, the loss of contact with a class teacher which this entailed meant that it was 'swings and roundabouts'. The continuity provided at the KS2–3 divide was also a strong advantage of the middle–upper school system. An issue for middle schools introducing the KS3 *Framework* would be that not all the teachers are English specialists and would resent having to give extra time and effort to the subject, since they had other curricular responsibilities.

Co-ordinator B was an advocate of the middle school. She felt they 'helped children grow up a lot faster in Year 5' in order to make the transition to KS3 eventually. Then, in Years 7 and 8, teachers were able to give a lot more individual attention and help to children in the family atmosphere of a smaller school, which they would not receive in a secondary school context. The middle school was better placed to follow pupils through from KS2 to KS3 and as a result there was no dip in performance in Years 7 and 8. Pupils encountered specialist teaching but on a small scale.

Co-ordinator C felt there was an argument that 'our expertise with literacy – which you only really get with dealing with children in Years 5 and 6 – could lend itself to developing skills in Years 7 and 8'. The LH was much easier to do in the primary school, she felt, because of timetabling and accommodation constraints in middle schools, and that was an argument against middle schools, but the KS3 NLS was an argument in favour of them, providing these constraints could be mitigated. The decline of middle schools was felt to be because they were expensive and if the contraction in middle school numbers continued there would be problems for the career development of middle school teachers, with potential recruits regarding middle schools as a 'dead end'.

At school D, the Co-ordinator 'believed fervently in the middle school set-up', in terms of children's personal development as well as the curriculum. A primary style approach to relationships with pupils was followed at KS3, support which would not be there in a very large secondary school where many children would 'fall through the net'.

Responses from advisory staff

Semi-structured, tape-recorded interviews were also conducted with KS3 advisory staff who dealt with middle schools in the two LEAs concerned. Questions referred to the position of middle school teachers in relation to the extension of the NLS to KS3. For reasons of space and to avoid undue repetition, responses here will be reported and summarized only briefly and in general terms rather than under specific headings.

The advisory staff in LEA 1, which contained schools B and D above, felt that middle school teachers were 'one step ahead' in implementing the KS3 National Strategy because of their experience with the KS2 version over the past three years. They were more confident generally in their approach to the NLS and had particular expertise, for example, in the following areas:

- providing differentiation for pupils in other ways than through outcomes
- organizing and teaching guided group work
- using demonstration and modelling strategies in whole-class teaching
- using techniques and resources specific to literacy teaching (e.g. use of whiteboards).

However, the advisory staff felt that middle schools themselves 'needed the KS3 Strategy' because of a lack of subject specialist expertise there, since frequently even the Co-ordinators were not English specialists. Middle schools faced the problem of having fewer teachers to implement the KS3 *Framework*, and there was also often a difficulty in achieving overall coherence in the middle school curriculum where Co-ordinators did not teach all year groups. The Advisers also felt that the introduction of Progress Units should help remedy a situation where pupils sometimes arrived at upper school in Year 9 with literacy problems not identified by the middle school concerned.

The LEA 1 Advisers felt that one benefit of the imminent extension of the NLS to KS3 was the increased liaison between middle and upper schools. Apart from the shared training they had experienced, upper school English teachers were now paying more attention to records from middle schools, both SATs results and teacher assessments. Middle schools had also benefited from exposure to the moderation practices employed in upper school English departments.

The Adviser in LEA 2, which included schools A and C, acknowledged the advantages that training for and working with the KS2 NLS had given middle school teachers. They had already had their attention drawn to key features relevant to the KS3 strategy such as:

- the specificity of teaching objectives
- the need for pupils to be able to articulate their learning
- the necessity for differentiation, irrespective of any setting procedures
- the emphasis on pace
- the need for short, sharp tasks in acquiring and applying skills learnt
- the emphasis on interactivity
- the role of the teacher in direct teaching (this was a feature which 'may not go down so well at KS3' with secondary teachers).

Although some colleagues in middle schools, having had their skills honed in these areas by their experience at KS2, could give a lead in training and offer support and advice, the LEA 2 Adviser thought it was not possible to say that *all* middle school English teachers were in this position: her answer was 'maybe', 'could be' but 'might not always be'. The 9–13 system, as opposed to say an 11–14 'high school' model, had weaknesses in its lack of the notion of a subject department; where there were subject specialists, learning was good, but non-specialists, who were not confident in their own literacy, were not best placed to move children forward. There was also still the need to develop 'that corporate responsibility and commitment' which was essential if literacy across the curriculum was to be picked up in the way required by the NLS and NC.

In LEA 2, the Adviser felt that middle and upper schools enjoyed good relationships already, but her advice on the implementation of the KS3 National Strategy had been that the schools should 'work together as if one Department'. Five days' training had been shared by middle school Co-ordinators and upper school Heads of Department and individual schools had got together to do initial planning and sharing of tasks. Transition in terms of literacy was all to do with the transfer of information and with trust between colleagues, and she was confident there would be no discrediting of previous teaching or programmes by upper schools. Middle schools in LEA 2 were 'key players' in the KS3 strategy because they had both Years 7 and 8, leaving upper schools with only two terms' input before end-of-Key-Stage tests at 14.

What can we learn from middle schools?

The Chief Inspector's Annual Report for 1999–2000, *Standards and Quality in Education*, comments that: 'Improvements in teaching have gone hand in hand with rising standards in pupils' attainment at all levels of education'. However, 'important problems' are said to remain and one that is singled out for specific comment is pupils' transfer from primary to secondary schools:

> In general, pupils make too little progress in Key Stage 3. They often start their secondary education enthusiastically, but may become disheartened if their basic skills are not firmly enough in place to make sense of all the subjects' demands or if insufficient account is taken of what they already know and can do. Motivation and behaviour tend to fall away in Years 8 and 9, and end-of-key-stage performance at times shows too little gain in knowledge and understanding. (OFSTED, 2001)

Similar observations about insufficiently high standards, low expectations and rising disaffection at KS3 form the basis for proposals to 'transform' this phase of secondary education in the Green Paper, *Building on Success* (DfEE, 2001a). Plans for greater diversity in overall secondary provision are the centrepiece of these proposals, although no mention is made of the future of middle schools within this development away from the 'bog-standard comprehensive' model, to use the words of the Prime Minister's Press Secretary.

The extension of the NLS and NNS into KS3, 'building on the success' of the primary initiatives, is put forward as the mechanism for raising standards for 11–14-year-olds, specifically, in the next three years. However, after 2004, a radical proposal is put forward for consultation which suggests shortening KS3 to two years and bringing forward the end of Key Stage SATs to Year 8, so that pupils would take them at 13. This, of course, would leave 9–13 middle schools ideally placed to take pupils from the end of KS2 to the end of KS3. One of the Co-ordinators I spoke to liked the idea of taking pupils through a complete Key Stage so that she could get the credit for their attainment levels, rather than just the blame when things went wrong! The Adviser in LEA 2 also felt 'it would make a lot more sense' and would make middle schools 'doubly accountable', at the end of both KS2 and KS3. As an article in the *Guardian* recently pointed out, in its coverage of the Green Paper and the remedies proposed for the problems of KS3:

> Some teachers would argue that middle schools addressed the problems of this age group much more clearly than ordinary secondaries . . . 'Middle schools were a good idea,' says Brian Schram, the headteacher of Southwood Middle School in Milton Keynes. 'The ages of 8–13 are a time when children go from more concrete to abstract thought and become more streetwise. We try to develop their independence but also their interactivity with other children.'
> (*Guardian Education*, 2001, p. 3)

Assuming the idea of the 9–13 middle school does not enjoy a late revival through the transformation and diversification of secondary education, what experience and expertise in literacy teaching at KS3 can the dwindling band of middle schools hand on to those secondary schools that will implement the National Strategy for the first time from September 2001 onwards?

First, all the Co-ordinators and Advisers interviewed for this research (selected anonymously and speaking in confidence) are very positive about the impact of the KS2 NLS, despite initial misgivings and teething troubles, and all welcome the advent of the KS3 *Framework* and National

Strategy generally. In the growing sense of ownership they feel towards the evolving primary NLS, they make an interesting contrast with the secondary Heads of English interviewed by Winston Brookes in his chapter. They also approach the introduction of the KS3 *Framework* with some feelings of agency, however limited: a confidence that they can take what is offered and make it work for them, in the way they have at KS2 over the past three years. They are committed to as broad and inclusive a definition of literacy as possible and actually see in the development of the KS3 *Framework* some advance, however small, from the narrow boundaries of the primary Literacy Hour as it was originally conceived.

The specific advice coming from middle school English teachers is both strategic and practical. Strategically, secondary colleagues need to overcome their initial and understandable distrust of the new *Framework* by trying it out gradually, adapting it to suit their department's existing strengths and weaknesses, and evaluating honestly what works for them and what does not. This may require an attitude shift in some secondary English departments where previous research suggests that the 'personal growth' model of English teaching is still the dominant one, and 'cross-curricular' and 'adult needs' models are less welcome (Goodwyn, 1992). According to middle school colleagues, secondary teachers should treat the *Framework* recommendations flexibly and not be afraid to experiment; all lessons should not follow the same format and timings. The Drama objectives included under Speaking and Listening, for example, need to be incorporated into literacy lessons to introduce variety and interest, activity and creativity, in approaching texts. Secondary English teachers need to work more collaboratively, planning together and pooling lesson resources more, as well as observing each other teach to the new *Framework*. They need to be more aware of what is achieved in an individual lesson and in a week, rather than over a half-term. They will have to realize the need for differentiation in planning even within an ability set, and have clear expectations for individual pupils, groups and sets. *Framework* objectives will have to be kept in the forefront of teaching: explicitly shared with pupils, possibly written down by them, and regularly returned to at the beginning and end of lessons.

Practically, secondary English teachers can learn from their middle school colleagues by keeping the class reader and the experience of a whole text it provides. They should go on using class sets of complete texts, rather than Big Books or anthologies of extracts, but will need to revise the selection of texts in the light of what pupils have already encountered at KS2. Whole-class seating arrangements may need to be looked at (where possible) to help facilitate more interactive work at the start of lessons, but seating Year 7 and 8 on the carpet is not an option! Individual work in the Development section of the lesson is recommended rather than independent or guided group work. Plenary sessions are seen as an important part of the lesson, but this need not mean having one at the end of every lesson; they could be more effective used every two or three lessons. One final but important recommendation from middle school teachers, bearing in mind teachers' energy levels as well as pupils': press for a morning timetable slot for your English lesson if you are hoping to have plenty of pace and interactivity, as prescribed!

Acknowledgements

I would like to thank very warmly the middle school teachers and Advisers who gave up precious time to talk to me for this research, when it would have been much easier to have politely (or impolitely) declined the invitation. Without their contributions this chapter would not exist. Thank you all again.

References

Blyth, W. and Derricott, R. (1977) *The Social Significance of Middle Schools*, London, Batsford.

Burrows, J. (1978) *The Middle School: High Road or Dead End?* London, Woburn Press.

Department of Education and Science (DES) (1983) *9–13 Middle Schools: An Illustrative Survey*, London, HMSO.

Department for Education and Employment (DfEE) (1995) *Statistics of Education: Schools in England. 1994*, London, HMSO.

Department for Education and Employment (DfEE) (1998) *The National Literacy Strategy: Framework for Teaching*, London, DfEE.

Department for Education and Employment (DfEE) (1999) *National Numeracy Strategy: Framework for Teaching Mathematics*, London, DfEE.

Department for Education and Employment (DfEE) (2000) *Schools in England 2000*, London, The Stationery Office or on web site www.dfee.gov.uk/statistics

Department for Education and Employment (DfEE) (2001a) *Building on Success* (Green Paper), London, The Stationery Office or on web site www.dfee.gov.uk

Department for Education and Employment (DfEE) (2001b) *Key Stage 3 National Strategy: Framework for Teaching English: Years 7, 8 and 9*, London, DfEE.

Department for Education and Employment (DfEE)/Qualifications and Curriculum Authority (QCA) (1999) *The National Curriculum: Handbook for Primary Teachers in England*, London, DfEE/QCA.

Edwards, R. (1972) *The Middle School Experiment*, London, Routledge and Kegan Paul.

Fox, P. (1990) 'Middle schools: a mid-life crisis?', unpublished MA dissertation, University of Reading.

Goodwyn, A. (1992) 'English teachers and the Cox models', *English in Education*, 26 (3), Sheffield, NATE.

Guardian Education (2001), 20 February, p. 3 'Young at Heart' by Luisa Dillner.

Hargreaves, A. (1986) *Two Cultures of Schooling: the Case of Middle Schools*, Lewes, Falmer Press.

Hargreaves, A. and Tickle, L. (eds) (1980) *Middle Schools: Origins, Ideology and Practice*, London, Harper and Row.

Lewis, M. and Wray, D. (eds) (2000) *Literacy in the Secondary School*, London, David Fulton.

Office for Standards in Education (OFSTED) (2000) *Update*, **34**, Winter, London, OFSTED.

Office for Standards in Education (OFSTED) (2001) www.archive.offical-documents.co.uk/document/ofsted/hc102/102.htm

Standards and Effectiveness Unit (2001) web site: www.standards.dfee.gov.uk/keystage3/transforming/slowprogress

5

Evidence from experienced practitioners

Winston Brookes

This chapter draws on a research project conducted over the past three years that has examined the perceptions of teachers and pupils as the literacy strategy has affected them. Of 120 heads of English who completed a questionnaire three years ago four were interviewed in depth in July 2001 in order to find out whether their perceptions had changed since that time. Their responses are recorded here in the form of monologues. They express their dismay and discomfort that, although the *Framework* allows some flexibility, it proposes a straitjacket for teaching that has not been adequately researched with teachers themselves. In particular, they feel that their own experience as accomplished and reflective practitioners is ignored in what they see as a political imperative to raise standards of literacy.

The research context

This section sets the research project firmly in the context of the lessons learned from school improvement research in recent years and suggests that English teachers are resentful that they have not been made party to the process that led up to the introduction and dissemination of the Key Stage 3 National Strategy. This unease in English teachers was noted by Webster, Beveridge and Reed in 1996 who concluded from their research that 'there is much yet to be done in the development of effective literacy strategies' and that 'many secondary teachers remain to be convinced of their responsibility, as subject specialists, for creating teaching contexts where literacy plays a significant and strategic role'. Similarly, Brookes and Goodwyn in their survey of 120 secondary school heads of English (1998) found considerable uncertainty in their knowledge of how to develop literacy teaching in their schools. Some of their uncertainty derived from a sense they had that they were not directly involved in the changes taking place and that they had not been consulted about them. This notion of shared ownership of a project is one which Webster, Beveridge and Reed strongly advocate and is one which is recognized in much school improvement literature ('every person is a change agent', Fullan, 1993) as yielding positive outcomes. It is argued that in order to move schools to change a different kind of leadership is required from the traditional, rational, structuralist, personality mode. Bill J. Johnston (in Maxey, 1994, p. 130) describes this as postmodern leadership in which everyone contributes to writing the school's story:

> Opportunities to share authorship have historically been denied teachers, which results in the cycles of failure that have marked the recent history of school reform. To share authorship does not mean, however, that teachers are invited simply to write a chapter already outlined by the administrator. To the extent that administrators attempt to 'overwrite' the story, ownership is denied to teachers and students. Under these conditions the administrator may be able to coerce compliance with the script but should not expect commitment. An alternative strategy is to seek original contributions that may lead the story in unanticipated directions.

Only recently (2001) a research project conducted by Matthew Horne for Demos and based on interviews with 150 teachers reported on 'a weariness often combined with a slightly suppressed sense of anger' that teachers believe they are not included in the wider debate about education. Commenting on the report, Matthew Horne (2001, p. 27) concludes:

> A way must be found to give that sense of control back to the entire classroom. Teachers want to experience comprehensible, coherent organizational transformation and play an active part in the process. This is very different from facing a continuous demand for improved productivity with a set of organizational constraints which have hardly changed.

Authentic stories

The main purpose of this chapter will be, therefore, to provide an opportunity for four of those original 120 secondary school English teachers to tell their authentic stories. It will also seek to identify common strands in their narrative. This approach embodies and reflects a belief that literacy is constantly moving and changing, and the meaning of literacy events and texts in those events are actively constructed by participants, especially teachers and their pupils, through their social and professional interaction. Indeed, these four 'original contributions' do lead the story in directions that policy-makers would do well to heed. This is all the more important at a time when there is an almost unprecedented shortage of teachers and an alarming drop-out rate which is directly alluded to by one of the heads of English.

Despite the known difficulties and the clear recognition that, as HMI put it, 'there is no quick fix for deficiencies in literacy' (HMI, 1999 p. 2) the government's determination to maintain the momentum of literacy development from the primary phase of schooling into the secondary has accelerated rapidly over the past year or so. In the summer of 2001 secondary schools were invited to regional training conferences at which they were introduced to the *Key Stage 3 National Strategy*, subtitled *A Framework for Teaching English: Years 7, 8 and 9* (DfEE, 2001). The approach of the strategy at this stage was to commend an explicitly formalized teaching and management methodology to secondary schools rather than to prescribe. However, there was an expectation that all secondary schools would make provision for in-service training for literacy during the course of 2001–2002 and there is clear evidence that future OFSTED inspections, both of schools and initial teacher training providers, will address literacy development with the Key Stage 3 Strategy in mind. Indeed, all initial teacher trainees in English received a copy of the *Framework* at the beginning of their courses in 2001. Equally, local education authorities (LEAs) are required to have a written policy for literacy development in the schools for which they are responsible.

The interviews

In this section the research method is described and the reason for presenting the findings in the unusual form of four monologues is explained. Four English teachers, each with wide experience of teaching literacy skills, were interviewed ('an opportunity sample', Wragg, 1978) in their schools in order to explore their perceptions of recent developments in literacy policy and practice. The interviews were framed around six 'statement clusters' that were directly derived from the findings of an earlier questionnaire in 1998. Each of the interviewees was invited to respond to each of the statement clusters as they wished and without prompting, so that the emphasis they placed on any of the clusters was entirely their own.

Statement Cluster 1
- Literacy is a major focus for your school.
- The definition of literacy is problematic.

- You are uncertain about how to orchestrate literacy improvement.
- Your English department is seen as having a central role.
- Your English department does not have a policy for literacy.
- Your school does not have a whole school literacy policy.

Statement Cluster 2

- You are not aware of a substantive LEA role.
- You do not know the name of your external contact for literacy.
- The quality of feeder school information about literacy is poor.
- You make good use of the information you receive from feeder schools.

Statement Cluster 3

- You use a range of literacy tests.
- You do blanket testing for literacy in Y7.
- Some testing is used to identify SEN pupils.
- You do not use blanket testing for literacy beyond Y7.
- Most testing is used to assess the progress of individual low attainers – usually in reading.
- SATs are used as a measure of literacy.

Statement Cluster 4

- There is no coherent pattern of INSET provision for literacy.
- There is no INSET for literacy over time.
- There is no INSET for literacy at all.

Statement Cluster 5

- You believe that you can raise standards of literacy.
- You do not know how improvement will be measured.
- You need support in your school's improvement of literacy.
- You see support in terms of workable ideas and strategies.
- You need training in the teaching of literacy skills.
- You would like to see a coherent cross-phase literacy framework.

Statement Cluster 6

- You have a positive view about the latest literacy improvement initiatives.
- You think that your school is an example of good practice in literacy improvement.

These statements were to provide the researcher with a semi-structured framework for the respondent 'conversations' (Burgess, 1984, cited in Cohen and Manion, 1994). The conversations are taken from the original transcripts with alterations made only to clarify meaning, to avoid repetition and to achieve a consistent length. They make compelling reading because they follow the train of thought of the speaker, in the manner of Alan Bennett's *Talking Heads*, and capture voice and emotion in a way that no reported speech can. Indeed, all four speakers feel, to some extent, that their voice is unheard or unheeded in the face of the official soliloquies about literacy to which they are obliged to listen.

A significant shift since 1998

There is little doubt that English teachers are less antagonistic to the introduction of the Key Stage 3 Strategy than they were three years ago, despite their feeling of being marginalized in the process. This small sample suggests that there has been a significant shift in the perceptions of heads of English since 1998. Literacy has now, perforce, moved centre-stage and English departments are seen clearly as playing the key part, reluctant Hamlets though some might be. How to direct literacy is no longer an issue, since the script has been written and the stage directions are clear. Time has been set aside for rehearsals, although the tight schedule is seen as one more appropriate to a regional repertory company than the National Theatre. Even so, there are some deep reservations, not least that the script 'though it makes the unskilful laugh, cannot but make the judicious grieve': a wooden performance is seen as the prescribed method that will have the effect of switching the audience off. The major concern seems to be that English teachers feel they are being reduced to bit players whose capacity for productive creativity is limited. They are particularly dismayed that learning support assistants (LSAs) are being hired as strolling players to play key parts in improving literacy performance. All four have serious misgivings about the integrity of the information they receive from primary schools and the general lack of coherence across the two phases. Furthermore, they express deep resentment that their views about what literacy is and how it should be directed in the schools are at worst ignored and at best patronized. Although the speakers were not wearing balaclavas when they were interviewed, they have been given fictitious names.

Although fictitious in name John, June, Anna and Ellie each make the point that they are real teachers working in real schools – at the chalkface. All have substantial experience of teaching and managing English in comprehensive schools. They are all successful teachers, if judged by OFSTED criteria: the performance of their respective departments is well above average national standards. Each can fairly be described as an extended professional: beyond their teaching they are either literacy trainers or contribute to postgraduate teacher training. One has published work on the teaching of English. Most importantly, they regard themselves as autonomous and reflective practitioners who resent the notion that they need to be told how to teach English. But now, lest further offence be given, let them, uninterrupted, speak for themselves.

John

> We know we have to do this, this is what teaching's like: some big initiative comes and we have to do it, we have no choice; it's no good saying this is ridiculous because you get accused of being old-fashioned, past it; whatever you say you are side-stepped.

This quotation from John's 'story' conveys very powerfully that 'suppressed sense of anger' referred to earlier in this chapter as he bemoans what he sees as a failure of the policy-makers to take account of the people, like himself, who are likely to be the most effective change agents in the schools. He also conveys a sense bordering on despair that his views and his professional circumstances are being deliberately ignored.

This school is still very uncertain about how to orchestrate literacy improvement. I know how to do it but they are not asking me at the moment. That's because the English Department is not seen as having a central role. The school does not have a whole-school literacy policy, nor does the English department. I think there are some issues here to do with the micro politics of the school and whose responsibility it is and who are the more important players in the game. I think one of the reasons is that the curriculum deputy who is a very strong force in this school is very nervous about the whole area of literacy. If this were to do with numeracy he would be in like a shot.

Oh yes, literacy in all respects, in everything, is problematic. Literacy is now English as far as the Key State 3 strategy is concerned. Literacy and English is not the same thing: there is a problem with definition, and resting on that is a much bigger academic issue. I think they've defined it as English and not as literacy, as they did for the Primary strategy, because they want to make sure it happens. After all, if you are going to manage change you have to take some constants of the existing structures and it would be a big decision to do otherwise. If you call it literacy, it is something new, something extra. People with long memories remember Language Across the Curriculum; people with shorter memories know what they think about various cross-curricular initiatives, of which there have been hundreds. If you are going to make it happen it's got to be within an existing subject because the forces of inertia are too strong.

Our school doesn't have a whole-school policy on literacy because senior management are chicken. When OFSTED comes they'll have something to say that will keep OFSTED at bay. I think they are understandably chicken. I think this is a really difficult area so I think they are keeping well clear because it's a can of worms. That's the cynical hard-line approach. I think that a lot of teachers really believe that they are teachers of English and they don't really think that focusing on language and meta-linguistics is actually going to improve pupils' knowledge of geography or history; nor do senior management either, so it's bad enough trying to drag other people along with you when you do believe in it, but when you don't it's very difficult.

The increasing need for greater coherence across the transition point

I think there is coherence in the overall literacy strategy. Whether there's intellectual coherence to it is a different matter, but it's at least organized. I would like to see greater coherence across the transition point from primary to secondary because it's essential to overcome problems of continuity. There's also the issue of 'the dip'. There's an attitudinal dip, which is often ignored. However, it seems to me in terms of test scores you've got to look over a broader period: it's no good looking at progress over six months, you've got to look at progress over three years. I dipped when I went to university, but I didn't over three years. It depends on where you start and where you look. But the other thing is to do with adolescence: there's one argument that says as their hormones kick in, they become disaffected and stroppy and there's nothing any of us can do; and there's the other attitude that says the trouble is, you in secondary schools bore the pants off them because there's all these excited little kids who are used to interactive, fast-paced stuff and when they come here they are expected to sit still and listen for large tranches of time and no wonder they go out of their heads with boredom.

The feedback I've got from the *Framework* training is, well, guarded. We know we have to do it because this is what teaching's like: some big initiative comes and we have to do it, we have no choice; it's no good saying this is ridiculous because you get accused of being old-fashioned, past it; whatever you say you are sidestepped. People are professional in any case and they want to adapt and use and move on.

Does the strategy have a valid intellectual basis?

I don't have time to breathe, you know. Where is the academic community on this? I want to hear lots of loud noises from the academic community about this. I haven't heard loud noises yet; I've heard one or two small noises and they are not big enough as far as I can see. I've read Mary Hilton's stuff, I've read Bethan Marshall who says bits and pieces. Maybe I haven't had time to, maybe you've got a better view of this, but I want to hear a serious intellectual challenge to the presuppositions of the strategy both in terms of what literacy is and also in terms of the pedagogy of it. If I had more power and a bigger voice and more time to think about it and prepare it, and write or whatever, I'd say something like there is a huge amount of resources here being devoted to a rather narrow behaviourist raising of performance in a narrow area. Now if you put in all those resources and all that effort and all that repetition you could raise performance in anything. Everyone could fry better eggs, everyone could run a hundred metres; now because it's literacy and people say basic, fundamental, and it's going to make the world of difference in education, and I don't buy that, that's what I don't buy. It is, I think, because children are trained to pass certain kinds of tests of grammar or reading or whatever. I don't think it's going to make that huge amount of difference to that later knowledge and understanding of other sorts of texts in all subjects. So that's what I don't buy, and there is of course the danger that, in devoting primary sources and effort to that, that there are other areas of English and literacy that we won't have time for. And the final thing I want to say about that is, those areas of English and literacy that we won't have time for are precisely those areas that are radical, challenging, make children think, question and challenge the order of things in society, so I'm actually deeply suspicious on ideological grounds about this. But, we have to do it.

The argument coming from them is that you are ignoring these children and disadvantaging the people who are disadvantaged already, and I can see that. There is an entitlement, oh absolutely, and we've devoted our professional lives to try and give an entitlement to children who don't actually have it from other sources. So it's not that I'm unwilling to do that, quite the reverse, but there is a kind of mechanistic, behaviouristic, instrumental kind of approach to this and I don't understand why that's going to make these kids' lives different, I don't. It seems to me that there are other models of English teaching that are just as likely to do that and there's a lot of evidence that it's worked, because you read that people say, 'my best teacher was this English teacher who didn't do all this kind of stuff but came in and made things alive in terms of inspiration'.

I'm very concerned about boys' writing. I read boys' writing from all over the country, every year. And there is a difference between boys' and girls' writing. We can't afford to ignore it, but I don't know of any cast iron connections between learning the sorts of modal verb stuff and actually improving writing. I would like to believe that it works because it would be relatively straightforward, it would be like training somebody to do the hurdles or something, but I don't think it happens like that.

Only two years ago people would say 'we are on our own here we are not getting any help from anybody' and that's changed. I know publishers are jumping on the bandwagon and everything's got literacy all over it at the moment, and some of this stuff is actually useful and underwritten by and, indeed, written by good people.

Patronizing for experienced teachers

However, I think it's patronizing at times to think that teachers need ideas about how to teach. When we understand the theory we can go and do it. I think that English teachers that I've met, almost instantly customize things, so they do it like that the first time and then the second time round it's modified and that's what will happen here, no doubt. I'm very apprehensive about the comprehensive breakfast list: when you look at the amount of planning that's apparently expected it seems to me that that is foolish in the extreme because the documentation is already published and you see on overheads the lesson plans, weekly plans, the medium-term planning, the planning for the term, planning for the whole year. There's a sheaf of documentation here that would be used once only because you'd move on and need to develop it from there.

You'd think wouldn't you that the writing of the materials would be the one thing that would be down to QCA but it isn't QCA's baby. QCA have got a kind of hold over all other areas, curriculum and that, and this is the biggest one to hit me for a long time. The pedalling has come from DfE and elsewhere and the Basic Skills Agency so that QCA are very much in the background. But you'd think that since they've gone to all the trouble to produce the *Framework* that they'd actually go a stage further and make it into a syllabus and a whole kind of teaching pack rather than leaving us with a half-built bridge. I mean if they are going to be as detailed and specific as that in their requirements, why don't they go further and say 'well this is what you have to do'. 'Teach this lesson and do it.' Just like the kind of mythical French model of the minister of education knowing what's happening on Monday morning. In this case though, we don't know who the equivalent of the French minister of education is: we don't know who is directing literacy.

Concern about the amount of documentation

I do have positive views if it is literacy across the curriculum and if colleagues take seriously the questions about the kind of language they use. I'm just concerned about the amount of documentation and getting people inline that I'm going to have to do and it's quite a big management headache, it will take a lot of time. I'm also apprehensive because I think it's going to cause fallout. I think it's going to precipitate the early retirement of some colleagues who are going to say 'I was going to do another two or three years, I can't be bothered to do all that'. I can think of one or two grafters in my department that's going to happen to and that would be a loss. If that were replicated all across the country that would be a big loss. So that's another reason I haven't got a positive view. I also don't think it's going to do what it's supposed to do which is make children read and write better. I think it's going to make them temporarily more knowledgeable about certain aspects of things. In the Key Stage 3 SATs this year, the chief examiners who read stuff from all over the country commented on the nature of some of the responses to reading and, particularly, how pupils are now talking about strong verbs and the degree to which more explicit language commentary is coming in. But whether that is actually opening eyes to aspects of writing or getting in the way of it, I'm not convinced.

June

June directs her strongest criticism towards the literacy training and what she sees as an artificial and inflexibly scripted approach. She also rails passionately about what she calls 'a nonsense model of teaching', particularly in its assumption that learning support assistants can take on the role of teachers.

Yes, literacy is a major focus now for our school. There's always that issue of ownership though: who thinks it's a major focus? The English Department do and the people who've read all the national literacy stuff on the management team do and some members of staff do literacy things within subject lessons, but I don't know whether there's a whole span feeling that 'oh, we're all going to work on literacy'.

Although it's called a National Literacy Strategy, the objectives are called *A Framework for Teaching English.* I think it's to direct the way English is taught because it's about how you teach as well as what you teach. The English Department is seen as having the major role. I think when it comes to the expertise and who's got ideas and who knows the framework, that's the English Department.

I don't think that's a debate about the meaning of literacy anymore. I think a lot of departments' interpretation of literacy is to do with basic skills, writing skills and spelling and I think we'll be quite surprised when we do some training next year and are talking about speaking and listening skills. And of course there are some departments and some members of staff who are more keen to take literacy on board and can see the benefits from that than others, and that will never change. The fact that it's been called an English framework actually makes cross-curriculum literacy more difficult because those people who want to say 'it's not my job' have now got a lead and can say just that.

Training from the script

The training's very mechanistic, you know. Our trainer actually had a script and it lacks commitment because they do not depart from the script. Very clearly they have been given this body of knowledge to impart. Some teachers attempt to challenge the approach, but there's a real move to just get through what they've got to deliver and sidestep any questions. I'll give you an example: on the last training I went on the trainer referred to Key Stage 2 results and then Key Stage 3 results and to the number of pupils who were only improving by one level in Key Stage 3 and questioned whether that is good enough. On this and other occasions Heads of English have raised considerable sort of doubts about the reliability of Key Stage 3 results and the comparability of Key Stage 3 results with Key Stage 2 because secondary school teachers know that the idea of continuity just doesn't work, because the way they are tested at Key Stage 2 is very different at Key Stage 3. In fact one level's improvement can actually mean more than one level in real terms and they just won't acknowledge that. They just keep coming back to the figures and they just keep saying 'yes we know that but', and so on.

Just to go back about the reliability of the Key Stage 2, we were told that the progress units were for pupils who were attaining a level 3. When I spoke to the adviser she said 'oh well they are levels 3 and "wobbly 4s" you see, and I said 'what's a wobbly 4?' So what we are being asked to do is analyse every level 4 result for its component part: sometimes a pupil may just have got a level 4 because they've got a very high mark in handwriting; or because they've got a very high mark in reading, but low marks in the rest of it. That's what you call a wobbly 4, somebody who hasn't got a very secure 4, apparently.

I think there's a real issue about all the key stage tests: frankly, I think they are more about assessing teachers. I've seen Key Stage 3 results used on teacher threshold applications and on value added. No pupil I know puts their Key Stage 2 and 3 results on their CV once they've got their GCSEs, do they?

The workload implication

I mean, at the very least, there's the workload implication of it: we are being asked with very short notice to do a huge amount of curriculum development. They launch it the week before half term and they expect to see evidence of it in the September: now that's eight working weeks over half a term. The cynical side of me thinks that they've done it so quickly so you haven't got time to raise objections, you know, thrust it on them and make them get on with it. Experienced teachers will find the material incredibly patronizing. It's not new, despite a lot of saying that it is. 'I know you are all very experienced here', is always followed by a 'but', and it's this sense that we are being told to do these things that are 'new', that we've neglected to do them and we haven't been bothering about our children. And being asked this question in this very sort of patronizing way 'are you happy with one levels improvement in three years? In primary school they go from 0 to 4 in six years and yet in three years in secondary school they can only go one level, are you happy with that?' And it's this assumption that our answer is that we are happy with that. This seems to be saying 'you know, these results aren't good enough, these children aren't good enough, literacy skills aren't good enough, you haven't been doing anything about it, so now we are going to tell you how to do something about it'. That's really quite insulting, because a lot of teachers have been doing a lot of things about it and have been trying to improve results.

And then when you are presented on the training video with a starter activity to teach the subordinate clause and they are using a sentence that actually hasn't got a subordinate clause in it, then there is a real problem with credibility. Several people on the training day said 'that sentence hasn't got a subordinate clause in' and what we were told is 'ah well, you will find grammar definitions have changed with the literacy strategy'. And not only has that sentence not got a subordinate clause but it's actually written on the front of the National Literacy Strategy folder as an example.

The measure of improvement, of course, is going to be SATs results, because they are not going to let the strategy fail, are they? They are now applauding the Key Stage 2 SATs results and they are saying since the literacy hour the SATs results have gone up and the literacy hour, the numeracy hour must be working because the SATs results have gone up. Well, to me, you know it's just that teachers are teaching the exam: after so many years of the SATs you know the SATs very well and you know what you've got to teach to get those levels.

I'm not completely down on the whole of the strategy. I think there are some good things in there. For example, in speaking and listening it says you know pupils should be taught how to talk collaboratively in a group, pupils should be taught how to make a presentation. That's actually something I've believed in passionately for quite a while, that too much speaking and listening work is not actually teaching them how to speak and listen, it's just giving them opportunities to speak and listen. I think there's a big difference there and I've always said that we don't do enough explicit teaching, what it means to speak and listen. I certainly think that that push to actually teach those skills would be no bad thing.

I still hold that if they spend all that money actually in schools so that we could have more LSAs and smaller classes, literacy standards would be improved. I think there's a feeling that this is not the way to improve literacy standards across the country, by diktat, by objective, by test. I sit here in a reasonably resourced school but I know, I sit with other Heads of English who are struggling for every penny, so when they get presented with these lavish videos and folders and everything and all these days training, it must be very difficult to bear.

A nonsense model of teaching

I have some misgivings about the role played by LSAs. I've been told that the school is going to receive some really fancy money for the English Department to have an LSA. I think that's the sort of investment that they should be making. But, then when she said it is to help them deliver the progress units I sort of jolted a little bit, because they are learning assistants, not learning teachers. Their notion of what teaching is about is take some prepackaged material, somebody else's formulation, simply deliver it via a set of instructions, and that transmission is then going to lead into the pupil learning, something that they've missed in six years of primary education. I just think that's a nonsense model of teaching, and you and I both know that teaching is more about interrelationships and constructs and adapting the materials to suit the pupils, and when the pupil still isn't responding to the material taking it a stage further. LSAs are not qualified to do that. You know, the Warnock Report years ago talked about learning support teachers, and the number of learning support teachers in schools is dwindling and the number of assistants is increasing, probably for economic reasons. This notion that you just receive a file and it's in there like a set of instructions is one of the things that's making teachers angry: that the art and the craft of teaching is actually being reduced to on Monday get out cards A to C.

And of course a lot of the training videos are not about good teaching but a crude transmission model. In the Literacy Strategy the wording of the objectives is 'pupils should be taught to', not 'pupils should learn'. Yet there is this confident notion that if you teach it, in this way, like we are telling you, then they will learn it.

Anna

Anna echoes the sentiments of John and June as she comments on the failure of the Strategy to take any account of what she calls 'the management of change theory' which would help persuade teachers of the merits of the new approaches. Like June, she thinks that the timescales are 'ludicrous, particularly in respect of the progress units'.

Literacy is a major focus for the school. Certainly the literacy strategy is going to up the focus for us. Everyone is already on board. I think actually the main reaction, because we introduced the Key Stage 3 strategy on Monday at the staff meeting, the main reaction is that people are now saying 'oh, so the English Department have got to do it now and really take the lead on grammar and various things' and in reality they have been doing that fairly much.

Who can rely upon the Key Stage 2 results? And there is a lot of cynicism there and it's hard not to be when you know that actually the capability of the markers and speed with which the whole process happens at Key Stage 3 is ultimately flawed. I mean that was why we sent the whole lot back. We don't have any faith in the ability to really moderate the marking at Key Stage 3 or Key Stage 2. I'm not sure whether there is any political interference that English teachers see. I think for too long they've used it as an excuse actually and they are a bit too defensive but, even so, the marking is insecure.

No thought about the management of change theory

The problem is you take a literacy consultant who's a practising teacher who's been through the training and is very good. Then you give them a training that doesn't allow them to think about their audience, just allows them to think about their material. They are not used to training whole groups of teachers anyway, and then they are thrown into this lion's den with this huge amount of notes with this alien language and expected to turn the teachers on their side. There is no thought about the management of change theory within it. You don't start by offending people by telling them they are not doing well enough and then give them a whole load of jargon and a whole pile of paperwork that is so mammoth that even the most dedicated and organized person is going to shy away in horror and then expect people to welcome it. That's been the problem with it. If it's put in a context where people know the teachers, understand how to open hearts and minds, get them on board, start from the point of where they are. Our trainer threw the script out the window on the second day. She said 'I'm going to start it with sharing best practice, I'm going to ask them what they are doing well and we are going to start with the premise that we've got a lot of things right and then we are going to say right don't worry about the alien language, we'll get familiar with that. Are we agreed in principle that we want to make things better at Key Stage 3? Yes, right, now let's move forward.' And if you put it that way people are prepared to go along with you.

Flexing and tagging

The alien language? It talks about 'flexing', and 'tagging' which is just the shortened versions of the teaching objectives. Flexing is, you can take the idea of what they are suggesting in terms of teaching objectives and you just are more flexible with it, you don't mechanistically follow perhaps the four part lesson, you flex it to suit you. It's being flexible, but it is a jargon that surrounds these teaching consultants. Tagging, is where you've got about five pages of teaching objectives, masses and masses of them, W7, R15 all the rest of it. The tagging is just the one page of A4 that just gives you one-word references to what W7, R15 is. If you actually look at just the tags they are completely meaningless. If you actually try and label the teaching objectives into any form of planning in their full version it becomes unwieldy, so the idea is you just tag the lesson.

There seems to me to be an idea of audience that certainly doesn't suit the audience we've got in my school. The audience seems to be people who are frankly not doing well enough. I mean the concept that teachers are teaching activities and not objectives is so offensive and untrue. I don't doubt that there are some teachers out there who are just doing that and that seems to be targeted at them. Tar everybody with the same brush and presume that they don't recognize good teaching causes problems. One gentleman who is obviously a very good teacher was very hung up with the fact that this was a political move. He didn't think that it was possible to take any more, particularly this load of paper that he felt he had to deal with and the strange language and, furthermore, he said 'who says this is the right way to teach? Who says this is good quality teaching? I don't relate that to my teaching.' And I must admit some of the video material where they are doing the demonstration of lessons and modelling writing, which I do think in itself is a very good way forward, but they presented it as a very lengthy, onerous task with a teacher at the front with a whiteboard with her back to a class, which is frankly ludicrous. Where's the use of ICT? If I model writing I model it with a laptop in front of me, looking at everybody and pulling in ideas and you can print off a copy afterwards, but this method is crazy.

One teacher said that she thought that was just such a banal lesson, a boring lesson and the heads of English were, well lying on their backs laughing and thinking that if this is described as a good lesson then I'll go to the foot of our stairs. It is a typical lesson where the teacher comes out thinking 'God, that was a good lesson' because she'd worked really hard, but the reality was that the children, for a good 15 minutes while she was working on the board creating this wonderful piece of language were sitting there doing nothing, so they wouldn't have come out thinking it was a good lesson, they certainly wouldn't remember it. I have to say I don't think that's very good practice at all.

The timescales have been ludicrous

I have sympathy with the intention behind the literacy strategy. I have sympathy with really pinning down and clarifying Key Stage 3 in English because I feel it's been woolly, I feel it's been too flexible. I know my best teaching is at Key Stage 4 where I have a very clear idea of the skills the children need to develop and then display at the end of that Key Stage. There isn't that sort of demand at Key Stage 3 and as a teacher who is pressured in all sorts of directions it is too easy to be undemanding and have a lovely time and give fantastic experiences at Key Stage 3, but actually not do the children a good enough service and move them forward. So I'm not against Key Stage 3 strategy at all. I think there are strengths in it but there just hasn't been enough consideration to the people who are receiving it, the timescales have been ludicrous. It needed a far more thoughtful approach because in order to plan in progress units the literacy across the curriculum next year we needed to have been able to deal with that as a school this end of term and plan for it. Our planning term is the Autumn term, that's when we evaluate and we decide what we are going to do for next year in September. They're still on the training today with the progress units, so although I've managed to pick, because I'm involved, what I think is happening and put into place some timetabling things that will allow us to target things sensibly, no other school has done that. They will not have systems in place and I know they're reacting really badly to that because they say 'how can I deliver three lots of 20 minutes to six children and I've got 20 lots of six children on different units? I can't do it.' They could if they had the time to plan that in, but to suddenly land that on the last week of this term and expect us to have in place things in September is just ludicrous.

I'm very concerned about LSAs being seen as teachers because although they may be given specialized training this has to be people who are really very good at delivery. What we have is a situation where we are going to be using three LSAs in the literacy teaching and then progress teaching. In our case all three LSAs have teaching certificates and will be paid as a teacher to do it and all of them are skilled enough to be able to do it. I know that they can teach.

Ellie

In her quietly reflective monologue Ellie, although she agrees with the basic principles underlying the Framework for Teaching English, *expresses her concern that the essence and the enjoyment of English is being diluted by an over-emphasis on performance-related literacy. Pupils are, to her surprise and dismay, now identifying English as a subject they do not enjoy.*

Literacy certainly is a major focus for the school: we are actually teaching explicitly literacy aspects in the various subjects. Obviously some subjects more so than others as you would expect but science, for example, has taken on the idea of literacy wholeheartedly and has developed strategies for supported reading.

There is one area in particular we are tackling: it is the area of Performing Arts, which takes in dance, drama, music and PE. We are looking at the concept of working on spelling and how you can make visual the building of words through dance, through drama, through photography and so on.

I think that we are very fortunate in this county that there are some very strong English Departments who know what they are about and are not prepared to be swayed by, dare I say, government speak. I think that we are agreed that from the Key Stage 3 strategy we will take what we need that's appropriate to our English Departments. We need to be selective and look at what enhances and actually can make an enrichment and an improvement, a shift of focus.

The reason why we use CATs tests is because the information provided by Key Stage 2 tests is not sufficiently informative: it's a snapshot of that pupil's performance and it does not show us the potential that that child has, it doesn't show us whether they have depressed verbal ability, in comparison to their real potential that's shown in the non-verbal. By doing the CAT testing we are able to actually plot pupil performance. And that's important because if you just use the Key Stage 2 test information you could so easily set pupils in the wrong area for the level of academic ability.

The dilution of English

We do diagnostic testing: we test for reading age and spelling age and we revisit that because there is again a belief that students coming in Year 7 undergo a significant dip in performance and we need to be able to see how much actual truth there is in that. Senior management would like us to investigate whether there is a dip and they want to be able to see the difference that actually made, because of the kind of teaching that we deliver. For example over the last two years, we have had Year 7 pupils coming in who, when they discuss things that they enjoyed from junior school, are now putting English on the list of things they did not enjoy. I think that trend is terrible. We have never seen this before and it seems to us that the prime reason for this is because of the dilution of English within the junior school curriculum.

I think that the shift in junior school has been much more specifically towards specific literacy teaching. The literacy hour has obviously had some significant benefits for some children, but it does not necessarily benefit everybody and it certainly does not provide for the breadth, the depth of exploration of all the many forms of language use. It is tied very specifically to performance at Key Stage 2. Everything else, and junior schools agree with this, is set aside in order to crib, cram, practise for SATs and I, you know, I look back and can remember that that was how my last year in junior school was, preparing for the eleven-plus, and I feel that this is where we have come now.

They don't do the private reading but they are constantly meeting assessment, always assessment and the love of writing, the creativity of writing, creating, talking, performing is what seems to be missing. I'm not saying that we have it right, necessarily, because we obviously need to shift focus a little bit to accommodate some aspects of the framework. We can see the purpose of that, but what we need to work at so hard, and what I think we do extremely well in order to gain results at 70 per cent by the time they reach GCSE, is to revive that joy in English. That's what we are about and this is why I've been told this year we have been able to take children who have come in significantly below the national average to meet the national average by Key Stage 3 and to exceed the national average by GCSE. We must be doing something right.

Criticisms of the training

On our first training day I have to say that we were quite unkind, not unkind, but difficult. We were like a difficult class because we wanted to know and we were asking and we were probing and some people behaved slightly . . . obstreperously. Well the thing that annoyed people on that first occasion was the rather patronizing assumption which tends to come across: they try to draw you in, like, I'm one of you, with statements such as 'you know what teachers are like', 'you know how difficult it is to get teachers to do', 'you know, you've all been there, it's almost impossible to get teachers to'. It purported to place teachers as a negative group of people who were reluctant to take on responsibility for areas such as literacy, but that was not our experience and it wasn't just us, there were other schools there who felt equally irritated at that kind of assumption.

We have no intentions of taking the framework and putting that in place fully to the exclusion of aspects of our curriculum. We will take aspects of the framework and build that into what we do and we'll shift the focus and will be using starters, we'll be looking at how we can use grammatical structures in exciting ways.

We believe there is a better way that teachers can demonstrate improvement or lack of improvement. I think that much more significant than what children are able to turn out on the day is what they are actually able to do. It's a huge issue. I don't pretend to have the answers but I don't think necessarily that testing children to death is the answer either.

Lack of attention to pupils' development

I think that the one thing that's clearly missing in both of these frameworks is a real recognition of the developmental stages of pupils: for example, while I see within the framework that although many of the strategies have been taken from the Stepping Out programmes, there isn't the attention to individual development. There isn't the same opportunity to be able to look at a piece of work and to identify what this shows about the stage that the pupil has actually arrived at and I think that that is a real weakness. There seems to be an assumption that it is a progression, that all children can quite simply move on this ever-moving escalator, but without taking into consideration the fact that children do develop at different rates and teachers need to be trained to recognize those levels of development and to be able to know what to do in order to be able to take them further.

Now LSAs are not qualified to do this, although I suppose we need to start somewhere. They are not qualified teachers and we don't know what the quality of training is. Now, the LSAs have been sent off to training but I haven't been party to that, so I don't know what that quality of training is, and yet my role will be to manage that system.

Conclusion

Several conclusions and lessons can be drawn from these talking heads of English. They convey a powerful sense of the despondency and anger that some English teachers feel about the government's seeming unwillingness, or 'selective inattention' as Donald Schon called it, to draw on their years of experience so that they can contribute to change in a positive way. These teachers feel rejected, pressurized and patronized, as is poignantly expressed in John's 'I don't have time to breathe' heartfelt cry. Schon (1971, p. 14), again, aptly describes this feeling of uncertainty in the face of change as 'anguish':

> The depth of anguish increases as the threatening change strikes at more central regions of the self. In the last analysis, the degree of threat presented by a change depends on its connection to self-identity.

Further, Schon observes, the centre–periphery model of innovation, of which the literacy strategy is a good illustration, does not take into account 'the dynamically conservative plenum in which information moves' (ibid.). As a consequence, 'the process resembles more nearly a battle than a communication'. Schon suggests, therefore, a 'groping and inductive process for which there is no adequate theoretical basis' (ibid.) in order to both ensure the transformation of institutions and to support the self identity of those who belong to them.

John's plea for more intellectual rigour in the implementation of the *Framework* is echoed by June who laments what she sees as a crucial failure to distinguish between teaching and learning, particularly where it applies to the role of learning support assistants. Ellie, like John, considers the focus on assessment to be a conceptually impoverished one that, apart from their concern over the reliability of the SATs as indicators of improvement, takes insufficient account of maturation. They both argue for a more common-sense approach to explaining the apparent dip in pupil performance in Year 7. Anna, along with June, reserves her strongest comments for the artificial nature of the literacy training, the 'ludicrous timescale', the new jargon and, most importantly, the poor modelling of teaching. All four heads are at pains to point out that they are not being negative about all aspects of the *Framework*, but in view of the cost in terms both of physical and human resources they remain to be convinced that it offers the most effective approach to raising standards of literacy in the secondary phase of schooling.

Several lessons can be learnt from these teachers:

- Major policy decisions must take more account of the circumstances of the schools and those who work in them. Nobody who visits schools regularly can be unaware of the very considerable pressure under which they work and its effect on teachers. There is no question that the timescales set by policy-makers and, in turn, by senior managers in schools are 'ludicrous' and the need to address this as a serious problem is long overdue.
- To begin the process of addressing the problem educational policy-makers should invest time in their most experienced teachers at least as much before decisions are made as after. They need to understand more clearly that professional people resent being told what to do, but can be persuaded by reasoned argument and convincing examples. In Falstaff's words, 'If reasons were as plentiful as blackberries I would give no man a reason upon compulsion'. In other words, professional people do not like to be told what to do in their own sphere of competence.
- As Anna very sensibly observes, 'You don't start by offending people by

telling them they are not doing well enough and then give them a whole load of jargon and a whole pile of paper work that is so mammoth that even the most dedicated and organized person is going to shy away in horror and then expect people to welcome it. That's been the problem with it.' There clearly needs to be a greater emphasis on what teachers do well, rather than a seeming obsession with what they are thought not to be doing.

- The quality of the training and the training materials needs to be closely monitored and evaluated. There is clearly an anxiety about the amount of paperwork and the nature of the training that needs to be overcome. This could be done by offering guidance on how to phase the implementation of the strategy over an agreed timescale.
- The heads of English involved in this project, including the 120 who completed the original questionnaire, all made some comment about the nature and content of English teaching and several harked back nostalgically to what they saw as the golden era of the Bullock Report. Now is the time perhaps for another enquiry into the teaching of English.

In his conclusion to *The Reflective Practitioner* (1982) Schon writes:

When societal predicaments are grasped only through institutionalised contention, where each contending party sees a piece of the reality and embodies his perception in a view which he treats as a battle-cry, then it is unlikely that a fuller and deeper understanding of the predicament will become powerful for public policy. In order for society's conversation with its situation to become reflective, individuals involved in adversarial processes must undertake reflective enquiry. The question is, are they likely to do so?

The reply from our talking heads would surely be, 'They have not done so far'.

References

Bennett, A. (1998) *Talking Heads*, London, BBC Books.

Brookes, W. and Goodwyn, A. (1998) 'Literacy in the secondary school', paper given at the British Education Research Association Conference, Queens University, and published in *English and Media Magazine* (NATE, Autumn 1998).

Cohen, L. and Manion, L. (1994) *Research Methods in Education*, 3rd ed, London and New York, Routledge.

Department for Education and Employment (DfEE) (1998) *The National Literacy Strategy, Framework for Teaching*, London, DfEE.

Department for Education and Employment (DfEE) (2001) *The National Literacy Strategy, Framework for Teaching English: Years 7, 8 and 9*, London, DfEE.

Fullan, M. (1993) *Change Forces*, London, Falmer Press.

HMI (1999) *Key Stage 3 Literacy: a Survey by HMI*, Autumn Term 1998, p. 2, National Literacy Trust web site.

Horne, M. (2001) 'Make teaching a desirable career', *Times Educational Supplement*, 31 August, p. 27.

Maxcy, S. J. (1994) *Post-Modern School Leadership: Meeting the Crisis in Educational Administration*, London, Falmer Press.

Schon, D. (1971) *Beyond the Stable State*, New York, Maurice Temple Smith.

Schon, D. (1982) *The Reflective Practitioner*, New York, Maurice Temple Smith.

Shakespeare, W. (c. 1600) *Hamlet* (Act 3, Sc. 2).

Webster, A., Beveridge, M. and Reed, M. (1996) *Managing the Literacy Curriculum*, London, Routledge.

Wragg, E. C. (1978). *Conducting and Analysing Interviews*, Nottingham, Nottingham University School of Education.

6

Classroom literacy and everyday life

George Hunt

This chapter draws on detailed research into the experience of pupils in Years 6 and 7 and reveals their views and feelings about literacy and specifically the literacy hour. We can see that they have strong and essentially mixed feelings about this experience. They can see certain benefits but we can also sense how the obsessive focus of the NLS on narrow approaches to texts in particular may eventually lead to profound disaffection. The chapter has plenty to say about how this dismal outcome may be avoided.

Introduction

The aims of this chapter are to discuss specific findings about how some pupils in transition from Key Stage 2 (KS2) to Key Stage 3 (KS3) perceive the purpose and quality of the English instruction that they have experienced, and to link these findings to more general ideas about relationships between school-based and everyday literacies. The chapter arises from an interest in finding out what pupils who have experienced three years of the National Literacy Strategy, and who are beginning to work within a subject-dominated curriculum, feel about the relevance of English.

It could be argued that the focused analysis of literature and language offered by the literacy hour and by KS3 English lessons has the potential to enhance pupils' awareness of the role of literature and language in society at large. On the other hand, there is the possibility that the marginalization of cross-curricular approaches, the use of canonical texts and the anatomization of language by such activities as grammatical analysis, could cause them to regard literacy as a set of self-referential practices that belong mainly to school.

While preparing the chapter, I sought the opinions of two groups of pupils, one at the end of Key Stage 2, the other at the beginning of Key Stage 3. Some of their responses are reviewed in more detail below, but the attitude towards English that was most prevalent in both groups, encapsulated in the following quotations, is worth considering now as an opening to the discussion:

> Well when you get to your Sats like we've just done, you've got to do all sorts of stuff like writing, and answering questions on things like reading, and doing all your spellings right and that, and if you didn't do Literacy Hour you'd be hopeless at all that stuff. (KS2 pupil)

> When you leave school you've got to get a job, and you're not going to get a good one unless you've got good results, and you need to be able to fill in forms and write applications as well. (KS3 pupil)

The highly utilitarian views expressed here, reflecting what the Cox Report[1] (DES, 1989) referred to as an 'adult needs' model of the purpose of literacy instruction, are perhaps a reflection of the assumptions prevalent in society as a whole. The rhetoric of educational policy frequently features demands that teachers should prepare children for the 'real world' by making schooling relevant to concerns outside of the classroom. These demands often reflect an uncritical acceptance of the idea that the purpose of education is to provide the current socio-economic establishment with an annual supply of recruits who will act as effective producers and consumers in order to maintain and strengthen this establishment. Thus, teachers are often told that they should be making their work more responsive to the needs of industry and commerce, a claim which invariably carries the implication that 'today's school-leavers' lack the requisite skills for serving within the national economy and keeping it competitive. This tradition has, of course, a long and ignoble ancestry, and most English teachers would probably condemn the narrowly functional view of education that it embodies.

However, the question of how pupils' experience of English in school relates to their everyday life outside school is a serious one, since it is well established that motivation to learn is maximized when learners are aware of the purpose of what they are doing (Mortimore et al., 1988). In the field of literacy, Downing, (1984) provides a convincing argument that in learning to read, 'task awareness' – the ability of the learner to discern the purposes and key features of authentic acts of reading- is a crucial variable. It might seem that this has been obvious for long enough to inform educational planning, but it is clear that a lot of the anxiety arising from some of the features of the NLS (for example, the use of technical phonological vocabulary at Key Stage 1, or the study of complex features of sentence grammar at Key Stage 2) can be traced to teachers' and pupils' bewilderment at why they should be teaching or attempting to learn this material. When pupils *are* aware of how 'classroom English' relates to the world outside of school, it becomes possible for them to make and share explicit links between their personal concerns, histories and interests on the one hand, and their explorations of oral and written language on the other (see McMahon and Raphael, 1997, for some interesting demonstrations of this point).

It is also possible to defend the demand that experience in school should reflect experiences outside school without accepting the rationale of the economic argument: we can instead defend this demand from the standpoint of critical literacy. This approach turns the utilitarian view back on itself by asserting that pupils do indeed need to be aware of the needs of industry and commerce, not in order to serve these masters better, but in order to resist being exploited by them.

In this chapter, I will suggest that a critical literacy approach can provide pupils with a coherent view of what English is for, and can help them to see how the texts and aspects of language explored in literacy lessons relate to everyday life. I will also suggest that such an approach can help them to become more active participants in the shaping of the worlds they will enter after schooling is over.

After attempting to justify a critical approach to literacy learning, I will refer to some outcomes from the small-scale investigation mentioned above. This was conducted in one primary and one secondary school in Reading. The in-school and out-of-school literacy experiences of a Year 6 class and a Year 7 middle-ability subject group were surveyed using a questionnaire, which also asked them for their opinions of literacy hours or English lessons and how they might be improved. Responses were collected from 24 primary and 21 secondary pupils. Subgroups of six to eight pupils from each of these larger groups were later tape-recorded while engaged in group discussion about the purpose and quality of literacy instruction, with their questionnaire responses as a focus. Each of the groups was mixed in relation to gender and attainment in English.

A rationale for critical literacy

A well-established model of reading (see, for example, DES, 1975) sees it as a process consisting of well-defined hierarchical stages. Learners are first taught to 'decode' graphic symbols into the spoken words that they represent. This is the foundation upon which later stages are built. These consist of comprehension skills, stratified into progressive levels such as 'literal', the recall of explicitly stated information, and 'inferential', the ability to use background knowledge in order to discern information implied but not explicitly stated by the author. A further 'level' of comprehension skills relates to the ability to bring one's own powers of judgement to the text in order to make evaluations about such aspects as relevance, veracity and quality of expression. All of these stages assume a straightforward, dyadic encounter between an autonomous reader and an autonomous writer, both of them deploying skills which are ideologically neutral.

Critical literacy reflects what the Cox model of rationales for English teaching referred to as the 'cultural analysis' model. The term is used to subsume instructional approaches which dispute the notion that reading and writing can ever be ideologically neutral. The basic assumption of critical literacy is that readers and writers are inevitably influenced by such factors as purpose, power relations, gender, historical period and affiliation to various belief systems. At the level of overall content, these factors determine which voices and positions authors include and which they omit. They also influence such structural aspects of the text as vocabulary choices and the patterning of grammatical elements. Everyday examples include the use of chains of vivid adjectives in food advertising; the inclusive 'we' pronoun in managers' memos to their underlings; the passive voice in statements where the agency of an action is deliberately omitted ('It has been agreed that . . . '). These influences are most obvious in material such as advertising, polemics and journalism, but it is a tenet of the critical literacy approach that *all* forms of text are trying to do something to the reader, and are structured accordingly. Legends and folk-tales convey traditional values about the morality of individual and group action within specific cultures; historical and other documentary texts recount carefully selected events to support privileged and contestable versions of reality; research literature foregrounds favourable findings while filtering out others; and, as Luke, O'Brien and Comber (2001, p. 113) point out: 'even a medicine bottle label features particular values and positions – a possible world where the reader (as prospective purchaser, medicine consumer and 'patient') is constructed and located'.

None of this obviates the need for people who are learning to read to acquire 'decoding' skills. Luke and Freebody (1999) point out that decoding is an essential part of the reading process, but it is only one aspect of a network of competencies that also includes text participation (understanding what the text means), text use (knowing what the text is actually for) and text analysis (working out how the text has been constructed to produce specific effects on the reader). Although these four aspects are discernible in the common-sense model of literacy outlined above, critical approaches do not regard them as sequential or hierarchical. Whereas the hierarchical model would postpone critical analysis until decoding and so-called lower-level comprehension skill have been secured, critical approaches insist that reading experience from the very beginning has to include all of them if the reader is to achieve independence. Comber (2001, pp. 92–3) asserts;

> I want to question any suggestion that critical literacy is a developmental attainment rather than social practice which may be excluded or deliberately included in early literacy curriculum . . . in the early years of schooling, students learn what it means to read and write successfully in terms of school practices. They need opportunities to take on this text analysis role from the start, as part of how culture defines literacy, not as a special curriculum in the later years of schooling or in media studies.

This point is particularly important given the quantity and variety of texts to which learners are exposed, and to which they contribute, in everyday life. In 1985, Masterman, writing before the use of mobile phones, email and the Internet became widespread amongst young people, estimated that

> When one considers pop music, radio, newspapers, magazines, computers and video games – in addition to TV – we are exposed to more mass media messages in one day than our parents were exposed to in a month. (Masterman, 1985, p. 3)

Luke (2000) compares the literacy experiences of young people to that of a surfer on a sea of signs: 'post modern childhood involves the navigation of an endless sea of texts'. In such an environment, reading instruction which neglects or postpones critical reflection will not necessarily prove empowering to learners:

> being able to construct and make meaning from text may appear empowering, but in fact may open one to multiple channels of misinformation and exploitation. You may just become literate enough to get yourself badly into debt, exploited and locked out. (Luke, cited in Fehring and Green, 2001, p. 8)

Critical literacy approaches attempt to equip learners with the ability to negotiate the rapidly evolving and expanding demands of their worlds. They go about this in various ways (see Fairclough, 1989, and Fehring and Green, 2001, for theoretical background and practical implications) but the following general strategies are characteristic:

- A recognition that texts are constructed in specific ways in order to influence the reader. This includes choices of lexis and syntax as well as selection of which voices to include and omit.

- An emphasis on the social production and consumption of texts; just as their writing inevitably reflects social factors, their reading in educational settings should involve collaborative investigation in which different readers' perspectives are brought to bear on them. This is in contrast with traditional instruction which gives more prominence to individual reconstruction through such practices as one-to-one reading aloud and individual engagement with comprehension and reader response tasks. Critical literacy seeks multiple interpretations rather than definitive meaning.
- Investigation of a wide scope of genres and their shared features, ranging from the classical and conventional texts of the official curriculum to those such as official forms, environmental print, popular culture, journalism and junk mail which have a direct or indirect bearing on readers' lives in the wider community.
- A commitment to social action; for example by writing to authors and publishers, creating alternative versions of texts, engaging in community publishing, and conducting research into issues raised by one's reading and writing.

Luke, O'Brien and Coomber (2001, p. 116) suggest the following framework of questions to guide critical investigations:

> What is the topic?
> How is it being presented? What themes and discourses are being used?
> Who is writing to whom? Whose voices and positions are being expressed?
> Whose voices and positions are not being expressed?
> What is the text trying to do to you?
> What other ways are there of writing about the topic?
> What wasn't said about the topic? Why?

Projects based on this philosophy and framework have been conducted with learners from a range of ages working on a wide variety of text types. O'Brien (cited in Comber, 2001) worked with 5–7 years analysing junk mail, including a comparison of mothers' and fathers' day catalogues to raise their awareness of age and gender stereotyping; Kempe (in Fehring and Green, 2001) showed how junior age children could make critical responses to the values presented in both traditional stories in old reading schemes and updated fairy tales; Alvermann and Hagood (2000) report how high school students were able to reflect on their own 'fandom' after examining song lyrics and pop group websites; Mellor and Patterson (2000), also working with high school students, explored the influence of historical conditions underlying images of gender and ethnicity in

Shakespeare's plays.

A promising aspect of such projects is that they provide opportunities for pupils to appreciate that the set reading and subject-specific tasks that they encounter in literacy hours and in English lessons relate to the texts and literacy demands of everyday life.

Rationales for literacy: the pupils' perceptions

As mentioned above, the majority of pupils subscribed to an adult needs model regarding the purpose of English, holding that its main purpose was to enable them to pass examinations in the short term and to help them find employment in the long term. It was interesting that many pupils took a 'word level' view of these objectives: they saw them as being realized through expanding their spoken and written vocabularies rather than familiarizing them with a wider range of genres or sharpening their critical skills.

> I think you get to know more and more words, and the more words you know the better you are at describing things. We do lots of work on adjectives and adverbs to make what you say more interesting. (KS2)

> When you're reading older books and harder books, you're always finding new words, really hard words or words they don't use any more. You've got to be able to think them out or use a dictionary and remember them for next time. (KS3)

These quotations, reflecting an awareness of the value of vivid language and of increasing competence and independence, perhaps suggest a 'personal growth' view of the purpose of English, showing that the adult needs model was not the only one that the pupils were aware of. The latter model was definitely the one that they were most ready to articulate, but they appeared to have a tacit understanding that there was more to English than *just* a preparation for working life. For example, some comments on the importance of vocabulary also suggested awareness of a cross-curricular rationale:

> You get more and more new words coming up in maths and especially science. If you know about how the words are made up, like with tri- in triangle and so on, it can help you to understand them. (KS3)

Hints of both 'personal growth' and 'cultural heritage' views were evident in the pupils' commentaries on poetry, which was the most popular genre for both KS2 and KS3 groups:

> Some of the poems we've done really make you think. We had to

put ourselves in the position of all the different characters in the poem and to write about how they felt. (KS2)

Poetry is brilliant. You've got rhythm and rhyme and it says every-thing in just a few words. Poets have got to be really brilliant. (KS2)

The cultural heritage view was also evident in the KS3 children's appreci-ation of *Treasure Island*, which had been read in a playscript format, and of *Romeo and Juliet*, which they had experienced in two video versions as well as in its original language. The comments of one pupil on the latter could be seen as evidence of the need for an approach that makes explicit the influence of classical texts on contemporary culture and language.

We saw the cartoon version and the modern one with Leonardo DiCaprio and they were great. But the original version was too hard. It's written in old English with all these hard words. (KS3)

What was noticeably absent was any explicit awareness of a cultural analysis view. Although one KS3 pupil did refer to the need for non-speakers of English to learn the language 'so that they won't get ripped off' there was no mention of the need for *everybody* to learn how to cope with the plethora of manipulative texts that envelop them. Both groups had had some experience of activities with the potential to activate criti-cal awareness. The KS2 group had been taught to take an appreciative interest in the poetic aspects of wordplay as it appears in headlines and adverts, and the KS3 group had worked on comparing different news reports of the same episode. However, this type of work seemed to be regarded by the pupils as marginal to the main business of expanding vocabulary and studying set texts.

This might reflect the role that critical awareness is given in the NLS. Although the framework of objectives for KS2 and *Language for Learning at Key Stage 3* (QCA, 2000) suggest investigations which would make promising starting points for critical literacy, they form only a small scat-tered part of the curriculum rather than providing a cohesive thread. They are positioned in the later years of both stages, and at Key Stage 2 they do not explicitly address issues of language and power.

Perhaps pupils' seeming lack of awareness of the importance of critical literacy arises from their teachers not having mentioned it to them, in which case there would be a case for making explicit to pupils of all ages the fact that there are conflicting views of why they study language and literacy. The five models offered by the Cox Report might make an acces-sible starting point. It is certainly interesting that the adult needs model was the only one cited explicitly by pupils (rather than being implied by other responses), though hardly surprising that teachers should stress to their pupils the need to be adept in literacy for future life. Given that many Key Stage 3 teachers at least sympathize with a cultural analysis rationale for English (Goodwyn and Findlay, 1999), one might expect that this could be communicated to pupils.

Links between schooled and unschooled literacies

Turning to the survey of out of school literacy experiences, the pupils' responses certainly supported perceptions about the quantity, diversity and complexity of the experiences that pupils participate in. More than 50 per cent of pupils reported recent participation in the following activities:

- sending and receiving mobile phone text messages (including the use of predictive and telegraphic text)
- sending and receiving email messages (including the use of emoticons)
- surfing the Internet
- reading and exchanging comics, magazines and games cards
- commenting on environmental print, such as adverts, road signs, shop-window notices and junk mail
- attempting to complete crosswords and other word games
- reading in the course of watching television and playing computer games.

Activities reported by fewer than 50 per cent of the pupils included;

- reading or writing graffiti
- writing out or parodying the lyrics of popular songs
- writing to famous people
- writing songs, poems and stories at home
- collecting and circulating jokes
- entering a competition
- writing a note to send round in class
- recommending a website
- using or discussing special vocabulary from books or other media (an example was 'quidditch' from the Harry Potter series)
- using Post-it notes or other formats as short messages or reminders
- keeping a diary.

Other practices mentioned by individuals during discussions included:

- writing captions for drawings
- writing letters and cards
- compiling address books
- consulting horoscopes

- reading material related to specific recreational interests, such as cookery books, model railway catalogues, Nintendo manuals and maps.

Perhaps the most striking thing about this list is its variety. Both print and electronic media are mentioned, solitary, dyadic and group actions, ephemeral and enduring texts, socially approved and socially frowned-upon customs. Of course, not all of the pupils engaged in all of the activities, but only two questionnaires mentioned no extra-curricular reading or writing activities. It is also notable that in the interviews, some pupils who were not described by their teachers as high achievers in English reported engaging in activities, such as the use of telegraphic text and emoticons, which involve fairly sophisticated skills which would not have been formally taught. This, and the participation by some of the pupils in activities which are clearly disapproved of by the school (such as graffiti-writing and note-passing) reflect the findings of studies of 'sub-rosa' literacies; those which thrive outside the mainstream of school culture, often engaged in by people who have been deemed to be under-achievers by official assessment procedures. Gilmore (1986), for example, showed how youths in working-class communities engaged in literacy activities (such as playing complex simulation games like Dungeons and Dragons) which involved a greater degree of linguistic sophistication than they had ever been credited with at school. Similarly, there is a long tradition of research into playground language (see, for example, Opie and Opie, 1959) which suggests that pupils classed as 'inarticulate' within the classroom can communicate with a great deal of fluency and expertise while at play.

The mismatch between these pupils' officially assessed competence in school-based literacy and their observed aptitude in informal settings has prompted some commentators to deny any simple distinction between the literate and the illiterate: 'the divide is rather between those whose literacy is recognized in school and those whose literacy is not' (Moss, Mabin and Street, 2000).

Even if one does not agree with so strong a statement of the implications of this mismatch, it should at least remind us of the possibility that 'underachievers' might live richer and more accomplished literacy lives outside the classroom than inside. The tendency to assert that certain pupils 'don't read anything outside school' is almost certainly based on too a narrow view of literacy, and risks creating self-fulfilling images of such pupils as academic failures.

The mismatch has also prompted many educators to attempt to transplant out-of-school literacy practices into the classroom in order to improve the appeal and the relevance of at least some school-based work.

While much fascinating and creative work, such as that of the National Writing and Oracy projects in the 1990s, has arisen from such synergy, the sub-rosa aspects of vernacular literacies complicates any effort to use them within institutional contexts. Hamilton (1998, p. 3) describes these literacies thus:

> Vernacular literacies are essentially ones which are not regulated or systematized by the formal rules and procedures of social institutions but have their origins in the purposes of everyday life. They are not highly valued by formal social institutions though sometimes they develop in response to these institutions. They may be actively disapproved of and they can be contrasted with dominant literacies, which are seen as rational and of high cultural value. They are more common in private spheres than in public spheres. Often they are humorous, playful, disrespectful, sometimes deliberately oppositional. When questioned about them, people did not always regard them as *real* reading or *real* writing.

These aspects of playfulness, privacy and subversiveness make vernacular literacies uneasy candidates for the type of formalized pedagogy that characterizes institutional practices like the literacy hour (though the ubiquity of rap-writing in KS2 and KS3 classrooms shows how some forms can be domesticated). The fact that the practitioners themselves are ready to adopt the traditional view that these activities are trivial (a view which might well be endorsed by pupils' parents in this context) also creates the likelihood of tissue-rejection if such transplants are attempted without due consideration for the social complexities involved in the operation. To illustrate this point, Maybin (in Moss, Mabin and Street, 2000) asks us to compare 'the defiant chanting of a rhyme in the course of a playground dispute, and the 'collection' of the same rhyme in a project folder in class'.

The pupils in both groups were well aware of this. Although all of the male members of the KS2 discussion group argued for the inclusion of football programmes, fanzines and sports reports in the reading menu for the literacy hour, all of this group and of the KS3 group wanted to maintain some degree of discreteness between classroom and extramural practices. The reasons that were advanced for this fell into three overlapping categories. The first reflects the role that reading and writing can play in constructing a safely private or even a secret life for oneself:

> Apart from homework, everything I write at home is private, and I want to keep it that way. I'd die of humiliation if anybody read my diary. (KS2)

Most of the stuff I read is about things I'm interested in, and everything I write about is just my own interests. Other people wouldn't know anything about it. They probably wouldn't be interested anyway. (KS3)

The second category reflects the subversive element:

We already study the stuff I read outside at school, except for graffiti which doesn't really have much on it, and that wouldn't be right for school anyway. (KS2)

Most of the things I read are unsuitable for school. They wouldn't allow them through the door. (KS3)

The third reflects pupils' insecurity about the value of their self-initiated activities:

I would be embarrassed, and scared that everyone would laugh at the stories I write and the books I read. (KS3)

I wouldn't want it studied in school because I like to keep my writing private. I don't usually like the songs I write, only parts of them. (KS2)

On the other hand, some pupils felt positive about instruction being shaped to their own interests:

I'd like to make my own writing better, and if I handed something in the teacher will give me tips on how to improve it and I'll see how well I'm doing. (KS2)

I would like to have some of what I read at home being studied because then it wouldn't always be a new thing and I'd already have some information about it. (KS3)

One pupil expressed the desire to enliven writing activities thus:

Most of literacy work is boring, but I can do some really wild and crazy stuff at my house in writing terms, and I wish I could do it at school. (KS2)

This ambivalence about the boundary between the public and the private, the socially sanctioned and the forbidden, the wild and the domesticated, is a phenomenon which could be explored through a critical approach. Questions regarding what lies on either side of the boundaries, of who polices the boundaries, and how the boundaries shift through time and across cultures, could be addressed explicitly, but with due sensitivity. This might help pupils to perceive that literacy is constructed, and that their private and personal explorations are as much manifestations of this as are the texts that they study at school. This is not to advocate a simplistic 'celebration' of diverse literacy practices, (which would hardly be appropriate, given that the values underlying many of the texts engaged in by pupils outside of the classroom are at least as questionable as those underlying the ones they encounter inside it) nor to rob children of the right to enjoy recreational texts by subjecting them all to dour and rigorous analysis. The point is rather to see how a range of literacy experiences impinge on everyday life by discerning their common characteristics and their points of difference. I would argue that it is important for teachers to model critical scepticism regarding *all* texts, but that this can be done in ways that are both appreciative and playful. (For practical accounts of how this has been done in the classroom see Marsh and Millard, 2000, and Schmidt and Pailliotet, 2001; for an exploration of children's own sceptical attitudes towards media texts see Tobin, 2000.)

Starting points based on the pupils' own responses and contributions might include the following:

- How do football fanzines maintain their audiences? Who finances them? What does the content and layout tell you about the producers' opinion of the consumer? How can this be related to other forms of persuasive text such as blurbs and advertisements? What characteristics does a sports report share with documentary and fictional accounts of other types of antagonism such as combat and romantic rivalry?
- What are the similarities and differences between the language of *Romeo and Juliet* and that of photo-romance magazines? Why is the one more highly regarded than the other? What influences has the language of *Romeo and Juliet* had on the rhetoric of romantic discourse in contemporary literature, humour and advertising?
- Why is it humiliating to have somebody read your diary or stories, but okay for people to read *Anne Frank's Diary of a Young Girl*? What 'selling points' differentiate Anne Frank's diary from that of Adrian Mole or Mr Pooter? Who are the real 'nobodies' whose diaries would never get published? Which aspects of private lives are customarily made public by publishers (for example, in newspapers and biography), and which aspects are always left out? What are the similarities and differences between these texts and diaries that pupils keep in secret for themselves?
- Why is it regarded as a criminal offence to create graffiti, but okay for publishers to promote it in a book such as Michael Rosen's *Culture Shock*? What are the similarities and differences between graffiti and more domesticated texts, such as advertising hoardings, traffic signs, piped music, announcements and junk mail, which are similarly

imposed upon audiences without their permission? How many different forms and functions of graffiti can be identified, and what other types of prose and poetry share them?

- Who decides what themes should be explored in children's literature and in children's own writing? How have these themes changed over the last hundred years or so? What can be learned by looking at the themes dealt with in the children's literature of other countries? What writing tasks are set for pupils in other countries? How has the degree of 'wildness' in children's fiction varied over time? For example, how does the treatment of episodes of violence and intoxication differ between a book such as Stevenson's *Treasure Island*, and one such as Burgess's *Bloodtide*?

Conclusion

If children and young adults have indeed become 'surfers on a sea of signs', then it is important for teachers to help them create charts of the prevailing currents and some strategies for steering their own way through them. At the same time, we should not assume that pupils are being pitched about helplessly at the mercy of these forces. We need to familiarize ourselves with the complexities of the literacy practices that pupils engage in out of class, and to negotiate ways in which the prescribed and potentially mechanistic elements of mandatory policy can be brought to life through interaction with these everyday practices.

Note

1. English 5–16 (DES, 1989), better known as the Cox Report, formulated five models or rationales for the study of English. These are summarized below.

- A personal growth rationale sees English as a humanizing influence on the child, nurturing imagination, empathy and communicative skills.
- A cross curricular rationale emphasizes that English, as well as being an area of interest in its own right, is a mode of communication in all subjects, each of which has its own lexicon and genre conventions. It is therefore the responsibility of all teachers to be teachers of English.
- An adult needs rationale is career and market driven, emphasizing that children need to be prepared for the communicative demands of the ever-changing world of work.
- A cultural heritage rationale emphasizes the child's entitlement to appreciate works of literature traditionally recognized as worthy of esteem.

- A cultural analysis rationale is aimed at the empowerment of the child. It seeks to develop in the learner a critical awareness of how language and literature of all kinds convey values and seek to affect the recipient.

References

Alvermann, D. E. and Hagood, M. C. (2000). 'Fandom and critical media literacy', *Journal of Adolescent and Adult Literacy*, **43** (5), 436–46.

Comber, B. (2001) 'Classroom explorations in critical literacy', in H. Fehring and P. Green (eds), *Critical Literacy*, Newark, International Reading Association.

Department of Education and Science (DES) (1975) *A Language for Life*, London, HMSO.

Department of Education and Science (DES) (1989) *English for Ages 5–16*, London, HMSO.

Downing, J. (1984) 'Task awareness in the development of reading skill', in J. Downing and R. Valtin (eds), *Language Awareness and Learning to Read*, New York, Springer Verlag.

Fairclough, N. (1989) *Language and Power*, London, Longman.

Fehring, H. and Green, P. (eds) (2001) *Critical Literacy*, Newark, International Reading Association.

Gilmore, P. (1986) 'Sub-rosa literacy: peers, play, and ownership in literacy acquisition', in B. Schieffelin and P. Gilmore (eds), *The Acquisition of Literacy: Ethnographic Perspectives*, Greenwich, Ablex.

Goodwyn, A. and Findlay, K. (1999) 'The Cox models revisited: English teachers' views of their subject and of the National Curriculum,' *English in Education*, **33** (6), pp. 19–31.

Hamilton, M. (1998) 'Becoming expert: using ethnographies of everyday learning to inform the education of adults', Papers from the 28th Annual SCUTREA Conference: Research, Teaching and Learning: Making Connections in the Education of Adults, web site http://www.leeds.ac.uk/educol/documents/000000719.htm

Luke, A. and Freebody, P. (1999) 'Further notes on the four resources model', *Reading Online*, web site http://www.readingonline.org /research/lukefreebody.html

Luke, A. (2000) Unpublished address to International Reading Association's 18th World Congress, Auckland.

Luke, A., O'Brian, J. and Comber, B. (2001) 'Making community texts objects of study. in Fehring, H. and Green, P. (eds), *Critical Literacy*, Newark, International Reading Association.

Marsh, J. and Millard, E. (2000) *Literacy and Popular Culture: Using*

Children's Culture in the Classroom, London, Paul Chapman.

Masterman, L. (1985) *Teaching the Media*, London, Routledge.

McMahon, S. I. and Raphael, T. E. (1997) *The Book Club Connection: Literacy Learning and Classroom* Talk, New York, Teachers' College Press.

Mellor, B. and Patterson, A. (2000) 'Critical practice: teaching "Shakespeare" ', *Journal of Adolescent and Adult Literacy*, **43** (6), 508–18.

Mortimore, P., Sammons, P., Stoll, L., Lewis, D. and Ecob, R. (1988) *School Matters: The Junior Years*, Wells, Open Books.

Moss, G., Maybin, J. and Street, B. (2000) 'Literacy and the social organisation of knowledge inside and outside school', *Virtual Seminar 2*, International Association of Applied Linguistics, web site http://www.education.leeds.ac.uk/AILA/virtsem2.mos

Opie, I. and Opie, P., (1959) *The Lore and Language of Schoolchildren*, Oxford, Oxford University Press.

Qualifications and Curriculum Authority (QCA) (2000) *Language for Learning in Key Stage 3*, London, QCA.

Schmidt, P. R. and Pailliotet, A. W. (2001) *Exploring Values through Literature, Multimedia and Literacy Events*, Newark, International Reading Association.

Tobin, J. (2000) *Good Guys Don't Wear Hats: Children's Talk about the Media*, Stoke-on-Trent, Trentham.

7

Literacy and Drama

Lionel Warner

Introduction

This chapter is intended to explore how valuable drama is to literacy, to explore the relationships between these two subjects in their various definitions, and to suggest ways in which teachers in Key Stage 3 might build on Key Stage 2 work. There seem to me to be two sets of questions underlying the relationship of drama to the teaching of literacy. First, there are the conceptual, philosophical questions and, secondly, the practical, or what I shall call situational, questions.

Can drama deliver literacy lessons? And should it? The answer to the former, a simple question of fact, is a resounding yes. Faced with such a clear affirmative there seems to be a moral imperative to answer the latter value question in the affirmative also; if you can, you must. It is a little like the rhetorical force behind the notorious title *Not Whether But How*, where the QCA is tacitly deploring any attempt to withhold grammar teaching from pupils. But just because something can be done it does not necessarily make it desirable. The role of drama needs closer examination. This leads to a second theoretical problem, that of definition of terms. Yes, drama can help us teach literacy, but we need to be clear what sort of drama and what sort of literacy. This matrix of possibilities will be the guiding structural principle of this chapter.

The situational questions centre on why this discussion is taking place at this time, and in what context. A SWOT (strengths, weaknesses, opportunities, threats) analysis of my own situation may be illustrative. I head the Department of English and Drama in a comprehensive school. Our strengths are that we have drama specialists in our team, that Drama is a successful subject at examination level, and that recent inspections and departmental review have been positive. Our main weakness is that as I write there is a considerable gap between the levels of planning recommended in the Key Stage 3 Strategy and our English scheme of work, which offers an outline core and a range of exemplar units of work in order to deliver the core. The opportunity is to give priority on our development plan to a reorganization of objectives such that the main elements of Literacy are addressed for all pupils, and to extend further the range of drama practices in the English classroom, of which I am firmly in favour. The main threat I can see is that the prescriptiveness of the English *Framework* may create disaffection amongst some experienced and much respected colleagues. The investigation of the contribution drama can make to the teaching of literacy is in part, then, a management issue; viewed from one perspective, a way of closing the implementation gap, from another, the adoption of a rational-empirical approach to curriculum planning (Becher, 1989). The advent of the *Framework* and the Key Stage 3 Strategy has caused us to make our first development plan priority the delivery of the word level and writing parts of the *Framework*. The situational questions are, then, how can our drama-specialist colleagues help us, especially with the starter activities in literacy lessons, and how far and in what ways can drama help pupils with writing? There are also questions about the state of expectation and preparation of our incoming Year 7 pupils; common experience and knowledge are perhaps a lot to ask for when there are more than 30 feeder schools. Our experience, that what may be broadly described as drama in primary school literacy lessons is a patchy provision, is supported by National Foundation for Educational Research (NFER) research (Sainsbury, 1998).

The availability of drama expertise cannot be guaranteed. There have been recruitment problems, particularly in the south-east of the country, in English and Drama as well as other subjects. Fortunately PGCE students trained to teach English at Reading University undertake a Drama module, and most are enthusiastic to use Drama in the English classroom when they arrive. But there are many other students and indeed teachers of long standing trained in other traditions in which the two subjects were kept firmly apart. It is for the good of both subjects first and foremost that I recommend the kind of integrative approaches which follow in this chapter.

To sum up the situation, I find myself reflecting on the many lessons I have observed and heard discussed, and even some that I have taught, in which drama and literacy were incontestably moving ahead in partnership. At the same time I am aware of vivid work linking the two in primary schools (see, for example, Ackroyd, 2000; Clipson-Boyles, 1998; Kempe and Lockwood, 2000). So we in secondary schools must be able to (statement of fact and value) build on it.

But first the matrix (see Figure 7.1). Since it is likely that drama in some sense can and does promote literacy in some sense, it is helpful, in order

LITERACY

	Reading and writing	Culture and range of texts	KS3 tests	KS3 pedagogy
DRAMA				
Means/method	1	4	7	10
Plays	2	5	8	11
Subject for study	3	6	9	12

FIGURE 7.1

Note: The numbers in Figure 7.1 refer to the order of the sections in this chapter, in each of which I try to make a practical suggestion for drama work to support literacy (to teach English?) in Year 7 or 8, to build on the Key Stage 2 curriculum.

to investigate further and to make recommendations, to offer some definitions.

Drama can be seen as a means of curriculum delivery, a method which may, incidentally, assist those pupils whose favoured learning style is not book and desk centred. The understanding that enactment can have an educational function goes back to Aristotle, who observed that man 'learns at first by imitation' (quoted in Neelands and Dobson, 2000, p. 14). Martin Esslin would go as far as to say: 'Drama has become one of the principal vehicles of information, one of the prevailing methods of "thinking" about life and its situations' (ibid, p. 1).

Drama can also be the performance of plays, reflecting an implicit understanding that the words on the page of a playscript are a mere blueprint for fuller vocal, spatial and technical realization. Thirdly, drama is, of course, a subject for study in its own right, with a body of knowledge as well as characteristic activities and practices. These activities may be organized into a curriculum in different ways. A GCSE Drama course will develop and assess knowledge and understanding of work done or seen, together with skills evident in practical work. Mike Gould's (2000) four elements of drama are setting, audience, otherness and story, which he urges students to remember in all aspects of their work. The framework for progression in the subject suggested by Kempe and Ashwell (2000) comprises creating, performing and responding. It is clear that elements of literacy are inextricably part of these elements of drama.

Definitions of literacy abound. The word permeates the titles of books and the discussions of teachers. This book as a whole faces up to the problematic nature of the term. What may be useful for the present discussion is a recognition of 'wide' and 'narrow' definitions of literacy. The latter is exemplified by Sue Hackman's reply to the question of what is literacy at a recent conference: 'Well, reading and writing.'[1] It is the commonsense view, implying both a set of skills to be mastered and an entitlement to be seized. The former, 'wide' definitions can be seen in the NATE position paper[2] and in the words of HMI Peter Daw (2001, p. 7):

> For me literacy has a much wider definition, related to the culture in which children are now growing up. It is about the ability to interpret, enjoy and produce a full range of texts, including media ones, literary ones and all the genres necessary for life and work in the new century.

The implication here is that literacy education can confer personal growth and cultural perceptiveness if it is not confined to the interpretation of others' print-based texts. The use of drama with adolescents may well be different depending on which definition is selected.

It may also be worth considering two instrumental, pragmatic aspects of literacy for teachers of English in Key Stage 3: performance criteria for success in the tests at the end of the Key Stage, and the pedagogical expectations of the Key Stage 3 Strategy. The criteria for performance at level 5, the 'expected level,' in the English tests include the ability to refer to the text in some detail, and this has to be done through the medium of writing. Literacy Hour lessons may well have sharpened pupils' awareness of language features, in extracts from texts negotiated in classroom talk, but at the end of Year 9 they will have to write down responses to what they have read with limited prompting on the question paper itself. Unsurprisingly, half the marks available in the test are awarded for 'Reading' thus defined. In my department we have chosen to focus our early development planning on writing, of which certain aspects become foregrounded under test conditions. The pedagogical expectations to which I refer are mainly the starter activities, but also the final plenaries to an extent. In the current situation in schools 'literacy' means teachers' classroom practices, in which drama could be an integral part.

It is not the intention of this chapter to repeat the lists of orders, objectives, programmes of study and strands which apply to literacy and drama, although occasional, partial mention is made of them. Nor is it intended to explore the explicit official links made between Drama and Speaking and Listening. At Key Stage 2 the National Curriculum for English requires scripted and unscripted work, and response to performance, in the Speaking and Listening Programmes; similarly Drama is a section under the same heading in the Key Stage 3 *Framework*, and comprises work in role, techniques, collaboration and evaluation. As Kempe and Lockwood (2000, p. 4) rightly observe, 'It is difficult to see how these requirements can be met without getting children up from behind their desks and trying things out in practice'.

1. Drama for reading and writing

My earliest experience of a drama INSET course involved a series of improvizations, concerning an accusation of theft, which led to each character writing a letter to another. My abiding memory is of the intensity of the atmosphere, both during the writing process and the process of reading the letters that followed. I have often tried to re-create that intensity in my own classroom by the same means, with variable success. The development of the role, perhaps over more than one lesson, has a liberating effect on students, freeing them from the personal revelations of the letter form, yet permitting them its immediacy. And, of course, everyone wants to read what someone has written about 'you'. The technique has been effective in GCSE Literature work to encourage students to respond empathically to characters in the texts: writing a letter from Sheila to Gerald based on *An Inspector Calls*, for example, or something like Lady Macbeth's suicide note. The preparation is helpful for possible questions of the empathic style in the GCSE examination itself.[3] The success of the writing, and indeed of the reading, depends on the active re-creation of the scene in the classroom or studio. When the drama works, then there is the need to express something. It is by now a somewhat traditional approach to English teaching to provide pupils with a stimulus. It is pleasing to see it rehearsed in current drama practice; Tina Moore is sure about the order of priority:

> Form and content are intertwined in improvizational work in order that children first have something to say and secondly have choices as to how best to say it . . . (quoted in Nicholson, 2000, p. 20)

The traditional approach is further endorsed by George Hillocks:

> people write arguments because they have something to argue. They write narratives because they have a story they want to tell. For most writing the substantive purpose comes first. (quoted in Hilton, 2001, p. 9)

This leads us to another favourite and valid English/Drama activity: the advocate's speech. The National Curriculum specifies that in Key Stage 2 pupils will work in role, and use dramatic techniques to explore characters and issues (DfEE, 1999). Exploration in role and proposing a point of view are specific strands within Year 7 Speaking and Listening in the Key Stage 3 *Framework for Teaching English* (DfEE, 2001). Generally Year 7 pupils enjoy their induction into the rule-governed game that is the formal debate. Even more challenging and engrossing can be the courtroom drama based on a studied text: the appeal of Shylock to the European Court of Human Rights (an activity I have conducted with equal success in Year 9 and Year 12), the trial of Dr Frankenstein for crimes against humanity (based on the Pullman playscript adaptation of Shelley's novel), or the court martialling (I am assuming that she failed in her quasi-military mission) of Grinny, the eponymous alien in Nicholas Fisk's (1975) novel, which I regularly teach to Year 7. All of these offer pupils the opportunity to argue a coherent point of view and to be challenged on points of fact and interpretation, perhaps in a less personally exposing way than if one's own beliefs, and therefore identity, were under scrutiny, but none the less searchingly and engagingly.

The current emphasis on the teaching of writing is far from the traditional, stimulus-based approach, however. The work of Debra Myhill and the Technical Accuracy Project (QCA, 1999) has specified for us the characteristics of successful writing in Key Stages 3 and 4. Myhill outlines some of the findings thus: 'the tendency is for the best writers at each key stage to use fewer finite verbs, to move away from the use of co-ordination towards the use of subordination, to manage the reader–writer relationship more effectively, and so on' (Myhill, 2001, p. 34). An important challenge is to apply drama techniques to the teaching of these strands of writing. The use of exemplar sentences and passages as scripts for, say, mime could well make vivid the difference between a plodding narrative loaded with finite verbs and a more sophisticated piece using descriptive clauses. And how better to manage the reader-writer relationship than to re-enact a scene for different audiences, evaluating the consequent differences in diction, body language etc. I would start with the old favourite, telling a friend about a fight on the school field, then describing the same event to the Head of Year. The follow-up writing could be a narrative in which the narrator had to tell the same event two or three times to different audiences. Paragraphing would become an essential feature of the piece, and would confirm what Peter Thomas (2001, p. 24ff) calls 'the pleasure and the power of the paragraph'.

2. Reading plays

Reading plays is, of course, an explicit requirement of the National Curriculum and the Frameworks: e.g. 'prepare, read and perform playscripts' (NLS Framework, Year 4 Term 1). In the Key Stage 3 *Framework* reading and performing scripts is rarely specified ('Response to a play' Reading 18, 'Collaborate on scripts' Drama 16, both from Year 7) but may be interwoven into other Reading strands.[4] As Head of Department I would want to see at least two full playscripts read and dramatized in each of the Key Stage 3 years, bearing in mind that the Shakespeare play will occupy a good deal of the spring term in Year 9. Both reading and responding to the plays should take a dramatic form. It is important to choose texts and editions appropriately. I favour editions which also supply resource material and suggestions for activities, such as *Oxford Playscripts* and *Collins Classics Plus*, partly to support the work of less experienced colleagues, and partly to give pupils ready access to matters of context. It is then important to treat the scripts as scripts. Gould (2000) suggests activities such as taking the text for a walk (p. 110), which I do regularly in Year 7 and Year 12, experimenting with pace (ibid., p. 48) and investigating subtext by means of thought-tracking (ibid., p. 78). Pupils should be given opportunities to experiment with ways of saying the lines, spaces and levels, placing of the audience, and sound and musical effects. Most classes contain able musicians who, with a little persuasion can be led to perform in unusual contexts. These pupils and their instruments are, in my opinion, an underused resource in English and Drama rooms. It is next important to reassemble awareness of the play. Performance of part of *Dr Jekyll and Mr Hyde* (Adorian, 1999) will demonstrate the role of the courtroom drama convention in mediating the horror story. Performance of any brief episode from *Frankenstein* (Pullman, 1990) will generate awareness of the fine line between melodrama and humour: all you really need is a classroom or studio door that will withstand numerous rushed and energetic entrances and exits! It is now appropriate to use spoken techniques such as hot-seating and conscience alley to investigate and respond to the characters in their contexts, and to combine these with elements of written response. Thought-tracking a character's dilemma could be scripts as a mini-morality play and performed to the class, who, when asked to comment, will be quick to point out inaccuracy and unlikelihood. This technique is very valuable for set text revision further up the school. Or short character-monologues could be written for characters at a particular point in a play, and then performed with the monologues intercut together, as a choric commentary on the action. These seem to me to be the kind of activities implied by Drama 15 'Explore in role' and 18 'Exploratory drama', both from the Framework for Year 7, and no doubt other strands too. The quality of understanding of plays is enhanced by this doubly dramatic treatment of them.

3. Drama concepts and language

There is the danger that drama may become instrumentalized and demeaned in the service of reading and writing. David Hornbrook (1998, p. 49) expresses the worry thus:

> uncouple role-play from the distinctive concepts, procedures, knowledge and traditions of the theatre arts and all that is left is a bag of pedagogical tricks . . .

Perhaps the pedagogical devices in Figure 7.2 deserve a little more serious consideration.

Drama technique	Literacy purpose
Mime	To assist memory through recap
Tableau	To provide a form for presentation
Dynamic duos	To practise particular speech forms
Script reading	To practise reading with expression
Dance drama	To give form to expression of feelings

Figure 7.2
Source: adapted from Clipson-Boyles, 1988, p. 12.

Nevertheless here are two further suggestions as to how the integrity of the subject can be preserved and children's reading and writing developed.

Margaret Cook (2000) suggests that oral and written work are enhanced when teacher is in role. Dorothy Heathcote (quoted in Neelands and Dobson, 2000, p. 194) is a major proponent of the activity, since it empowers pupils: 'opposition to a role places the class in a very safe position from which to disagree'. The argument is, in part, that it is the pupils' right to be able to oppose. There can be little doubt that the extra impetus given by means of teacher in role to the imaginative inhabitation of a fictional world can only increase understanding at whole text level. The point is developed in 11 below.

Response to texts, under Reading, and evaluation of presentations, under Drama, are strands within the Key Stage 3 *Framework*; pupils are also expected, each year, to undertake writing to analyse, review and comment. Kempe and Ashwell (2000) show how progression in written responses to performances can be mapped using drama-specific strands. For example if theatre language and terminology are taught pupils responses can be judged in terms of their use (which is also Year 7 Word Level 21: 'Subject vocabulary'). Similarly, pupils can be encouraged to make links between the piece of drama they have seen and others in a variety of media in terms of genre, style and tradition (which is clearly 'Critical evaluation', Drama 15 in Year 9, and doubtless several other *Framework* strands). Violence is done to neither Literacy nor Drama in teaching secondary school English in these ways.

4. Drama and cultural literacy

Drama as a means to promote wider cultural literacies could well begin by building on the awareness of written genres pupils have acquired during Key Stage 2. Their sense of the language conventions of reports, persuasive and discursive texts and so forth can fruitfully interact with what they know of television conventions. A report presented on the evening news will have different, though similar, conventions from those on *The Big Breakfast*. The notion of a balanced argument in a discursive text is inflected very differently in a *Newsround* report and a chat show such as *Trisha*. My experience teaching Year 7 suggests not only that pupils work collaboratively in groups to enact a Trisha/Jerry Springer/Oprah-style show with great willingness and parodic skill, but also that they can be led to reflect on persuasive strategies such as rhetorical questioning and the use of evidence. Although I do not use the large cardboard television recommended by some primary teachers,[5] television-style presentations are a feature of my work with the objective of media as well as verbal literacy.

There are many commentators who would expect literacy to include aspects of media education, and it is pertinent to observe how often elements of role play feature in media work with older students. Our GCSE Media Studies specification (AQA) includes a written simulation as a controlled test, i.e., the examinable component. Here students have to work in role, as members of a television production company, for example, submitting a detailed proposal to a cable channel for a new soap opera or documentary series. It is a very valuable exercise, for the sake of speaking and listening as well as the realism of the media preparation, to make the proposals to a board of students representing the cable channel in a class simulation/presentation. On a recent course at the Language and Media Centre in Islington I and fellow teachers of AS Media Studies (OCR) worked on interactive and creative ways of teaching the institutional and industrial background to modern technologies. Yes, of course students need access to hard information, but dynamic student-led role play and simulation, rather than didactic, teacher-led sessions were felt to be more appropriate, because this is a new subject where there are few traditional certainties, and more effective. Ask groups of students to promote a new mobile phone package of their invention for a specific age group, to another group of students (as journalists? parents?). Try this in Year 9 if you have time, again in Year 10/11, and in Year 12 with some specific information about the competition if you are teaching AS. The principle of handing over ownership of the subject and the discourse, albeit merely partially, is central to drama and effective for literacy, especially when 'literacy' includes an understanding of how the 'texts' are produced in the real world.

I hope when Peter Daw (above) spoke of genres necessary for life in the twenty-first century he meant to include poetry. Pupils in Year 6 will have had to 'evaluate the style of an individual poet' and 'comment critically on the overall impact of a poem, showing how language and themes have been developed' (NLS *Framework*), and the dramatic presentations of poems, in groups to the rest of the class, is a valuable way of building on these. Work spent in the English classroom on mime and tableau, for example, is a profitable investment in adding to the range of language pupils have in which to convey their appreciation of the poems they have read. For further suggestions, see Figure 7.3.

Drama technique	Purpose	Notes on use
Tableau based on whole poem	To capture the essence of the poem in a still image	Pupils should be encouraged not necessarily to go for the most obvious, literal picture
Tableau based on single lines or images	To make the imagery more memorable and accessible	If the poem is full of visual images, the pupils can create each mime as they read aloud
Monologue	To explore the voice of the poem, filling in gaps and experimenting with possible intrpretations	Could be the central voice or the voice of an observer
Voices in the head	To articulate inner conflict	Two people standing behind a third . . .
Time shift	To examine contexts and alternative outcomes	The drama looks to the past and/or the future
Incongruity	To invite a fresh examination of the language	Lines of the poem are incorporated into an unlikely context

Figure 7.3
Source: adapted from Fleming, 1999.

5. Drama and range of texts

Pupils generally have a substantial experience of dramas, through television and film. It is interesting that one aspect of progression under reading in the Key Stage 3 *Framework* is that context appears in Years 8 and 9. I use a scheme of work in Year 9 which considers treatments of the Frankenstein story in general, and the monster in particular, in prose, playscript, television sitcom, and cinema films from different eras.

English teachers are adept at introducing intertextuality into lessons and tasks, even if they do not introduce the term itself until post-Key Stage 3. Just as favourite soap operas exist in a web of trailers, listings magazines and tabloid news items, so plays in performance are promoted and reviewed. The task of designing a new cover for a playscript or a poster for a production should not be a relative afterthought set for administration by the cover teacher, but instead prepared for and taught, using real exemplars in the classroom and aiming to distil important elements of the play concerned. It is also valuable to focus pupils' attention on the blueprint nature of the playscript. Stage directions in Shakespeare are often inscribed in the speeches, for example this from *Macbeth*:

Is this a dagger which I see before me,
The handle towards my hand? Come, let me clutch thee –
I have thee not and yet I see thee still . . .
I see thee yet, in form as palpable
As this which now I draw.

Year 9 pupils (much more than half the country will probably study this play for the Test) when presented with this speech ought to be able to find and demonstrate four or five movements or gestures implied by the written text. A similarly fruitful passage is the following from *Romeo and Juliet* (most of the country used to study this play for the test in Year 9; we now use it happily in Year 8):

What's here? a cup, clos'd in my true love's hand?
Poison, I see, hath been his timeless end.
O churl! drunk all, and left no friendly drop
To help me after! I will kiss thy lips;
Haply some poison yet doth hang on them,
To make me die with a restorative.
Thy lips are warm!

Other playscripts are more explicit about stage directions, and plays by Arthur Miller and George Bernard Shaw often seem overwritten in this regard. The issue is worth spending class time on, especially in view of the Shakespeare requirement at the end of the Key Stage. Scripting for television or film is, of course, a very different matter, and encountering such scripts on the page can be a stimulating extension of reading plays and moving image literacy.[6]

6. Drama and culture

Drama could be said to promote literacy in the widest possible sense. When working together in a drama context pupils negotiate both the message and the medium, drawing on their existing repertoire and developing it all the time. It is this social aspect of literacy which is one of Gavin Bolton's four aims of the subject (quoted in Kempe and Lockwood, 2000, p. 6). McGregor, Tale and Robinson (1977, p. 14), arguing for a central place for drama in the school curriculum, put the same point thus: 'In drama the child negotiates meaning through social interaction at what we have called the "real" and the "symbolic" levels.' Perhaps literacy is an aggregation of these symbolic levels.

There is a strong echo here of David Buckingham's view of television literacy. He makes the point that television is an integral part of the daily lives of most young people, that the meanings of television are constructed through discussion, and that 'the competencies which are involved in making sense of television are . . . socially distributed' (Buckingham, 1993, p. 34). The social negotiation of meaning and the pedagogical imperative to widen social distribution are shared aspects of drama and media education, and arguably what literacy fundamentally entails.

7. Ways into Shakespeare

As we have said, half the marks in the tests (the 'SATs') are given for Reading, and the higher levels will be gained by pupils who can quote and comment on the language of what they have read.[7] How can drama help? On a recent English Shakespeare Company course teachers were encouraged to enact the imagery within the line or the phrase. For example, when saying 'the multitudinous seas incarnadine, making the green one red' you had to make a movement or gesture appropriate to each part of the imagery: you needed to respond to 'multitudinous' and 'incarnadine' separately, and your own interpretation of the last three words would become evident from the chosen actions to accompany them. This technique certainly focuses pupils' attention on the metaphorical density of their Shakespeare, and is recommended as an approach to key substantial speeches in the prescribed scenes. Another helpful approach to a prescribed scene is a group scaled-down adaptation of it, where key original phrases and lines have to be preserved, amidst newly invented script. Even when there is bathos and humour, the original words are thrown into relief and made memorable. A third approach worth considering is the choric one. To work on the banquet scene in *Macbeth* (Act III, Sc. 4) the scene is played by the chosen actors with the rest of the class joining in, for example to underline references to blood or violence, or with one group echoing Lady Macbeth's attempts to be the 'honour'd hostess', another stage-whispering her desperate asides to her husband, and two other groups playing the two sides of Macbeth himself. Such an approach not only makes aspects of the language familiar and confers ownership, but also draws attention to the dramatic structure of the scene. I can see no reason why these approaches should be reserved for Year 9. The techniques could well be practised using, say, Helena and Hermia exchanging insults in *A Midsummer Night's Dream*, in Year 7 (supported by the relevant part of the BBC *Shakespeare Shorts* video) and the *Romeo and Juliet* party scene in Year 8.

Drama can foreground quotation in other ways. I would want pupils throughout Key Stage 3 to practise writing about their reading using quotations, and a useful preliminary to this is role-playing the chat-show style interview with a character in the text. This works particularly well when the text concerned is a relatively short non-fiction text, a newspaper article or an extract from an autobiography, for instance. The interviewer has, as it were, been given the text by the programme's researcher, and is therefore asking questions based on particular words and phrases. The follow-up written task's requirement to include quotations is usually easier to fulfil as a result.

8. SATs Shakespeare I

This section concerns the reading of plays to prepare for the 'SATs.' I will not attempt to summarize the huge outpouring of in-service training and published material there has been to support the study of the prescribed Shakespeare plays and scenes. Marking test scripts gives me and my colleagues some insight into the use that has been made of such material. It is evident that in some schools 'critical' responses to the prescribed scenes are virtually rote learned. The aim, presumably, is to secure some sort of test success for the pupil, but the actual result is that test performance is undermined, for three main reasons: the demotivating nature of this approach to Shakespeare, the exposure of limitations of understanding brought about by the adoption of others' language, and the problem of relevance, of failure to address the terms of the question set. It is also evident that some schools look closely at Shakespeare's words only in the two prescribed scenes, and sometimes only in one of them. By contrast, the overview of and enthusiasm for the play to be seen in the work of many schools suggest the use of dramatic ways into Shakespeare and ways to reflect on the plays (see Section 2 above). To start *Macbeth* I recommend cutting up a large print version of Lady Macbeth's sleepwalking speeches in Act V Scene 1, giving each pupil a phrase or so, and ask them to practise saying their 'speech', to themselves and to each other, in different ways. It is helpful if they can walk round a space while doing so. Then, in a circle, each pupil says her/his line; probably some questions about meanings will be generated, but ask them what they think it means.

Also ask them which of the lines seem to go with others; reorder the circle, and hear them all again. Ask them how many episodes are being described here, as well as generally what is going on. Ask them then which event they would like to find out about first: the old man with 'so much blood in him', the wife of the Thane of Fife, the buried man that cannot come out of his grave, the hand that will not be cleaned. Start the play there, where they choose; by now there should be sufficient interest in a lurid sequence of supernatural violence. Themes, tragedy, natural order and indeed order of events can come later, together with the comparative use of video extracts. Do not rely on a showing of one video to convey the spaces around the prescribed scenes, or pupils will be guilty of the mark-losing 'Romeo on the beach with a gun' syndrome.

The value of comparing different video versions of key scenes, whether prescribed or not, is not only that pupils do not see any one version as definitive, but also that they see the possibility of a range of meanings. A comparison of the opening witches' scene (for example, the satanic church atmosphere of the Royal Shakespeare Company (RSC) McKellen version as compared, say, with the primeval monoliths in the BBC) reveals different readings of these most ambivalent figures. Lady Macbeth in one version may well be 'fiend-like', but in another a bereaved mother or a conspiratorial adolescent. Not only do we thus address 'Analyse scenes' (Study of literary texts 14) and 'Compare interpretations' (Drama 13, both Year 9) but also increase the likelihood of *engagement with the text*, a Level 7 criterion, being demonstrated in the test. It is worth remembering that the Introduction to the Test Mark Scheme says this:

> Some pupils will base their answers on a study of a text of this scene while others may focus in detail on a performance. The performance criteria can apply to both these and equal credit can be given to both.[8]

As long as pupils are aware that it is a performance, one of many possible, markers are untroubled if the performance alluded to in the answer is on film.

9. SATs Shakespeare II

It follows from much of 8 above that Test performance will be supported by the fullest possible operation of drama in this part of the Key Stage 3 English curriculum. To refer back to a definition of drama in the introduction to this chapter, pupils are tested on their response to the play, but logic and experience suggests that response needs to be preceded by creation, or at least re-creation, and performance. Text-based ways to do this have been suggested in earlier sections.

10. Drama and literacy pedagogy

In this cell we are considering drama activities as means to implement NLS pedagogy. Judith Ackroyd (2000, p. 2) argues that drama makes literacy learning more enjoyable and therefore more effective: 'finding a fictional reason for the children to learn literacy makes a significant difference to that learning experience. The literacy areas are taught in disguise as something else!' At word level, spelling rules and word families can be the basis of 'Crystal Maze' style games and competitions. Adverb games are effective; adverbs can be formed from adjectives and then enacted, e.g. *She came into the classroom quiet/noisy/hurried/lazy*, etc.

Paul Hitchcock[9] has created a language of hand mime to facilitate a range of grammar teaching games and activities. The NLS style starter activities are intended to have an element of the dramatic; 'dynamic' is perhaps the favoured official term. But increasingly drama teaching techniques are being seen in these starters, which, incidentally, do not have to be at the beginning of the lesson; a teacher in role activity would need a little preparation. At sentence and text level the mantle of the expert is recommended by Mills and Evans 'to lure pupils into the process of reading and writing'. The scheme of work involves a case study concerning a refugee child which gives 'a dramatic immediacy to which the children must respond'. The language elements are made specific by the tasks and audiences that must be addressed (Mills and Evans, 1999, pp. 14–15).

11. Plays and literacy

The main elements of the recommended NLS pedagogy, the dynamic starter activity, working in like groups, and the plenary in which key learning points are reinforced, are practical suggestions for good lessons, whatever subject you are teaching. They may take on a particular inflection in drama, with role play and shared fictional contexts. Some detailed suggestions as to how this might play out are made in Sections 10 above and 12 below.

We are told (e.g. by Rudduck, Chapman and Wallace, 1996) that 'the dip' in pupil performance early in Key Stage 3 is in part motivational; children become bored and disaffected, particularly when they are expected to sit and listen for long periods of time. At primary school they were encouraged to be up and active more often and with less delay. Clearly this is not the whole story, and two equally important factors are adolescence and the level of difficulty of the programmes of study. Nevertheless, there is an active and physical kind of learning which can take place in drama which can address the 'dip'.

12. Drama skills

In many ways the activities in the above sections do not undermine the integrity and identity of drama as a discrete subject. Consider the practice of teacher in role as an example. This could be practised as part of a word level starter activity or a fuller delivery of the Reading groupings in the Key Stage 3 *Framework* for Year 9: 'Reading for meaning', 'Understanding the author's craft', and 'Study of literary texts'. I have several times found myself hot-seated playing the role of Prince Escalus in *Romeo and Juliet*, fielding some very awkward questions from 'journalists' and 'citizens', as well as 'young lovers' and their 'parents'. Dorothy Heathcote's justification for the technique has been referred to in Section 3 above. The development of real personal response to texts and reader autonomy relies on such strategies. Bear in mind that in Key Stage 5 we will want students to, for example, explore their own responses to the character of Shylock in the context of Elizabethan as well as modern notions of race and usury.[10] Progression is always a consideration.

A further consideration is that drama skills are transferable. Children, as was suggested earlier, do not all respond best to desk and book-based learning. Drama often makes children proactive in their approach to learning, and the key drama elements of creating, performing and responding have application in other areas of the curriculum. Drama aims to 'reinstate the physical' (Denise Margetts, in Nicholson, 2000, p. 41). Shane Irwin makes the same point (op cit in Ibid, p. 26ff) in his discussion of 'Physical Theatre'.

Conclusion

I think the message is proceed with confidence, though the situational and conceptual questions with which I started still remain. My note of hesitation is because I hear dissident voices. I should make a thought-tracking morality play out of this situation: on the one hand drama is 'a potent force in the development of literacy' (Kempe, 1999); the days have truly gone when a teacher in this field could address language issues that are raised in the classroom or studio 'at another time when the atmosphere is more conducive to these matters' (Barrett, 1995, p. 6). Teachers cannot afford to leave such matters to chance, and should plan for drama to raise language awareness. On the other hand teachers, especially English teachers, are very good at 'mediating practices' (Bousted, 2000) to retain what they value when faced with prescriptive curriculum pressures. Drama is a contested site; there is no doubt that it is being officially colonized.[11] And we may yet have to face the limitations of drama in the face of conceptual frameworks for literacy derived from media education; as Cary

Bazalgette (2000, p. 49) says, in defining a 'wide' notion of literacy:

> We need to be developing a far better and more rigorous account of
> what it will mean to be literate. Literacy won't just be a competence
> in a range of specific media from verbal language to time-based
> texts . . .

But Hornbrook (1998, p. 48) is impatient of the polarization of his subject
into 'service of the revolution' versus 'training programmes of the new
utilitarianism'. As we have seen, drama can retain its identity and
integrity while fostering a range of literacies. At the same conference
referred to above Julia Strong of the National Literacy Trust made the
point that her list of 'What works with boys' (Strong, 1999, p. 21), which
includes reference to drama, could equally be headed 'Good teaching'
and should be invoked in order to address the needs of other/any
underachieving groups, such as EAL pupils.[12] We should probably, therefore, be happy to embrace strategies which generate enthusiasm in
our pupils, confident in the knowledge that we are all stakeholders in
literacy.

Notes

1. 'Literacy in Transition', Reading University School of Education,
   June 2001.
2. Available on-line at the NATE site, www.nate.org.uk
3. For example, from OCR 1501/22, June 2001:
   4. You are Marge, just before arriving at Diana's and Paul's house
      for the tea with Colin.
      Write your thoughts. (Ayckbourn, *Absent Friends*)
   1. You are Jem. You have just heard of the death of Mrs Dubose.
      Write your thoughts. (Lee, *To Kill a Mockingbird*)
      I would recommend to question-setters to try specifying in the
      question *to whom* the thoughts are to be addressed.
4. For convenience, KS3 references are to the Management Summary
   of the *Framework* (DfEE, 2001).
5. See www.tagteacher.net Discussion Forum on-line.
6. The camera script and the stage script of the beginning of *Shakers* by
   Godber and Thornton are available in photocopiable form in Kempe
   and Warner (1997, p. 63ff).
7. Test Performance Criteria for Level 7:
   Paper 1 'Pupils . . . select appropriate references to support their
   points. They make some comment on the effect of the writer's
   choice of language.'
   Paper 2 'Pupils . . . justify their comments by the use of carefully

selected references to the text' English Test Mark Schemes (QCA, 2001).

8. See Introduction, on p. 8 of the Mark Scheme for Paper 1 (QCA, 2001).

9. See the Grammimes web site www.btinternet.com/~paul.hitchcock
See also http://english.unitecnology.ac.nz/resources

10. A valuable resource to support the study of *The Merchant of Venice* at Advanced Level is Kinder and Harrison's *Pre-1770 Drama: Elizabethan & Jacobean*, in The English and Media Centre's Advanced Literature series.

11. See 'Drama in the KS3 National Literacy Strategy' on *The Standards Site*, www.dfee.gov.uk

12. Or highly able girls (see Freeman, 1996).

References

Ackroyd, J. (2000) *Literacy Alive!* London, Hodder.

Adorian, S. (1999) *Dr Jekyll and Mr Hyde* (adaptation as playscript), London, Collins.

Barrett, S. (1995) *It's All Talk*, Carlisle, Carel.

Bazalgette, C. (2000) 'A stitch in time: skills for the new literacy', *English in Education*, **34** (1), pp. 42.

Becher, T. (1989) 'The national curriculum and the implementation gap', in M. Preedy (ed.), *Approaches to Curriculum Management*, Milton Keynes, Open University Press.

Bousted, M. (2000) 'Rhetoric and practice in English teaching', *English in Education*, **34** (1), pp. 12–23.

Buckingham, D. (1993) *Children Talking Television: The Making of Television Literacy*, London, Falmer.

Clipson-Boyles, S. (1998) *Drama in Primary English Teaching*, London, Fulton.

Cook, M. (2000) 'Writing and role play: a case for inclusion', *Reading,* **34** (2), pp. 74–8.

Daw, P. (2001) 'Peter Daw: subject adviser at Ofsted' (interview), *Secondary English Magazine*, **4** (5).

Department for Education and Employment (DfEE) (1999) *The National Curriculum for England: English*, London, DfEE.

Department for Education and Employment DfEE (2001) *Key Stage 3 National Strategy, Framework for Teaching English: Years 7, 8 and 9, Management Summary*, London, DfEE.

Fisk, N. (1975) *Grinny*, Harmondsworth, Puffin.

Fleming, M. (1999) 'Not waving but drowning', *Secondary English Magazine*, **2** (4).

Freeman, J. (1996) *Highly Able Girls & Boys*, London, DfEE/NACE.

Gould, M. (2000) *The Complete GCSE Drama Course*, Dunstable, Folens.

Hilton, M. (2001) 'Writing process and progress: where do we go from here ?', *English in Education*, **35** (1).

Hornbrook, D. (2000) *Education and Dramatic Art*, second edn, Oxford, Blackwell.

Kempe, A. (1999) www.literacytrust.org.uk/Pubs/drama

Kempe, A. and Ashwell, M. (2000) *Progression in Secondary Drama*, Oxford, Heinemann.

Kempe, A. and Lockwood, M. (2000) *Drama in and out of the Literacy Hour*, Reading, RLIC.

Kempe, A. and Warner, L. (1997) *Starting With Scripts*, Cheltenham, Stanley Thornes.

Kinder, D. and Harrison, J. (2001) *Pre-1770 Drama: Elizabethan & Jacobean*, London, The English and Media Centre.

McGregor, L., Tate, M. and Robinson, K. (1977) *Learning Through Drama*, London, Heinemann/Schools Council.

Mills, C. and Evans, I (1999) 'Mantle of the expert', *Secondary English Magazine*, **2** (4), pp. 14–15.

Myhill, D. (2001) *Better Writers*, Bury St Edmunds, Courseware.

Neelands, J. and Dobson, W. (2000) *Theatre Directions*, London, Hodder.

Nicholson, H. (ed.) (2000) *Teaching Drama 11–18*, London, Continuum.

Pullman, P. (1990) *Frankenstein* (adaptation as playscript), Oxford, Oxford University Press.

QCA (1999) *Improving Writing at Key Stages 3 and 4*, London, QCA.

Rudduck, J., Chapman, R. and Wallace, G. (eds) (1996) *School Improvement: What Can Pupils Tell Us?*, London, Fulton.

Sainsbury, M. (1998) *Literacy Hours: A Survey of the National Picture in the Spring Term of 1998*, Slough, NFER.

Strong, J. (1999) *Literacy at 11–14*, London, Collins/National Literacy Trust.

Thomas, P. (2001) 'The pleasure and the power of the paragraph', *Secondary English Magazine*, **4** (4) pp. 24–8.

8

Literacy and Modern Foreign Languages

Cynthia Martin

Summary

This chapter focuses on recent initiatives in both the primary and secondary sectors, which make links between literacy and modern foreign languages (MFL) in line with changes in current National Curriculum documentation, which now encourages links between subjects. It seeks thereby to demonstrate the contribution that the learning of a foreign language in primary school, at both Key Stage 1 and Key Stage 2, can make to the overall literacy of young children. It argues that the teaching of a foreign language complements the aims and objectives of the National Literacy Strategy (NLS). It goes on to consider work being carried out at Key Stage 3, which makes connections between English and the MFL curriculum and illustrates ways in which the transition between Key Stages 2/3 is being bridged. Finally, it gathers together some implications for practice from initial findings emerging both from the joint Centre for Information on Language Teaching and Research (CILT)/Qualifications and Curriculum Authority (QCA) Modern Foreign Languages and Literacy Project (CILT/QCA 2001) and related work in other initiatives.

Introduction

One of the dilemmas facing those wishing to implement a foreign language programme in the primary school, is how to find a place for modern foreign languages within an already full primary curriculum (Low, 1998). This chapter advocates meeting this challenge by viewing the foreign language as part of the language curriculum as a whole (Martin, 2000a; 2000b). It suggests that in view of the now well established National Literacy Strategy (NLS) in primary school (DfEE, 1998b), and the coming on stream in September 2001 of a NLS for Key Stage 3, we need to continue to explore ways of making links between foreign language learning and English teaching, rather than allowing MFL in both the primary and secondary phases to be squeezed out by additional statutory requirements. It also suggests, that where fruitful collaboration between English and MFL departments in the *secondary* phase occurs, this is likely to lead to work in literacy that children are doing in the *primary* school increasingly being taken into account, with subsequent dialogue across the transition. Where links are made between literacy in English and *primary* foreign language work, the ensuing need to build on primary achievements also has the potential to benefit continuity between the phases.

In this context it should be noted that MFL is itself 'in transition', as secondary MFL departments seek to come to terms with the increasing numbers of primary pupils entering the secondary phase with an early foreign language learning experience. Furthermore, one of the major problems confronting primary modern foreign languages (PMFL) is to find ways of ensuring continuity at the point of transition between the phases. Currently, there is often lack of co-ordination from the primary sector to the secondary, and even where the foreign language started early, is carried on in some way, the discontinuities of teaching approach or change of language at secondary level, inhibit progress.

Background

Currently, MFL is not a National Curriculum subject at Key Stages 1 or 2, and is the only foundation subject with a delayed statutory start at age 11. Traditionally, English and MFL have been viewed and taught as two discrete elements of the secondary curriculum and MFL teachers have become accustomed to their subject being 'new' to pupils in Year 7. However, the last decade in particular, has seen an increase in the provision of early MFL programmes (CILT, 1995; Driscoll and Frost, 1999), some supported by local education authorities, and others more ad hoc at the level of individual schools. In April 1999 the government announced the start of the DfES (Department for Education and Skills, formerly DfEE) Early Language Learning Initiative, to promote and develop the provision and quality of the learning of MFL in the primary sector (*Early Language Learning Bulletin*, 1999). The first phase was completed in March 2001 and government funding has since been extended to a second. Accompanying the growing numbers of pupils experiencing some kind of introduction to a foreign language before the age of 11, has been a change in attitudes across what in the 1970s was termed the 'space between' the English and MFL curriculum areas (CILT, 1974). As the 1990s drew to a close, it became evident that in a small number of primary schools in which a class teacher was responsible for the whole curriculum, links were being made between English and the early teaching of a MFL, using the NLS *Framework* as a basis. This chapter reports some of that work.

Curriculum 2000

As a prelude to discussion about these literacy and MFL links, it is important to note that the revised National Curriculum 2000 actively advocates a more integrated curriculum through making connections between subjects, as a perusal of the orders for English and MFL both indicate. Indeed, each of the separate subject booklets incorporates a section entitled 'Use of language across the curriculum'. The MFL curriculum is self evidently different from that of other subjects in the requirement to develop skills of this kind through the target language (the MFL pupils are learning). Nonetheless, in line with other curriculum areas, explicit links are made to the English programme of study alongside the programme of study for MFL. Thus, in contrast to earlier versions of the MFL National Curriculum, learners are permitted to use English 'when discussing a grammar point or when comparing English and the target language' (DfEE/QCA, 1999, p. 16) and to 'use their knowledge of English or another language when learning the target language' (Developing language-learning skills 3(c). Statements of this kind acknowledge the instances when pupils' understanding may be consolidated through the medium of English. Similarly, the opening section of the revised National Curriculum for MFL entitled 'Acquiring knowledge and understanding of the target language' requires that pupils should be taught the:

- principles and interrelationship of sounds and writing in the target language (MFL 1(a)
- grammar of the target language and how to apply it (MFL 1(b) (DfEE/QCA, 1999, p. 16).

Each subject booklet contains non-statutory information in the margin on potential ways in which requirements in one subject can build on the requirements in another in the same key stage. Requirements 1(b) and 3(c) of the MFL National Curriculum cited above are therefore linked to English 1/5, 2/6 and 3/7, which state that pupils should be taught to:

- use the vocabulary, structures and grammar of spoken standard English fluently and accurately in informal and formal situations (En 1/5)
- draw on their knowledge of grammar and language variation to develop their understanding of texts and how language works (En 2/6)
- the principles of sentence grammar and whole text cohesion and use this knowledge in their writing (En 3/7).

Similarly, both the MFL Schemes of work at Key Stage 3 (QCA, 2000b) and the non-statutory schemes at Key Stage 2 include examples of ways in which links can be made with pupils' prior learning in English, through the NLS and language awareness work. Indeed, the Teacher's Guide for the non-statutory schemes of work at Key Stage 2 states that:

> In Key Stages 1 and 2 children will have followed the National Literacy Strategy and will have knowledge of English, including grammatical awareness and knowledge of some grammatical terms. The scheme of work takes account of this and consolidates and builds on this work ... Children are encouraged to increase their knowledge of how language works and to explore differences and similarities between the new language and English or another language. (QCA, 2000a, p. 7)

The same document goes on to indicate the opportunities for links to be made with other curriculum areas, the most substantial being with English, through the development of

> speaking and listening skills, knowledge and understanding of grammar and sentence construction. Opportunities to compare the foreign language with English or another language can be exploited through use of the new alphabet, phonemes, rhyming patterns, sound/spelling links, dictionary work, formation of structures (such as singular/plural, gender, negatives, question forms, position of adjectives, imperatives), intonation, dialogues, poetry, different text types, formation of complex sentences. (QCA, 2000a, p. 11)

Making the link in practice

Currently, there are a variety of different models of provision for the introduction of a foreign language in the primary phase, each with its own particular aims and emphases. Broadly speaking, primary MFL programmes focus on either the development of language competence, typically in a single foreign language, or sensitization or encounter with several foreign languages, or language awareness. Interestingly, experience of offering a language competence programme without making explicit links with English as in the early years of the now well established Modern Languages in the Primary School (MLPS) programme in Scotland, indicated the importance of developing children's knowledge about language (Low, 1998).

Alternatively, sensitization or encounter programmes aim to develop children's understanding of language learning by giving them a taster experience of more than one language (Mitchell, Martin and Grenfell,

1991). Earlier versions of the National Curriculum for English (DfEE, 1998a, p. 2) acknowledged that the 'richness of dialects and other languages can make an important contribution to pupils' knowledge and understanding of standard English'. Indeed, the Nuffield Languages Inquiry (2000, p. 43) recommended that modules of language awareness should be introduced into the National Literacy programme in primary schools with content designed to bridge the gap between English, literacy and foreign languages.

The non-statutory Guidelines for MFL at Key Stage 2 comment that through learning a foreign language in primary school:

> Pupils develop communication and literacy skills that lay the foundation for future language learning. They develop linguistic competence, extend their knowledge of how language works and explore differences between the foreign language and English. Learning another language raises awareness of the multilingual and multicultural world and introduces an international dimension to pupils' learning, giving them an insight into their own culture and those of others. The learning of a foreign language provides a medium for cross-curricular links and for the reinforcement of knowledge, skills and understanding developed in other subjects. (QCA, 1999, p. 32)

Each of these teaching approaches tends to be supported by different teachers: so, for example, a language competence model is often, though not always, delivered by a language specialist, since it emphasizes performance and progression and tends to be based on the concentrated study of a single language. In other programmes, it is the primary teacher, rather than a visiting specialist, who delivers the foreign language element in the primary curriculum. Particularly where this is the case, there are opportunities to explore ways of making the links advocated in the preceding paragraphs between teaching a MFL and extending work in English and literacy. It is to these that we now turn.

Current developments at Key Stages 1/2 to link English and MFL

The starting point, as we have seen, is one of a variety of practice. Even within clusters of primary schools feeding similar secondaries, there can be inconsistency, with individual schools using a range of systems to develop good practice. This situation, combined with concerns expressed by local head teachers about children's low levels of literacy, led teachers within South Gloucestershire education authority to agree to develop a common Literacy and Early Foreign Language Learning (EFLL) Framework for a group of 10 primary schools working in partnership with a special-ist secondary language college. Initial development work and joint plan-ning began in 1996, as part of a strategy to promote language and literacy learning in schools. The intention was to provide a curriculum outline for Years 5 and 6, using a choice of models based on a weekly language and literacy plan. However, class teachers of children in Key Stage 1 have also been involved, basing their foreign language sessions on 5 to 10 minutes of daily, planned French, using counting games, music, story and song (Cole, 2000). This approach grew out of the recognition that the NLS is something with which primary teachers are now familiar, which has been seen to 'work' and with which they feel comfortable. Using the NLS *Framework* as a basis, key skills and learning objectives were identified, and set in a similar framework for MFL. The Literacy and EFLL Framework (SGC, 1999) was also a means of establishing a shared system to help schools survive staff turnover. This initiative later became one of the 18 Good Practice Projects participating in the DfEE Early Language Learning Initiative, without the support of which it would not have become embedded.

According to Mary Rose, Senior Adviser, Research and Development, for South Gloucestershire, abundant opportunities already exist within the effective primary classroom for the successful development of lan-guage – mother tongue or foreign, a view endorsed by Driscoll (1999) and Sharpe (2001). 'The methodology is firmly founded on primary philoso-phy and best primary practice' (Thomas, 2001, p. 6). The primary teacher is therefore well placed to develop children's confidence and competence in oral expression and responsive listening. It is therefore primary teach-ers who have been called upon to implement the joint strategy, with support from the specialist language college, without whose sponsorship the initiative would never have taken place, linking and extending current successful practice already established in the Literacy Hour.

At this point it is important to note that primary teachers have been supported in their delivery of the joint curriculum through a planned sequence of professional development, which has comprised a three day course led by an experienced Language Teaching adviser from CILT to induct teachers into the approach. This MFL adviser worked in close col-laboration with South Gloucestershire's Senior Adviser, Literacy Consultant and the primary teachers to devise and trial the Literacy and EFLL Framework. Experience of the MLPS schemes in Scotland has demonstrated that ongoing support is required, to back up the initial in-service training of teachers. In South Gloucestershire an annual extension course is offered to participating teachers.

Sharpe (1992) stresses the need to develop primary teachers' confi-dence alongside their foreign language competence. On account of the unique characteristics of early MFL work and the need to incorporate the target language, from 1999 two native speaker student teachers from a French teacher training institution partnered with the specialist language college, the *Institut Universitaire de Formation des Maîtres* in Tours, have had annual placements as foreign language assistants. They have worked alongside primary teachers, modelling pronunciation in the target language and providing a strong cultural influence for the children. Twilight language learning sessions have also taken place, supported by access to multimedia facilities at the specialist language college.

The native speaker foreign language assistants enable pupils to see for themselves that the foreign language they are learning is actually spoken by real people. This realization is enhanced for some pupils by class-to-class projects between primary schools in the South Gloucestershire cluster and partner primary schools in France, with whom they exchange cultural boxes and posters. As Sharpe (2001) emphasizes, these kinds of activity, as well as providing a context for the kinds of language and literacy related tasks described later in this chapter, also help initiate children into the concept of Europe as a community of which they are a part.

According to the Literacy Task Force (1997, p. 15), the intention of the Literacy Hour was to make 'initial and continuing progress in reading and writing a central objective of the school'. However, the NLS also states that as well as uniting the skills of reading and writing, literacy 'involves speaking and listening . . . which are an essential part of it. Good oral work enhances pupils' understanding of language in both oral and written forms and of the way language can be used to communicate' (DfEE, 1998b, p. 3).

The NLS *Framework* does not, however, include speaking and listening in the planning of work for literacy, despite the fact that the quality of interaction is of central importance within the Literacy Hour. Significantly, the South Gloucestershire Literacy and EFLL Framework stresses that a range of listening and speaking opportunities must be planned, to ensure that learning activities with a high 'talk' potential are provided, promoting individual and shared learning (SGC, 1999, p. 1). Although speaking and listening skills are not separately identified, they are considered an essential part, and it is recommended that the daily dedicated time should contain three elements, the first of which should always develop simple listening and responding and/or speaking skills. The Literacy and EFLL Framework (SGC, 1999, p. 23) states, 'Good oral work enhances pupils' understanding of language and communication. Effective teaching of reading and writing is achieved within a strong oral context.'

Adapting the National Literacy Strategy *Framework*

The Literacy and EFLL Framework offers a common structure based on the same teaching approach as for L1 literacy. The structure of the Literacy Hour as set out in the NLS *Framework for Teaching* (DfEE, 1998b) consists of four elements. It is suggested that it begin with 15 minutes of shared text work, followed by 15 minutes of focused word work for 5–7-year-olds, and for 7–11-year-olds, a combination of either focused word- or sentence-level work, 20 minutes of 'independent reading, writing or word work' for 5–7-year-olds, or sentence level work for 7–11-year-olds, whilst the teacher works with at least one ability group on guided text work. It ends with a 10-minute plenary, for whole class review, reflection and consolidation. In South Gloucestershire the Literacy Hour framework has been used as a model for EFLL sessions, which are perceived flexibly as consisting of either five 15-minute sessions, three 20-minute sessions, or two 30-minute sessions over a week. A recent review of practice (summer 2001), indicates that schools are now confidently adapting the suggested time blocks to match their individual curriculum plans.

During each of these sessions previous objectives are revisited, new objectives introduced and the session finishes with a plenary. Examples demonstrate how to use a range of activities and resources to teach and assess word, sentence and text level objectives, focusing on skills in listening, responding, speaking and reading. This has ensured an integrated approach to EFLL within the primary curriculum, allowing teachers to develop learning on a 'little and often' basis. The 1999 Literacy and EFLL Framework has provided a sound foundation for teachers' work and is acting as an effective bridge as teachers move into the next stage of building curriculum programmes which incorporate the QCA Schemes of Work and which will link to work at Key Stage 3.

The following sections indicate some of the activities undertaken in the primary schools, starting with word-level work focusing mainly on phonics, spelling and vocabulary. Strategies with which teachers are already familiar, using the 'searchlight' approach (DfEE, 1998b), have been developed to enable children to discriminate between the separate sounds in words, both by listening to a variety of sounds in the language(s) which with they are working, and by enunciating these sounds themselves. Throughout, the foreign language is a point of comparison with pupils' own language, so for instance, pupils have been encouraged to compare the use of intonation in English and French to signal a question.

Riley (2001) suggests that successful readers have to distinguish aurally between the constituent sounds of words (phonological awareness) as well as becoming increasingly familiar with the letters and groups of letters on which these sounds map (orthographic awareness). Researchers such as Goswami and Bryant (1990) hold the view that learners' phonological development follows a pattern from becoming aware of syllables, to an awareness of onsets and rimes within syllables. Finally, beginner readers become able to discriminate between the smallest sound units, phonemes, although they find it hard to detect phonemes, except when the phoneme coincides with a word's onset. In South Gloucestershire, word-level work has involved clapping and counting the number of syllables and grouping words together with the same number of syllables, using familiar words from introductory themes typical of early foreign language programmes.

Martin and Cheater (1998), and Cheater and Farren (2001) suggest that working with a foreign language at primary school can help ensure that pupils acquire the full range of decoding skills, as they practise recognizing, exploring and working with rhyming patterns through nursery rhymes and songs. As mentioned earlier, writers such as Bryant (1993) are also of the opinion that children first become aware of the larger sound units of language, recognizing rhyming words in their mother tongue, and then alliteration. Activities such as discriminating 'onsets' from 'rimes' in speech and spelling, identifying alliteration and onomatopoeia in poems and songs, finding particular words or phrases in a text by listening or reading, holding up text flashcards with matching key words which rhyme with a word spoken by the teacher, have been extensively trialled within Good Practice Project schools. There are indications that work of this kind helps train pupils to listen carefully, as it focuses on the small details of language such as sounds in words and intonation. Talking about familiar words in rhymes makes children more aware of the critical features of words, such as their shape and length. Goswami and Bryant (1990) also point out that children's pre-school knowledge of nursery rhymes in their mother tongue is strongly related to their later sensitivity to rhyme. Detecting rhymes and alliteration in foreign language nursery rhymes would appear to at least have the potential to complement this.

Work with the Literacy and EFLL Framework has shown that in order to support and reinforce learning in English, it is advisable for activities highlighting grapheme–phoneme correspondence to begin by considering phonemes and graphemes, which are the same in both English and the foreign language. Through a variety of parallel activities, some carried out in English and others with foreign language examples, children have been taught to signal using a simple action, whenever they hear a word beginning with the chosen sound(s), which may be formed of single letters or combinations of letters, and be vowels or consonants. As well as using familiar expressions such as greetings, or children's names, teachers have incorporated well-known rhymes in both English and the foreign languages. These have been used repeatedly, to enable learners to listen out for and respond to many different sounds, initial, final and medial as appropriate. As children have become familiar with the activities and the sounds, the foreign language examples have been extended to not only reinforce similarities with English, but to give practice in listening for sounds, which are not found in English, or to talk about 'silent' letters such as the 'h' in *'j'habite'*.

Teachers in primary schools have also developed strategies to consolidate alphabetic knowledge in both English and the MFL. They have found that once children are secure in their knowledge of the English alphabet, the foreign language alphabet can be used to develop spelling skills even before the whole alphabetic sequence in the foreign language has been learned. Blatchford et al., (1987, cited in Beard, 2000) has noted a link between children's early letter-name knowledge and their subsequent reading development. Tasks have included naming each letter of the alphabet in lower and upper case, in both English and the foreign language, writing letters in response to letter names, spelling and reading on sight a small bank of familiar words, for instance, colours, names of pets, and words repeated often in favourite rhymes, songs or storybooks. Multisensory approaches such as finger tracing in the air, and writing on backs have been used alongside articulating.

Children will have made class dictionaries and glossaries in English and work indicates that they can be taught to apply alphabetic and phonic knowledge through understanding alphabetic order. As Cheater and Farren (2001) state, this knowledge is crucial for the effective use of either mono-lingual or bi-lingual dictionaries. However, experience has shown that learners must be very secure with the vocabulary and associated items before dictionary skills are practised. Some teachers have discovered that even before they are accustomed to using real dictionaries, children in Key Stage 1 have been able to place toys into dictionary order, and they can sort and sequence words according to the sound of the initial letter of the words, using familiar objects. It has been possible to introduce the notion of gender through sorting, say, the *'un'* toys from the *'une'* by placing them on separate mats or in different boxes, as suggested in the QCA (2000a) French scheme of work, before learning the dictionary 'code' later on. Older learners in Key Stage 2 have been willing to practise dictionary skills in the foreign language, where these have been 'covered', but, as Cheater and Farren (2001) point out, not necessarily mastered, in the mother tongue. Using high frequency words from the primary MFL classroom, Key Stage 2 learners have successfully located headwords in a dictionary, found out the gender, searched for the meaning or organized into dictionary order sets of words beginning with the same two letters.

The NLS expresses the hope that literate primary pupils should have an interest in words and their meanings. Although referring primarily to the English curriculum, aspects of work in MFL are suited to promoting this basic curiosity about language and enjoyment in working with words, so, as suggested for instance in the QCA (2000a) schemes of work for French, pupils can explore the origins of the names of countries.

Sentence and text level

Short texts often provide the context for foreign language literacy supportive activities at sentence level. At sentence level teachers have helped pupils to use some of the knowledge and skills they are acquiring at word level to focus on grammar and punctuation and begin to put words into a meaningful context. Through work in the foreign language, children have come to realize that syntax used in English is not necessarily the same in other languages. By discussing similarities and differences, children have been helped to identify features of syntax in English.

It is evident that by learning poems, rhymes and songs by heart, children are gradually acquiring the ability to link words in a meaningful way. By reciting what they have learnt using appropriate intonation, rhythm and expression, their ears become attuned to how the foreign language should sound. Children enjoy reciting individual words, and also poems in the 'mood' of different adjectives, developing and reinforcing an understanding of the function of adjectives in language.

Text-level work focuses on the comprehension and composition of language. Participation in regular storytelling activities has provided children with the opportunity to hear and see extended pieces of language, either in aural or visual form, within a familiar context (Tierney and Dobson, 1995). Indeed, OFSTED reports have suggested that good progress is characterized by pupils quickly understanding the conventions of print and enjoying stories and books (OFSTED, 1998). The Teacher's Guide for MFL at Key Stage 2 (QCA, 2000a) also encourages the use of techniques developed during children's work in literacy and English under attainment target 3 Reading and Responding. Big books are increasingly being used in early MFL learning, some created by teachers, using books they already have in English language versions, with a simple foreign language text placed over the English with Post-it stickers. Publishers are producing other foreign language versions. Teachers have also displayed text and illustrations on an overhead projector or transcribed large format text onto a flip chart. In South Gloucestershire, the Literacy and EFLL Framework includes a section offering titles of appropriate storytelling and reference books, mirroring the support available in the NLS for English.

Very often the stories are already familiar to children from their English language versions. Listening to foreign language stories read aloud by their teacher or a foreign language assistant, has also built up learners' confidence, as they have become aware that they can *understand a story* without understanding the meaning of *every word*. As Holdaway (1982) has noted, successful shared book experiences need to be based on texts which children enjoy. Similarly, Adams (1993, p. 208) has pointed out that to learn to read, a child must first learn what it means to read and that he/she would like to be able to do so.

Telling a story provides a model for pronunciation, particularly when learners participate through actions or a verbal response during 'shared' reading. Listening to stories in the foreign language contributes to developing children's listening skills, which have been neglected by the exclusion of English attainment target 1 from the NLS *Framework*. Suggestions from the NLS about ways of using texts in shared reading have proved to work equally successfully when a big book or story is shared in the foreign language, including for example, tracking the text by pointing and making one-to-one correspondences between written and spoken language. Using foreign language as well as L1 resources helps children understand the conventions of written language and recognize printed and hand written words in a variety of settings at text level. Sentence level work has included developing the understanding that words are ordered from left to right, from line to line, from page to page, and that reading proceeds down the page, and beginning to use the term 'sentence' to identify sentences in a story or poem text.

By hearing a variety of stories children become familiar with storybook language in the foreign language, and are able to select familiar elements as they watch and listen. Shared reading in the foreign language also allows the teacher to draw children's attention to the correct terms about books such as cover, title, page, line, sentence, word, letter, beginning and end. As Donaldson (1993) reminds us, shared reading encourages the notion of language as something to talk and think about.

Although often disregarded in MFL classes at Key Stage 3, young learners need frequent opportunities to read aloud themselves, to enable them to put appropriate expression into their speaking. Starting with short sentences in songs, poems and stories, pupils gradually read familiar texts aloud with pace and expression, pausing at full stops, raising the pitch of their voice to indicate a question. Teachers have started by encouraging first whole-class choral reading, followed this by small groups, and eventually, individual children on their own. They report that reading familiar foreign language stories aloud helps develop the self-confidence of those children with a poor self image of themselves as readers, who would be unwilling to read a similar text aloud in English.

Repeated exposure to familiar rhymes and stories permits learners to locate and read names of key characters, rhymes or enlarged words and to recite stories and rhymes with predictable and repeating patterns. Even very young learners at Key Stage 1 have been shown to enjoy re-enacting traditional stories, such as Little Red Riding Hood (Cole, 2000), inventing simple mimes for each character, and responding imaginatively.

Listen and respond activities have focused on spotting how many sentences there are in a poem, extended to include work on punctuation within texts, recognizing capital letters and full stops, and counting the number of words in sentences. On other occasions, the features of question forms in different languages, the use of speech marks and their style, have given rise to interesting discussion. Children have also used text flashcards, including some featuring punctuation symbols, to reassemble stories, poems, or songs together from jumbled versions, so that they make sense.

The NLS aims to make learners more aware of the names and functions of different parts of speech, and words such as noun, adjective, verb, pronoun and adverb can be taught in both English and the foreign language, and accompanied by physical responses (Cheater and Farren, 2001). Pupils have also compared the position of colour adjectives in French with their position in English. It has been shown that talking about language can help to reinforce the most frequently used technical terminology from the NLS *Framework*, increasing children's linguistic awareness and their desire to experiment with language. Teachers have also used non-fiction texts such as recipes, instructions, letters, advertisements and children's messages from the internet to develop grammatical awareness.

Work at Key Stage 3 linking English and MFL

Through the CILT/QCA MFL and Literacy Project and within other initiatives, such as the Pilot Schemes for the Key Stage 3 Literacy Strategy, connections have been established between secondary English and MFL departments. This section briefly considers three examples.

Under the auspices of the former project, one study explored ways of developing a group of Year 9 pupils' understanding of sentence level work in both English and MFL (CILT/QCA, 2001). The starting point was the administration of a questionnaire, which investigated pupils' knowledge of word classes. Pupils were asked whether they had heard of a range of linguistic terms such as nouns, pronoun, adjectives, past tense, preposition, definite article, phrase, main clause, dependent clause, in English, French or German and whether they thought they could identify these parts of speech in a sentence. Pupils also had to try to actually identify examples in a number of sentences.

Analysis of the questionnaire responses showed that pupils claimed to have come across very few technical terms in MFL lessons. However, discussion with MFL teachers indicated that the concepts were used but not necessarily described using the associated meta-language. Consequently, grammatical terminology relating to sentence structures was incorporated little and often into English lessons and comparisons made from time to time with French or German. The questionnaire was readministered at a later date. Findings indicated that this low-level but consistent focus on sentence level terminology appeared to have succeeded in enabling both boys and girls to identify a wider range of grammatical features in English and in MFL than on the first occasion. However, knowledge of the terminology did not *necessarily* match the confidence and accuracy with which pupils actually could identify and use the terms. Verbs and adjectives (which tend to be emphasized in MFL lessons) continued to be the forms which caused most problems (CILT/QCA, 2001).

A second strand to the study involved investigating ways of developing understanding between the English and MFL departments in order to make connections between the ways in which both curriculum areas used grammatical terminology at sentence level. This latter element was similar to the focus for investigation in another mixed 11–16 comprehensive school, which also participated in the MFL and Literacy Project.

In the latter, the rationale included a shared interest in the teaching of grammar in both the English and MFL departments, with the aim of raising attainment further in both subject areas. The joint curriculum project was piloted in September 1999 in one Year 7 class, extended in 2000 to all Year 7 classes, all of which were mixed ability. This project demonstrates the effectiveness of starting small: the initial Year 7 pilot class was taught by one English and one MFL teacher, between whom a link was established. Collaborative work on developing a common approach to the teaching of grammar through analysis of the English and MFL schemes of work was undertaken. This involved comparing the schemes of work in both departments and making a note of key grammatical concepts (definite and indefinite articles, verbs, subject and object pronouns, adjectives, and the infinitive). Timing for teaching these key elements in both languages was identified, leading to a modification of the English schemes of work to ensure that specific aspects of grammar were taught by both the English and French teachers during the same term, although not necessarily at the same time (CILT/QCA, 2001).

Noteworthy features of this project are the paired observations, which allowed the English and French teachers to learn from each other and identify similarities and differences in approach (CILT/QCA, 2001). Outcomes included agreement on a common terminology between the two departments and the development of teaching materials.

The MFL teachers reported (CILT/QCA, 2001) that pupils in the pilot French class grasped grammatical concepts more quickly than previous cohorts and other control groups in Year 7. English teachers commented that their pupils' understanding of key concepts was reinforced by 'coming at it from both angles'. Since the pilot, liaison between the two departments has increased and all English and MFL teachers have become involved.

Similar adaptations of schemes of work in English and MFL have also been undertaken by secondary schools within the Key Stage 3 Literacy Pilot in Berkshire. In one girls' school, for instance, statements about literacy are included in the MFL schemes of work. Here the MFL department has encouraged pupils to use conjunctions to link sentences, staff actively make learners aware of syntax, and use prepositions, quantifiers and grammatical terms. Question and answer technique forms a focus for work on question structures. Particularly successful has been the incorporation of a large number of writing frames, skeleton outlines of starter, connectives and sentence modifiers to model letters and help scaffold other forms of creative writing. Mind mapping with or without pictures is used as a tool to support the development of ideas for stories in the target language. Grammatical terms are displayed in classrooms and marking includes pointing out literacy aspects of class and homework.

Making an effective transition to Key Stage 3

It is clear that where collaboration between English and MFL departments is taking place in the early years of secondary school, as in the above examples, it will be advisable to build on literacy work in the primary phase. Indeed, this will be the case, even where joint work at Key Stage 3 has yet to be explored. Where there is MFL teaching in the primary school this too will have to be built on, especially where literacy and MFL links have already been established. This has been recognized in the South Gloucestershire initiative cited earlier, which is working in collaboration with a specialist language college.

Here, not only have the Year 7 schemes of work for French been reconsidered but extra-curricular activities in French are also laid on for the half year group which starts out with German. French as a second foreign language starts in January, preceded in the autumn term by a language awareness course linked to both MFL and English/literacy. The links between the two subject areas remain throughout Year 7. Following the language awareness programme, work in the foreign language is done in tandem with what is being taught in Year 7 English lessons throughout the rest of the year. Programmes are being modified to bring further coherence to the development of literacy in both English and MFL.

It is reported that pupils arriving in Year 7 with only a year's French experience appear to have an enhanced understanding of structure, knowing 'what a verb and an adjective are, and what they do'. This improvement is seen as a direct outcome of the LEA's decision to base its approach on the NLS *Framework*: 'Instead of compartmentalising foreign languages, pupils see language as a whole' (Thomas, 2001, p. 6).

As suggested in the White Paper (DfEE, 1997, p. 45) 'teachers need to have opportunities to exchange ideas and best practice'. Since September 2000 the language college has funded the secondment of a primary teacher to act as Literacy/EFLL co-ordinator one day a week. Not only does the co-ordinator meet regularly with the Senior Adviser, key staff from the language college, the Head of MFL, and the primary link teacher from the MFL team, but he also leads a teachers' network which meets monthly, attended by the LEA Literacy Consultant and the Curriculum Director for International and Cultural Studies at the language college.

Evidence from the initiatives cited in this chapter, as well as others, indicates that making an effective transition across Key Stages 2/3 depends on the interface between teachers in primary and secondary school. As Jones (1998, p. 54) has stated: 'To enable pupils to transit smoothly from one stage of learning to the next and in order to build appropriate teaching and learning bridges, we must create positive, instructive and mutually supportive dialogues'.

Implications for practice

In this chapter, we have described aspects of literacy and MFL links from several projects. From these a number of implications for practice can be identified, as follows.

A characteristic of the most effective initiatives has been that of strong partnership between teachers and schools. This may be horizontal liaison across several primary schools within a cluster and vertically, between the cluster and associated schools in the secondary phase. In this context it should be noted that the Nuffield Languages Inquiry (2000, p. 42) recommended financial incentives for primary and secondary schools to form groups in order to agree a common pattern of provision for early language learning, including choice of languages and continuity arrangements.

Even where there are *no* MFL programmes in place in feeder primary schools, where possible at least one secondary MFL teacher needs to

- read NLS documentation to familiarize themselves, at a minimum, with the content, format, terminology and activities pupils will have encountered during the Literacy Hour in Key Stages 1 and 2
- find out how the NLS is being put into practice in local primary

schools. This can be achieved in part by visiting primary schools, to observe the Literacy Hour in English. The period in the summer term after Year 11 have left may provide opportunities

- establish on their arrival in secondary school, the extent of Year 7 pupils' meta-language retained from the NLS at Key Stage 2.

Where *some* pupils have experienced a foreign language,

- it is essential for the new MFL teacher to have identified who has already learned a foreign language at Key Stage 2 and which foreign language concepts children are already familiar with
- where the local context permits, it is helpful if Year 7 MFL teachers can teach Year 6 pupils. The period after SATs in the summer term is a good starting point
- a bridging topic, which can be literacy related, is a means of making a practical link between the primary and secondary phases
- when some foreign language work is being done at primary, it is useful for primary teachers to observe Year 7 MFL classes.

Currently there are very mixed views about whether to record progress and prior learning in MFL, with some primary teachers strongly against any kind of assessment, which they feel would undermine the enjoyable nature of the subject and lead to excessive demands. One of the reasons for retaining the non-statutory nature of primary MFL stems from its 'novelty' status as a non-National Curriculum subject, without the pressures for monitoring, assessment, recording and reporting that becoming one might bring. For this reason, the situation exists where even flourishing primary MFL initiatives have no liaison arrangements in place with secondary schools, or where the secondary schools appear to ignore any information on primary MFL which comes their way. Contexts in which information transfer across the Key Stage 2/3 divide is taken most seriously are often those in which a secondary school, typically a language college, is obliged to work with its feeder primaries and therefore establishes procedures. These show that to facilitate the transfer of data from Key Stage 2 across the transition to Key Stage 3, it is advisable

- to establish common practice between schools, so that there is some consistency between feeder primary schools. A portfolio such as the European Language Portfolio, which includes pupil self assessment, can be helpful as a means of tracking linguistic experience and making pupils interested in their own progress
- to disseminate information early enough to be of use at the start of Year 7. As well as being timely, data must be user-friendly and not too time-consuming
- lastly, secondary MFL departments must make use of the information.

Where a joint literacy/MFL framework is being developed,

- where a primary MFL is being offered, joint literacy/MFL links are most sensibly started in the primary school
- the primary class teacher is in the best position to promote a shared experience of literacy and MFL. This is because of their understanding of children's learning in the mother tongue and ability to take children's learning styles into account when structuring similar teaching programmes in the foreign language
- there must be a solid infrastructure of support from English and MFL advisers, from literacy consultants at both Key Stages 2 and 3, from literacy co-ordinators in primary school, and from MFL language specialists
- a member of staff in the secondary school needs to be designated to assume responsibility for linking with participating feeder primaries
- where funding permits, a Literacy/MFL co-ordinator from within the primary schools can help give ownership to primary teachers
- participation by primary teachers in piloting joint literacy/MFL approaches and resources is crucial, as is their ensuing commitment to implementation
- provision of a programme of professional development for primary teachers centred on the joint Literacy/MFL framework is a key element
- to enhance the MFL component, language learning sessions for primary teachers are helpful
- funding is needed for supply cover to allow teachers to attend liaison meetings and in-service training sessions
- the presence of native speaker foreign language assistants (FLAs) adds an intercultural dimension within which the literacy/MFL work can take place
- aspects of literacy and early foreign language work can be taught within the context of the international and European dimension, as well as Citizenship education.

Similarly, within secondary schools, English and MFL staff can achieve a community of purpose by:

- finding out what is being taught at particular times in both subject areas
- providing an account of how it is being taught, supported where possible by mutual observation between English and MFL colleagues
- auditing schemes of work and comparing their content, looking for elements common to both programmes, which could be referred to in English and MFL
- agreeing a systematic common core of linguistic terminology,

applicable to English and to the foreign languages, to be mutually used.

At both primary and secondary level, it is essential that any framework becomes a useful working document, offering genuine practical guidance. As one teacher commented, 'The (Literacy and EFLL) Framework provides me with a clear plan and stops me just "pick-and-mixing" activities' (cited in Cooper, 2000, p. 10). But documentation alone will not improve children's literacy development, in either English or the foreign language. A positive feature of all the Literacy/MFL initiatives mentioned in this chapter is that of implementation underpinned by internal support from headteachers and senior management, and by external support from local education authorities, advisory personnel, and investment in staff development and training (see Joyce and Showers, 1995, cited in Beard, 1999).

Conclusion

At this early stage, we must be cautious in making over ambitious claims about what can be achieved through efforts to link English and MFL. Nonetheless, work under way does indicate that teaching approaches similar to those adopted by the National Literacy Strategy can be incorporated effectively into MFL teaching both at primary and secondary level.

In the primary phase, the focus is likely to be on developing listening and speaking skills, and making links between literacy and MFL at word level. As Sharpe (2001, p. 86) has pointed out, oral/aural learning of MFL in the primary phase is *par excellence* an inclusive subject, in which children's early learning of both literacy and the foreign language can be supported by imitation, pronunciation, intonation, patterning and rhythm. It should be noted, in this context, that once the oral form is secure, many primary teachers (unlike some of their secondary MFL counterparts) are happy to incorporate judicious exposure to the written form of the foreign language in the early stages of MFL learning through reading and copy writing familiar words. Secondary specialists, in contrast, have tended to advise postponing these skills at primary level. Shared reading of rhymes, poems and stories can form a meaningful context for simple sentence and text level work. On the other hand, extended and creative writing, which is an important strand of the NLS for English, does not feature very strongly in Key Stages 1 and 2. This is partly because skills in early MFL naturally lag behind those in the mother tongue and work in the foreign language will always reinforce work previously covered in the NLS *Framework*. Thus many of the aspects of the NLS *Framework* for English in Key Stage 1 will be revisited by children beginning a foreign language in Key Stage 2 (Primary Languages Network, 1998). Also, the time available for primary MFL, as we have seen, is extremely limited, and may be put to more efficient use if primarily focused on oral/aural skill development.

At Key Stage 3, links have tended to be made at sentence level, considering comparative aspects of grammar, punctuation and syntax, and have focused on compositional features of extended writing in the foreign language, including drafting and revision. Reading of extended foreign language texts continues to be a somewhat neglected skill at early secondary level.

Adopting an objectives-based approach within a flexible framework for Literacy and MFL provides a practical structure which has the potential to support primary teachers. By being based on what Crandall *et al.* (1986, cited in Beard, 1999) termed 'craft legitimisation' through consultation with teachers and their involvement in trialling, educational change is more likely to be brought about. And even if primary teachers do not wish to go so far as to conceptualize their MFL teaching in word-, sentence- and text-level terms, bearing these links in mind, as suggested throughout the QCA non-statutory schemes of work at Key Stage 2, will help provide literacy-supportive experiences which consolidate work in English. Well taught, primary MFL can also positively affect children's attitudes to literacy in general, including confidence to listen, speak and engage in communication (Sharpe, 2001).

At secondary level, MFL classrooms already display several of the features which have made the NLS effective, such as oral, active and interactive teaching with pupil participation, and the use of mime, gesture, modelling and visual support to create a supportive learning environment. Secondary MFL lessons are typically highly structured around the whole-class teacher-led presentation and practice of new language, followed by pair and group work. MFL teachers are usually skilled at using graded questions offered in sequence to help pupils learn new vocabulary and structures. However, these sequences are conducted in the target language. In the early years of the National Curriculum for MFL the emphasis was on operating in the target language, not on using English nor on the explicit teaching of grammar. Secondary MFL teachers are therefore likely to need to plan carefully for skilful use of questions and interventions in English, to direct literacy and grammar-related discussion and more direct, explicit talk about language.

As the CILT/QCA (2001) MFL and Literacy Project Report indicates, these developments provide evidence that it is not only desirable, but actually possible to open up a number of channels of dialogue between the two subject areas of English and MFL, thereby bridging the 'space between'. Doing so appears to be beneficial to both learners and teachers on both sides of the transition, with children in these contexts acquiring a curiosity about language. As Cheater and Farren (2001) point out, through literacy related work in both English and the foreign language, early learners realize that literacy is not confined within one language but exists in foreign languages as well. It will be interesting to research in what further ways English and MFL departments at Key Stage 3 continue the task of making links between literacy and foreign language learning in the coming years.

Acknowledgements

I should like to gratefully acknowledge information provided by Mary Rose, Senior Adviser, Research and Development, South Gloucestershire on the South Gloucestershire Literacy and EFLL Good Practice Project. Also by Patricia McLagan, Language Teaching Adviser at the Centre for Language Teaching and Research and Co-ordinator of the Good Practice Project, on the CILT/QCA MFL and Literacy Project.

References

Adams, M. J. (1993) 'Beginning to read: an overview', in R. Beard (ed.), *Teaching Literacy. Balancing Perspectives*, London, Hodder and Stoughton.

Beard, R. (1999) *National Literacy Strategy. Review of Research and Other Related Evidence*, London, DfEE.

Beard, R. (2000) 'Long overdue? Another look at the National Literacy Strategy', *Journal of Research in Reading*, **23** (3), pp. 245–55.

Bryant, P. (1993) 'Phonological aspects of Learning to Read', in R. Beard (ed.), *Teaching Literacy. Balancing Perspectives*, London, Hodder and Stoughton.

Cheater, C. and Farren, A (2001) *The Literacy Link*, London, Centre for Information on Language Teaching and Research.

Centre for Information on Language Teaching and Research (CILT) (1974) *The Space between . . . English and Foreign Languages at School*, London, Centre for Information on Language Teaching and Research.

Centre for Information on Language Teaching and Research (CILT) (1995) *Modern Foreign Languages in Primary Schools*, London, Centre for Information on Language Teaching and Research.

Centre for Information on Language Teaching and Research (CILT)/Qualifications and Curriculum Authority (QCA) (2001) 'CILT/QCA Modern Foreign Languages and Literacy Project 1999–2001', unpublished draft report, London, Centre for Information on Language Teaching and Research.

Cole, J. (2000) 'South Gloucestershire LEA', *Early Language Learning Bulletin*, **5**, pp. 2–3, London, Centre for Information on Language Teaching and Research.

Cooper, A. (2000) 'Celebrating the launch of the Literacy and Early Foreign Language Learning Framework in South Gloucestershire', *Early Language Learning Bulletin*, **4**, p. 10, London, Centre for Information on Language Teaching and Research.

Department for Education and Employment (DfEE) (1997) *Excellence in Schools* (White Paper), London, Department for Education and Employment.

Department for Education and Employment (DfEE) (1998a) *The National Curriculum for English*, London, HMSO.

Department for Education and Employment (DfEE) (1998b) *The National Literacy Strategy: Framework for Teaching*, London, DfEE.

Department for Education and Employment. Qualifications and Curriculum Authority (DfEE/QCA) (1999) *Modern Foreign Languages. The National Curriculum for England*, London, Department for Education and Employment/Qualifications and Curriculum Authority.

Donaldson, M (1993) 'Sense and sensibility: some thoughts on the teaching of literacy', in R. Beard (ed.) *Teaching Literacy. Balancing Perspectives*, London, Hodder and Stoughton.

Driscoll, P. (1999) 'Teacher expertise in the primary modern foreign languages classroom', in P. Driscoll and D. Frost (eds) *The Teaching of Modern Foreign Languages in the Primary School*, London, Routledge.

Driscoll, P. and Frost, D. (eds) (1999) *The Teaching of Modern Foreign Languages in the Primary School*, London, Routledge.

Early Language Learning Bulletin (1999) May, London, Centre for Information on Language Teaching and Research.

Goswami, U. and Bryant, P. (1990) *Phonological Skills and Learning to Read*, Hove, Lawrence Erlbaum Associates.

Holdaway, D. (1982) 'Shared book experience: teaching reading using favourite books', *Theory into Practice*, **21** (4), pp. 293–300.

Jones, J. (1998) 'Teaching diaries: an exercise in reflexivity', in G. Barzanó and J. Jones (eds), *Same differences. Intercultural Learning and Early Foreign Language Teaching*, Torre Boldone, Grafital.

Literacy Task Force (1997) *The Implementation of the National Literacy Strategy*, London, Department for Education and Employment.

Low, L. (1998) 'To enhance or inhibit? Is there a place for English and knowledge about language in Primary Modern Languages', *Studies in Modern Languages Education*, **6**, pp. 49–66, University of Leeds School of Education.

Martin, C. (2000a) 'The way forward – a reassessment of MFL at primary school', *Early Language Learning Bulletin*, **3**, pp. 16–17, London, Centre for Information on Language Teaching and Research.

Martin, C. (2000b) 'Modern foreign languages at primary school: a three pronged approach?', *Language Learning Journal*, **22**, pp. 5–10, Rugby, Association for Language Learning.

Martin, C., with Cheater, C. (1998) *Let's Join In! Rhymes, Poems and Songs*, London, Centre for Information on Language Teaching and Research.

Mitchell, R., Martin, C. and Grenfell, M. (1991) *Evaluation of the Basingstoke Primary Schools Language Awareness Project (1990/91)*, University of Southampton, Centre for Language in Education Occasional Paper 7.

Nuffield Languages Inquiry (2000) *Languages: The Next Generation*, London, Nuffield Foundation.

Office for Standards in Education (OFSTED) (1998) *Standards in Primary English*, London, Office for Standards in Education.

Primary Languages Network (1998) Linking the National Literacy Strategy with Primary Foreign Languages. London, Centre for Information on Language Teaching and Research

Qualifications and Curriculum Authority (QCA) (1999) *Non-Statutory Guidelines for MFL at Key Stage 2*, London, QCA.

Qualifications and Curriculum Authority (QCA) (2000a) *Modern Foreign Languages: A Scheme of Work for Key Stage 2*, London, QCA.

Qualifications and Curriculum Authority (QCA) (2000b) *Modern Foreign Languages. A Scheme of Work for Key Stage 3*, London, QCA.

Riley, J. (2001) 'The National Literacy Strategy: success with literacy for all?' *Curriculum Journal*, **12** (1), pp. 29–58.

Sharpe, K. (1992) 'Communication, culture, context, confidence: the four 'Cs' of primary modern language teaching', *Language Learning Journal*, **6**, pp. 13–14, Rugby, Association for Language Learning.

Sharpe, K. (2001) *Modern Foreign Languages in the Primary School*, London, Kogan Page.

South Gloucestershire Council (SGC) (1999) *Literacy and Early Foreign Language Learning Framework*.

Thomas, A. (2001) 'Complete cohesion', *Times Educational Supplement*, MFL Curriculum Special, 15 June, pp. 6–7.

Tierney, D. and Dobson, S. (1995) *Are you Sitting Comfortably?* London, Centre for Language Teaching and Research.

9

Literacy and subject knowledge

Margaret Perkins

Teachers and student teachers do not approach literacy in some neutral mode. This chapter probes the thoughts, feelings and attitudes of student teachers from both phases as they become 'teachers of reading'. We learn about the differences between the phases and also about their shared perceptions. Most importantly we are able to see how they have been to some extent 'formed' by their backgrounds, education and training and how this provides real strengths but also some potential blind spots.

Introduction

What do you need to know to be an effective teacher of literacy? Does it matter how you use literacy in your own life? Will that influence how you teach literacy? Can you teach pupils to behave as readers and writers in ways which you do not behave yourself? Does that matter?

Questions such as these are important for teachers who want to improve their practice and for intending teachers who want to learn, not only how to do it but how to do it well. It is these issues which are the subject of this chapter. The relationship between the personal and the professional is explored and so I attempt to explore the question 'How can I improve my practice as a teacher of reading? What do I need to know?'

Literacy has always been given a high profile but it cannot be denied that the closing years of the twentieth century were ones in which the profile of literacy across the educational spectrum has been raised even higher by a government eager to improve standards. It is not just the individual teacher who wishes to improve his/her practice but the government which attempts to improve practice nationwide.

Does the teaching of reading need improving?

In their *Review of Secondary Education 1993–97* (OFSTED, 1998) Her Majesty's Inspectors of Schools found that standards of reading were unsatisfactory in about one in seven schools. They specified that pupils were not given tasks which challenged them as readers. Amongst many recommendations about practice in secondary schools concerning literacy, HMI recommended that 'work on the teaching of reading and writing should be made a requirement in all secondary teacher training courses' (ibid., para. 117). In autumn 1997 HMI surveyed all schools who were involved in literacy development initiatives and identified seven key points which seemed to them crucial to successful practice. One of these affirmed that literacy development is inextricably connected with the development of the whole person and is part of a person's perception of themselves and their place in the world. Her Majesty's Inspectorate made this statement with reference to pupils but in this chapter I want to apply it to teachers. In so doing I will argue that, as teachers support pupils in their literacy development, the perceptions those teachers have of themselves as people and as readers will affect the way in which they teach and relate to their pupils and the curriculum.

The introduction of the National Literacy Strategy has led to a decrease in the schools' and teachers' autonomy. Although it was not a statutory requirement teachers were required to attend training which stipulated what and how literacy should be taught and it was a brave school which decided to swim against the tide to go its own way. More common were those teachers who complied but tried to carry on with certain elements of their past practice in which they strongly believed, e.g. hearing individual children read. As the twenty-first century progresses, schools and the NLS 'authority' are beginning to relax and teachers are beginning to reclaim their professional knowledge but in those early days the top-down model cascaded with force. It is clear that telling teachers what to do is felt to be the way to improving practice. Is this true?

Professional subject knowledge

At this same time, Circular 4/98 came out and gave teacher education institutions a curriculum which they must follow. Possession of this knowledge it was felt would enable students to become effective teachers of literacy. As a result of this central government involvement, the present world of teacher education is dominated by a discourse that sees knowledge as certain, predefined and based on a set of competencies, which, once acquired, will make the student into a professional and 'competent' practitioner. The National Curriculum for Teacher Education

(DfEE, 1998a) sets out this knowledge clearly and unproblematically. This is what students are required to know; they must provide evidence of their knowledge and once this is done they will be deemed able to be teachers. It is not so clear to me, however, that this type of knowledge is all that is required by effective and professional teachers in the context of the classroom and the school.

It can be argued that this type of knowledge reduces everything to its minimum and fails to recognize any sort of existential nature to the process of knowing. Thus knowledge becomes an abstraction of reality and so is desiccated and unrelated to the complexity of human life. Reid acknowledged this issue:

> It is indispensably important to have knowledge of facts of all kinds and to have, and increase, intellectual understanding of the world. But our beliefs, our beliefs in values, what of them? . . . Can we not validate it in experience, without reducing it to argument or proposition making? (Reid, 1986, p. 32)

and so did the HMI in the survey of 1997, when they claimed that the development of literacy is inseparable from the development of the person.

As teachers of English, literacy and/or reading it is vital that students know 'how to teach the essential core of phonic and graphic knowledge explicitly and systematically' (DfEE, 1998a, Annex C B5d) or 'how to teach literary and non-literary texts to whole classes and groups' (DfEE, 1998b, Annex F B6), but on its own that knowledge is not enough for effective teaching of reading. The teacher needs to know those texts and the reading process in a living vital way; it is bound up with my own personal experience, which makes me the person I am.

The dilemma occurs when there is a mismatch between personal knowledge and the knowledge required by an external authority and this might be said to be happening as the National Literacy Strategy extends its influence from the primary school into Key Stage 3. It is widely accepted that reading is the bedrock of the Key Stage 3 curriculum and yet, outside of the remedial department, it is rarely explicitly taught (Dean, 2000). The teaching of reading is considered to be the prime function of primary schools. How far is this common conception borne out by teachers who are beginning their teaching careers? Surely the introduction of the National Literacy Strategy into Key Stage 3 has foregrounded the teaching of reading.

This chapter reports some research which put these two issues together: the teaching of reading and teachers' understanding of reading in relation to their own personal experience of reading. What do beginning teachers know about reading? How does that impact on their views of teaching reading? The answers to these questions will help identify what we need to know to be effective teachers of reading.

From the past to the present and into the future

I am arguing that teachers' own experiences of reading play a crucial role in their developing understanding of the teaching of reading. Often, in their training, students are required to draw on their own experiences of learning to come to conclusions about teaching but only superficially are they required to look at their own reading to develop an understanding of what it is they are teaching when they teach reading. That issue is not seen as a problematic on courses or in schools but I want to argue that a student learning to be a teacher of reading must draw on past experiences of reading to understand what it is that is being taught. In order to move forward to become a teacher of reading the student needs first to cross the boundary into the past of his/her own reading experience. This is a difficult process; it is easier to be given a body of facts than to adopt a new role but if one is to 'become' rather than just 'act', one needs to be able to deal with the complexity of the past as well as the uncertainty of the future.

This chapter describes work done with intending teachers during the year in which they were studying for a Postgraduate Certificate in Education. Some were intending to be primary teachers and others to be secondary English teachers. They were all graduates but not all were English graduates. The secondary students had degrees which included American History and Literature, English, Sociology and Latin, and the primary students had degrees in a wide range of fields, including Home Economics, Biology, Early Childhood Studies, Psychology, English, History and Geography.

I was interested in finding out how the students perceived both reading itself and the teaching of reading. The predominant means of data collection was interview. The interviews with different participants are analysed to identify the different ways of perceiving the particular phenomenon. There is a strong relationship between how I experience a phenomenon and how I understand it. My experience of being taught to read is related to my understanding of teaching reading; my experience of reading impacts forcefully on my understanding of what I am teaching when I teach reading.

I interviewed each of the secondary students once; each interview lasted between an hour and an hour and a half, and was recorded and subsequently transcribed. The primary students were interviewed three times, at the end of each term of their course. Each of these interviews lasted about an hour and the interviews were also recorded and

transcribed. I also looked at an assignment which the secondary students
had written on their own reading biography and the teaching of reading
in their first placement school.

Each of the interviews followed a similar pattern; there was a schedule
of topics and opening questions for each topic but individual responses
were then followed up. Typically questions began with the phrase 'Tell
me about . . .' As interviewer, I made no comment or validating response
to the students' answers.

I analysed the interviews by looking for commonalities and identifying
categories of response. I analysed the primary and secondary interviews
separately and then compared the two. I drew up a hierarchy of responses
related to students' perceptions of reading and of the teaching of reading.
Each category was mutually exclusive and described in the students' own
words.

Perceptions of reading

For all students reading was primarily an enjoyable experience. All the
secondary students and the majority of the primary students said that
reading was something which they enjoyed.

I really enjoyed reading and talking about books.

When asked to define a reader one student replied,

A reader is someone who loves to read, who enjoys reading, who
gets something out of it, engages with the text when reading.

The students from both courses saw enjoyment both as a key purpose of
reading and a required output of any reading experience. Some saw
enjoyment as a prior condition of reading and would not persevere if
enjoyment was not immediate:

I have to enjoy the book I'm reading.

I just read for pure enjoyment.

The use of the word 'pure' seemed to imply that the reading was unsul-
lied by and excluded by any other purpose. What was described as 'enjoyment reading' was seen as unchallenging and easy to read.

For all students then enjoyment was perceived as a crucial quality of
reading and all other perceptions of the reading process stemmed from
and were related to this. It is from this point, however, that differences
began to emerge in how the primary and secondary students perceived
reading and how they experienced it in their lives.

A primary escape

Nearly all the primary students would agree with Alex when she said,

> Books are special. That feeling of being able to go into another world. Getting lost inside some of the things that someone had held in their imagination or memory and written down.

The idea of being 'lost in a book' was common amongst the primary students and they perceived reading as being a way of 'switching off' from the pressures of life. Many read in order 'to lose myself'. When inside the book they were safe from the external world, because as Jane said,

> I had my own space.

Inside this space 'your imagination goes wild' and 'you just get swept away by the story.' The phrase 'getting into a book' was frequently used in a way that implied an almost physical transfer from real life into the life of the book. All this inevitably has an effect on your emotional well-being.

A secondary essential

The secondary students would agree with much of those views but there was a subtle difference in the place reading held in their lives. For them, reading was an essential and integral part of their lives; rather than an escape from the reality of life, reading *was* the reality of life for them. They cannot imagine life without reading,

> I think it was just something I always did.

> I've got a feeling I would have been the sort of child who would have been a bookworm anyway.

> It's always been there and always will be there and is very important.

Contemplation of life without reading raised strong feelings,

> I would be very angry if I couldn't read anymore – it's very important.

The students even used texts as a reference point when talking about experiences and feelings. Theresa was talking about the centrality of reading in her life and identified strongly with an incident in a favourite text,

> he reassures her that they will carry on reading in spite of what the teacher says and Scout says something like I didn't realize what I was going to lose – you know it's like grieving. You don't realize how

bad it is – I think that just about sums it up really – if I wasn't allowed to read any more what would I do then?

A primary relationship

For the primary students reading tended to be a whole experience connected with time, space and other people. Many read in bed as their last activity before they went to bed,

> I often read before I go to bed because it helps me to relax and switch off

and yet others became so engrossed with a book that it went everywhere with them,

> It even goes to the bathroom with me when I need the toilet. And in the bath I'll be reading it – I can never put them down.

For these students reading was an affective experience which involved a complete submission to a book within a special place and a specific time, and also frequently involved other people. Gemma was perhaps unique in the rather extreme Waltonesque scenario she described but not in the sentiments behind it.

> We'll have evenings when perhaps other families will be sitting watching the telly and not talking, we're sitting with gentle music on reading our own books for hours on end just relaxed and enjoying it. I come from a really nice reading background.

She is almost here describing a type of parallel play. Others discussed the books they had read with family or friends and these conversations were significant influences on them as readers.

> I find it very pleasurable personally . . . it's nice for me to have some time when I'm sitting down with the girls . . . sharing books.

For these students talking with other people about books was an important part of being a reader. This contrasted strongly with the negative views held about reading aloud,

> I remember in secondary school having to read out loud in English and I used to hate that.

> The first thing I even remember about reading was standing up at the teacher's desk and reading aloud and I absolutely hate reading aloud.

Reading was about relationship but about equal relationship not one where the reader is put under pressure in a test situation.

Secondary singularity

The secondary students did not talk much about reading as a social event; for them the relationship in reading was between them as reader and the text. This relationship was private from the outside world. Within this intimacy the meaning of the text is created by author and reader in an exclusive and creative partnership:

> I'm part of the creative process, bringing things to the text.

> I think reading is a very personal thing and everyone's got their own personal response to books or to a particular book.

Reading is a time when a reader can be alone and the book itself becomes a location,

> It's a place where I could read by myself. I was essentially a loner once more much preferring to have my head in a book.

Reading is something which is an essentially personal process and for these students they did not mention talking about books, reading aloud or even reading alongside others. Reading was private and individual.

The secondary text

It is perhaps a function of this singularity that the secondary students talked predominantly about specific texts when asked about their own reading behaviours:

> I can remember sitting there listening and thinking this is a wonderful book.

It was usual, when asked about their reading, for the secondary students to list books that they had read during the interview and frequently they could list books they had studied from GCSE through to degree level. Most of them could not remember books they had read as children and only started talking about books which they had studied for academic purposes. They talked about favourite texts and texts which were significant to them.

One student had been working as a librarian and when asked why she decided to become a teacher she replied,

> I used to find it a little bit limiting that role as a librarian a little bit frustrating at times because you're obviously involved with books

but coming from a different angle and I would see English teachers there and think well they're actually really involved with the books because you're in that classroom with that text ... I suppose I wanted to cross that divide and go from one side of the text to the other.

This student saw her relationship as being with the book; she wanted to change the nature of that relationship but still saw herself as a reader in partnership with specific texts. These students did not consider reading as an entity in itself but spoke only of individual texts. For the most part, when I asked the secondary students to talk about their experiences of reading they named specific texts. Frequently, they struggled when recalling books they had read as children but were able to, and did, list all the books they had studied for examinations at school and university. They talked at length about specific texts which were their favourites and held significance for them. They talked fluently and with feeling about texts they had known, loved or even disliked but did not talk about a reading process. For them reading was the text and teaching reading was about introducing children to those texts,

Teachers must have enough ways of approaching a text that will capture children's imagination and make it real to them.

Texts are imbued with almost a persona and the relationship is with the text. The privateness of reading involves a particular relationship between the reader and the text where a third party would definitely be a crowd. That relationship is, however, an active one and the reader, while engaging with the book, plays an active role within that world.

Primary process

In contrast the primary students talked about the process of reading. They remembered learning to read but they remembered people rather than texts:

I would say it was my Gran. I used to spend a lot of time with her and it was her who actually taught me to read.

I remember we had a supply teacher in school once ... she was there for about a term and she brought these books to read, she was very keen on reading to us as a class at the end of the day ... it was people like that, that made me love books and appreciate them and look for them.

The latter student had not been read to at home and it was the memory of a teacher who shared enjoyment and motivation that remained a driving force.

When asked about their own reading behaviour the primary students talked about the process of reading and how they go about it. They talked about people, places and specific occasions. For them reading seemed to be something which was concerned with particular occasions. Often, they could not remember specific texts but they remembered the experience of sitting on a grandma's lap and reading to her or of lying on the deck of a boat reading. They recalled talking about texts with others and of reading series by one author. They also talked explicitly about how reading was much more than the words they read:

> He seemed to know what words were and the fact that they were doing more than they actually looked like.

Students talked about what they did when they read challenging texts, how they understood difficult words and the feelings created by the reading process:

> I have a vague recollection of having to read in primary school – in fact I can actually see the teacher there now – with us having to read some sort of word test and just going down the page and reading out words and actually the thing that sticks in my mind is not necessarily the exercise of doing the reading but the way I felt and the feeling that you know I've got to get this right.

Primary and secondary reading

The contrast between the primary and secondary students seems to lie predominantly in how they position themselves in the intellectual, social and emotional landscape of reading. For secondary students reading is about them and the text in a unique and creative partnership. For the primary students reading is about how it makes them feel and that is as much to do with the physical, social and emotional context as the text itself. How did this difference in perception of reading affect what they saw themselves doing when working with children in school? What do primary and secondary trainee teachers think they are teaching when they teach reading?

Learning to teach involves gaining skills

For both primary and secondary students there was a concern in knowing what to do in the classroom and this involved learning skills and teaching strategies. However, there was a key difference in how this desire to gain skills manifested itself.

The primary students were concerned to find the 'way to do it'; they wanted to get their teaching right and perceived that somewhere out there in the schools was the system of teaching reading:

> I don't want to be offering the wrong sort of teaching programme.

They perceived that there was one way of doing it and it mattered to them that they followed the approved system. They felt relieved when they were told they were successful,

> The head came in to watch me do it and as a result of that several other members of the staff came in to watch me do it and were all very enthusiastic about it and I think it helped ... I found it a very positive experience ... people coming in and saying it's working.

This student was working just as the National Literacy Strategy was being introduced into primary schools and she was being regarded as the expert by the teachers in her practice school. This boosted her confidence and confirmed to her that she was 'doing it right'. Other students talked to their class teachers and OFSTED inspectors and were eager to gain approval of what they were doing,

> Having the OFSTED lady say to me you've got this sussed ... it always helps when you've got an adult saying you're doing this well ... it's like someone high up there saying I'm OK – it's just that reassurance.

Confidence was also boosted in these students by the realization that they were developing skills and as they progressed through the course they had many more strategies under their belt than at the start,

> There's stuff I did on this teaching practice that I didn't even think about doing on my first teaching practice.

For the primary students learning to teach reading was about finding the system and gaining the skills and this involved reconciling theory and practice and coming to their own understanding of the reading process:

> I think it's actually applying the knowledge which worries me – when you look at the notes you think oh yes I know all this but actually putting it into practice is another thing altogether really,

Learning to teach reading was seen by some students as something that is learned in the classroom,

> I don't think you can learn to teach reading from a lecture in college.

but for Phil it was first understanding what reading was

> I think you're teaching children about decoding print and linking that to sound – that's at a very mechanical level. You're then teaching them to make sense of what they're reading and to extract meaning from what they've read and then probably an extension of that is to teach them to engage and to think about what they have read rather than just absorb it.

The secondary students did not talk about the reading process in such a way. When asked about teaching reading, for all of them, their first response was to talk about working with children who had not reached the required level in reading. This was considered to be the work of the special needs teachers and was not their prime concern. One student said, when asked what teaching of reading went on in her placement school,

> The pupils that weren't to level 4 they were given half an hour or an hour a week and they went to a class in the library and they were actually taught reading and taught how to read.

These pupils were taken out during English lessons and when asked what the rest of the pupils were doing the student replied that they were reading and discussing Shakespeare. She had not considered this to be the teaching of reading. For her reading was the first aspect that Phil identified above – decoding print and linking that to sound; the other aspects, extracting meaning and engaging with a text, was teaching English and not teaching reading. It can be argued that the difference is just one of the terminology used but I want to argue that the terminology reflects an underlying belief about what it means to teach reading. For the secondary students intending to be English teachers, teaching reading was not a key element of their role because,

> Most people who come into secondary school unless they've got special needs can read.

One secondary student actually articulated this difference between primary and secondary perspectives,

> If you're a primary teacher I think that obviously the focus is on the process of reading but at secondary more on the side of fostering a love of reading and encouraging them to read a range of literature and encouraging them to do different types of reading and introducing them to different genres.

This was typical of a clear distinction in secondary students' minds between process and work with texts which involved a particularly limiting view of process as decoding. The former was seen as the work of the primary school and the latter of the secondary school. They seemed unaware of much of the work of people like Meek (1992), Bearne (1995) and Barrs and Cork (2001).

Secondary introductions

The secondary students saw their main role as introducing children to different texts, an idea which related very closely to their notion of reading as concerned with texts. Comments they made included many like the following,

> I'd like to get over my love of literature to the pupils.

> . . . encouraging them to a range of literature and introducing them to different genres.

> That's teaching reading – bringing enthusiasm to it.

They wanted their pupils to enjoy reading as much as they did and this is the essential element of their role as teachers. For them, reading is an essential element of life and they want it to be the same for their pupils.

> One of the main reasons that most teachers of English chose their particular career is because they experienced such pleasure from reading when themselves pupils. (Dean, 2000, p. 19)

The secondary students saw their teaching responsibility as being to introduce pupils to different texts and so enthuse and inspire them. For them, the teaching of reading was the teaching of texts.

> if you have to do a class text to make it as stimulating as possible, not just to do the dry bones of going through line by line.

There is a problem, however, concerned with the interrelationship of the teacher's enjoyment with the pupils' and it is one which was expressed by Juliette,

> I feel to some extent a negative thing is if I had to teach a text that I didn't really like. I mean I'm not a science fiction fan and I think it would be quite hard to teach science fiction with a great enthusiasm. I think I would find it hard to pretend I had that enthusiasm so I think I would find that quite hard.

For Juliette, her view of reading as an essential part of life and of reading being a personal and intimate relationship between reader and text meant that for her as a teacher of reading her role was almost that of an introduction agency. She wanted to create that intimate relationship between the pupil readers and the text but if she did not see much in a text to commend it she would find it difficult to make a valid and credible introduction.

A primary model

The primary students also saw an important part of their role as being to motivate and enthuse their pupils about reading but they saw this in different ways. They saw themselves as being a role model for the children. This came about not through introducing children to specific texts, though this is a part of it, but as showing children through their own behaviour what it means to be a reader. This came across in different ways:

As a teacher you are a role model.

If children see me as a model for reading I think that's good.

You can teach anything really by your own attitude.

The students saw reading to the children as being very important because then they were almost showing the children how it should be done. Secondly, the teacher acting as role model was seen as having an impact on teaching methods and, thirdly, on the books used within the classroom. One primary student echoed Juliette's remarks when she said,

I think it is very difficult to read to somebody else a book that you have problems with.

However, again there is a subtle difference. For Juliette the problem lay in not being able to broker a relationship between pupil and text when there was not a relationship between teacher and text. For the primary student the problem lay in not acting as an effective role model of what it means to be a reader.

Heather was a student who had had real problems with reading as a child and as an adult did not enjoy reading at all. She, however, was conscious of being a role model for the children and wanted to counteract her own natural feelings.

I don't particularly enjoy reading and I hope to make a conscious effort to reverse that in the classroom.

I think that this is a good indicator of the difference between primary and secondary attitudes to the role of the teacher. The primary students saw it as a much more conscious thing; they could learn how to behave and what to do in order to be a positive role model and it did not matter so much what they really felt. Secondary students found it difficult to separate their personal responses from what they were doing and how they behaved with their pupils. For them, reading was a personal integrated part of themselves as people.

Implications

The National Literacy Strategy has had a huge impact on the teaching of English in primary schools particularly in raising the standards of reading as defined by statutory testing (HMI, 2000). It seems fair to assume that it will have a similar impact on Key Stage 3, perhaps an even greater one. Dean makes a startling claim when he says,

> Reading is not taught in most secondary schools. Considerable numbers of activities in connection with books and other sorts of texts take place in classrooms, but these are not usually directed towards the improvement and growth of pupils' reading, except in a very limited sense. (Dean, 2000, p. 1)

That view, however, would appear to be supported by the perceptions of what is involved in the teaching of reading held by the secondary students who were the subjects of the research reported in this chapter.

Allan and Bruton (1997) looked at the perceptions of reading held by teachers and pupils in three secondary schools in Scotland. They found that teachers recognized the central importance of reading to pupils' learning but did not have explicit knowledge of how to develop pupils' reading. They also found that some teachers held some concerning misconceptions about reading which often reflected views expressed in the popular press. An example of such a view is the teacher who said, 'TV, video and computers are destroying reading'.

Lewis and Wray (1999) argue the importance of secondary teachers understanding what is meant by literacy and what can be expected of pupils in practical terms. They describe a Key Stage 3 pilot literacy project where the teachers themselves took a Year 6 English SAT test and were surprised at the expected level. Many a secondary teacher has looked at the Year 6 teaching objectives from the National Literacy *Framework* (DfEE, 1998b) and expressed surprise at what is requested.

Collins and Dallat quote a comment from a secondary English teacher,

> I have taught English for over twenty years and attended teacher training college before that. I do not consider myself trained to teach secondary pupils to read. (Collins and Dallat, 1998, p. 468)

Research seems to be telling us that secondary teachers do not have and do not perceive themselves to have the required subject knowledge to be teachers of reading. So the questions must be asked: What do they need to know and how can they know it?

Putting reading at the front

For most primary teachers the teaching of reading is seen as one of their prime purposes but in the secondary school it becomes an assumed vehicle for learning and is not given much attention in its own right. Where it is given attention it is seen as the responsibility of the English or Special Needs departments. This research has shown that intending secondary teachers of English do not see teaching reading as their prime role.

It may well be that in foregrounding the teaching of reading the introduction of the National Literacy Strategy will give teachers a vocabulary for talking about reading and so help them to make explicit what they already know implicitly. This could be done through an analysis of teachers' own reading behaviours. The secondary students in this research were experienced and effective readers, and could talk fluently about the texts they read. It could be that if these experiences were used to identify the reading process and to give them a language for talking about reading it would be the start of foregrounding reading in its own right. Phil, a primary student, described this process well,

> There's two strands to learning to read – there's one that you can engage with texts for your own enjoyment, and you can learn from it and you can gain a wealth of knowledge. And the other side is there are developing strategies and ways of understanding and extracting meaning.

The secondary students in my sample were very good at talking about their engagement with texts but they found it harder to talk about the strategies they used for making meaning. A stronger focus on these strategies, in the way in which their own reading is discussed, might help them to help pupils develop as readers.

Traves (1994) argues that teachers need to address the questions, 'What does it mean to be a reader?' and 'What is involved in the process of reading?' It is in answer to the second question that the secondary students in this sample had a lot of important things to say about reading but had no theoretical model underpinning their knowledge.

An understanding of such a framework gives students and teachers a metalanguage for talking about and analysing texts and the reading process. Palinscar and Brown (1984) have argued that thinking about *how* we learn as well as *what* we learn is an essential element of successful language and literacy learning. Increased metacognitive awareness along with the language needed to make it explicit will help teachers to support and extend learning. However, a note of caution needs to be expressed as the NLS is introduced to Key Stage 3. Many primary teachers went through a period of feeling very deskilled and undervalued as the rigid cascade model of training swept down on them in full force (Frater, 2000). They felt that much of what they had been doing before was wrong and so rigidly applied the dictates of the NLS, even to the extent of having timers in their classrooms so that they did not exceed the time limit of each part of the literacy hour. As time has passed and teachers grow in confidence, they are treating the framework with much less reverence and adapting it to best suit their circumstances. Secondary teachers would do well to learn from this experience. D'Arcy argues that equally important to this knowledge about linguistic analysis and processes is the knowledge of

> how a text is constructed through the thoughts and feelings of the writer and also how a text is interpreted through the thoughts and feelings it evokes in the mind of a reader. (D'Arcy, 2000, p. 3)

The secondary students I talked with were strong in their understanding of this aspect of reading and they need to hold on to that, strengthening it with a more explicit understanding of the theoretical reading process.

Definitions of text and reading

In these early years of the twenty-first century we are beginning to realize the impact of technology on our lives in general and our reading in particular. Gone are the days when the notion of the text was restricted to the book and reading is restricted to word by word identification.

Marsh and Millard demonstrate how the nature of texts and so of the reading process is changing,

> we are currently living through a period of rapid transition from a linear, print-based and page-bound culture, which developed from the introduction of the printing press, to a screen-based, hyperlinked mode of communication. Here, information is in a constant flux and is only arrested for the moment of reception, when a deliberate act is made to save in a semi-permanent version on disc or paper. These changes to the way in which we communicate with each other to express our intentions and even feelings is having a profound effect on the way we respond to texts and make meanings from them. (Marsh and Millard, 2000, p. 5)

Most of the students interviewed in this research talked about reading traditional narrative texts. A few of the primary students mentioned comics and newspapers but for the secondary students most of their reading experiences were concerned with classic fiction. One even distinguished between that which she perceived to be 'good' and that which she read for relaxation and described as 'pulp fiction'. They did not make the connection between reading and other types of text, and yet, for many of the pupils they teach, classic fiction is not a part of their immediate world.

Heath's (1983) work demonstrated how children from different cultural groups experience literacy in different ways. It was the middle-class white children who were more successful in school because their home experiences of literacy matched more closely the way in which literacy was defined in the classroom. Other research has echoed this within Britain (Gregory and Williams, 2000; Minns, 1990). Teachers of reading need to broaden their definitions of texts and reading to encompass the experiences of all the pupils in their classes.

So – what do we need to know to be better teachers of reading?

This research seems to me to provide several answers to this question. They might be tentative at this stage but I believe they are worthy of further consideration. I propose three main issues which I claim matter if a teacher wants to improve her practice.

It does matter what we read

Teachers need to have a wider definition of text – to recognize the variety of texts there are in the twenty-first century. This means that they will use all sorts of texts in their teaching and will find those which resonate with the experiences of their pupils. It means that we will think about how texts are constructed and why they are constructed in this way. We will no longer feel guilty that we are not 'well read' but will read well those texts we do read.

However, effective teachers of reading also need a wide eclectic experience of texts. They need to know a huge variety of texts; to have read and considered them. This means they will have read texts they enjoyed and texts they hated; texts they understood and texts which remained impenetrable to them. One of the most powerful reading lessons I 'taught' was when a 5-year-old explained to me the implicit understandings needed to read a Pokemon story.

It does matter how we read

Teachers of reading need to know about the process of reading so that they can talk about that process with their pupils. The effective teacher of reading is one who can make explicit what is essentially an implicit and often invisible process. It is not helpful to the immature reader to enthuse about a text and discuss the understandings that come from an awareness of intertextual allusions and authorial techniques. The reading lesson needs to be the time when pupils are taught how to read; when they are shown how to relate what they are reading to prior experiences and how to look at the language used. In order to do this they need a vocabulary and a 'way of looking'; in order to give them this, teachers need to be able to articulate the process of reading. I have been involved in many different kinds of reading groups and they have all been powerful learning experiences. I used to belong to a group of teachers which met once a month to discuss children's books they had read; for all of us this was one of the most meaningful experiences of professional development we experienced.

It matters what we use reading for

Teachers of reading tend to be people who enjoy reading and we need to accept that this will not be the case for all pupils. Reading for pleasure and for escapism is not the only reason for reading and neither is it the highest form of reading. Effective teaching of reading recognizes reading for finding information, for communication and for memory. It validates these reasons for reading and teaches pupils how to read in these ways more effectively as well. Teachers need to be honest about their own reading and recognize the many purposes reading serves in their own lives and the many different ways in which they read.

The notion of autobiography is a powerful one in exploring teacher development and knowledge. It raises awareness of teachers' experiences and values. Our understanding, knowledge and our teaching practice are directly related to our experience. If our practice is to be transformed then our experience must be also.

References

Allan, J. and Bruton, A. (1997) *Squeezing Out the Juice: Perceptions of Reading in the Secondary School*, Edinburgh, Scottish Council for Research in Education, web site http://www.scre.ac.uk/spotlight/ spotlight61.html

Barrs, M. and Cork, V. (2001) *The Reader in the Writer: The Links between* the *Study of Literature and Writing Development at Key Stage 2*, London, CLPE.

Bearne, E. (1995) *Greater Expectations*, London, Continuum.

Collins, J. and Dallat, J. (1998) 'Reading at Key Stage 3: a Northern Ireland survey of provision and need', *Journal of In-Service Education*, **24** (3), pp. 467–74.

D'Arcy, P. (2000) *Two Contrasting Paradigms for the Teaching and Assessment of Writing: A Critique of Current Approaches in the NC*, Loughborough, National Association of Advisors in English, National Association for Primary Education and National Association of Teachers of English.

Dean, G. (2000) *Teaching Reading in Secondary Schools*, London, Fulton.

Department for Education and Employment (DfEE) (1998) *Teaching: High Status, High Standards*, London, DfEE.

Department for Education and Employment (DfEE) (1998) *The National Literacy Strategy: Framework for Teaching*, London, DfEE.

Frater, G. (2000) 'Observed in practice. English in the NLS: some reflections', *Reading*, **34** (3), pp. 107–12.

Gregory, E. and Williams, A. (2000) *City Literacies*, London, Routledge.

Heath, S. B. (1983) *Ways with Words: Language, Life and Work in Communities and Classrooms*, Cambridge, Cambridge University Press.

Her Majesty's Inspectorate (HMI) (2000) *The National Literacy Strategy: The Second Year*, London, HMSO.

Lewis, M. and Wray, D. (1999) 'Secondary teachers' views concerning literacy and literacy teaching', *Educational Review*, **51** (3), pp. 273–80.

Marsh, J. and Millard, E. (2000) *Literacy and Popular Culture: Using Children's Culture in the Classroom*, London, Paul Chapman.

Meek, M. (1992) 'Literacy: redescribing reading', in K. Kimberley, M. Meek, and J. Miller (eds) *New Reading: Contributions to an Understanding of Literacy*, London, A. and C. Black.

Minns, H. (1990) *Read It To Me Now! Learning at Home and School*, London, Virago.

OFSTED (1998) *Secondary Education 1993–1997: a review of secondary schools in England*, London, HMSO.

Palinscar, A. M. and Brown, A. L. (1984) 'Reciprocal teaching of comprehension-fostering and comprehension monitoring activities', *Cognition and Instruction*, **1**, pp. 117–75.

Reid, L. A. (1986) *Ways of Understanding and Education*, London, Heinemann Educational.

Traves, P. (1994) 'Reading', in S. Brindley (ed.), *Teaching English*, London, Routledge/Open University Press.

I

Index

DATE DUE

GAYLORD   #3522PI   Printed in USA